DISCARD

New Perspectives on
Contemporary Chinese Poetry

New Perspectives on Contemporary Chinese Poetry

Edited by

Christopher Lupke

palgrave
macmillan

NEW PERSPECTIVES ON CONTEMPORARY CHINESE POETRY
Copyright © Christopher Lupke, 2008.

All rights reserved. No part of this book may be used or reproduced in any manner whatsoever without written permission except in the case of brief quotations embodied in critical articles or reviews.

First published in 2008 by
PALGRAVE MACMILLAN™
175 Fifth Avenue, New York, N.Y. 10010 and
Houndmills, Basingstoke, Hampshire, England RG21 6XS
Companies and representatives throughout the world.

PALGRAVE MACMILLAN is the global academic imprint of the Palgrave Macmillan division of St. Martin's Press, LLC and of Palgrave Macmillan Ltd. Macmillan® is a registered trademark in the United States, United Kingdom and other countries. Palgrave is a registered trademark in the European Union and other countries.

ISBN-13: 978–1–4039–7607–9
ISBN-10: 1–4039–7607–4

Library of Congress Cataloging-in-Publication Data is available from the Library of Congress.

A catalogue record for this book is available from the British Library.

Design by Newgen Imaging Systems (P) Ltd., Chennai, India.

First edition: January 2008

10 9 8 7 6 5 4 3 2 1

Printed in the United States of America.

*To all contemporary Chinese poets who have
suffered in the steadfast pursuit of their art*

Contents

Part II Contemporary Poetry of Mainland China

Foreword

Muddy Rivers and Canada Geese

Lyricism has come to mean several things, including the playing of emotions as if they are the lyre and are capable of music without stringed instruments. When accompanied by music words can be challenged, or they can so dominate the space that the music cannot be other than subordinate. The power of the poet is in his sensitive nature, a nature that remains mysterious. Hopefully, this will always be a mystery, this business of why a poet must be so sensitive, so open to experience. We ask whether a poet's work can be assessed according to the depth of this gift, this whirling. The poet is more likely to ask this question of himself or herself at various points in life. I have asked it of myself when I have felt weighed by the whirling, and as someone who appreciates Chinese poetry and culture, I have turned to that tradition in considering questions of *lyricism and the sublime.*

My thoughts on the subject of lyricism and the sublime have taken me to T.S. Eliot's later thoughts on the sublime in poetry and Stevens' efforts toward the same in poems such as "The Snowman." Although each speaks to a profound moment of maturity in their lives, a reckoning Yeats called "the foul rag and bone shop of the heart," I suspect there is more light to be shed on this from the perspective of Chinese poets, traditional and contemporary. There is a translator's space, a river of forgetfulness between the two traditions where the difference between Chinese traditional spirituality and Western Judeo-Christian ways ask that we look more closely at the sublime and what it may mean.

Blues musicians with their emergence from the Mississippi Delta bring us one image of the struggle of the wellspring of emotion and experience to rise above emotion and manifest as art that survives sentimentalism, as I think now of America's struggle to define itself even as it possesses so much power. The American poetic is full of elegies, and I wonder if the dead were to talk would they urge the American poet to go on with claiming the land. The image for me is much like the rivulet in Boston's Fenway Park, an emblem of the marshland this whole area was before landfills and construction. Often a flock of Canada geese add a feathery component to spring and autumn blossoming and to deciduous change, and one can forget for a while the artery of muddy water coursing through the park where mud persists like the heart's slippery flesh. The whole image can be likened to the ancient Chinese character for poetry, the soldier over the heart, which may say all there is to say about poetry: that it is the struggle to make artistic sense of life's complexities, taking the soldier now as the sublime.

There is something in the river's own heart that is the heart inside the heart, which longs to transcend its own self, to acquire the ability to fly.

Yu Guangzhong has written that the poet can describe the sage's experience but cannot be the sage. If the poet becomes the sage, he must shed himself of his poetic effect in writing, going beyond the bone to the marrow inside, which is not the sludge but the electric soil that feeds the light of dancing with the moon. The image here is from Li Bo.

This dance with the moon is part of the experience of deeper meditation, where one acquires the strength of mind known in Chinese as *ding li*.

定力

In deeper states of meditation that come after some years of disciplined practice, relaxation becomes so deep that the calmness of the mind will go undisturbed in the midst of various kinds of turmoil and chaos. This stillness is spoken of in Daoist and Buddhist texts. While all is whirling about you, you are rooted where you are, watching all else go by, unmoved but moving on the inside according to the rhythms established by several years of concentrated thought. Alongside this deep relaxation comes a clarity that is also quite sparse. Daoist and Buddhist meditation methods produce this state after a while, and in the stage known as Samadhi it is more of a constant state of awareness. The mind is cleaned daily so as to approach this clarity. In the blues, emotions are still too strong to allow this stillness as transcendence in the blues is more a surrender to struggle—an acceptance of it as a quality of life. In that way Yeat's shop may be seen as something of a blues poetic.

The price of this ticket known as Buddhist or Daoist stillness is a shedding of poetic effect such as we see in the work of Han Shan, the Zen poet. The ticket allows the dance with the moon. One is so rooted in serenity that as one approaches self-realization there is a connecting directly to all that exists in material reality and in that way a connecting to the harmonious motion of nature's harmony. From there one may grasp the truth, which is that reality is not real; here we find the image of the slipping of muddy water over small banks and the indolent nonchalance of geese waddling to the trees, unmindfully stopping traffic as they thus waddle. This is where a poet can go into stasis and thus a crisis.

The beauty in these realizations rivals the poetic. Such is bliss.

The poet describes the experience of the sage as he looks out from inside his own heart at the bare lines that configure the sublime's victory over the mud as it were, but the poet is not totally envious. The mud has its own attractions, the accoutrements of fame, the heart indulging itself, seeking and giving itself pleasure, perhaps even possessing a higher wisdom, which is that the geese themselves are not the sublime. No, the heart's own higher wisdom says the absence of both muddy river and waddling geese are the sublime. Knowing this, what poet would wish to be simply air? We have a definite purpose, struggling to create the art and live with the relative anonymity of fame that is the reality of contemporary life for the poet.

There is the strike of the pen or the brush to paper, the creative act that resists the sublime. What is it that we poets do and why do we persist in so doing?

We waddle as we go, some of us hoping that our work will make a difference in the world, although we cannot see the end of good intentions. A gesture made now toward producing positive change in the world could in several decades bring untold misery, chaos, and suffering. We simply cannot see the end of good intentions, nor can we ignore this need to bring a blossoming to a place struggling with the lack of the same, a place that lacks even the gift of a sluggish rivulet. To make it more complex and thus challenging we can say that these places are often spaces in the human heart. What are we to do with this gift of ours, this poetry? What we receive compassion tells us we should also give, a blues kind of generosity.

Yeats' foul rag and bone shop of the heart is the crisis brought on by a poet's maturity, when self-awareness and self-knowledge replace the blind ambition of the younger poet. Here a poet must decide what the other priorities are for what remains of his or her life. This is a more serious matter than simply saying that, as a poet ages, more is less or that one carves a single letter at a time in a word as opposed to a single word at a time in a line, a simplistic reading that is more the linear determinations of a material society.

Maybe Eliot was feeling a need to give out of poetic compassion as he tried to lay to rest Wordsworth's ideas of the place of emotions in the poetic consciousness as he wrote "Tradition and the Individual Talent." It is tempting to think he was simply being egotistical, looking to conquer the crown of King Poet, or that it might have been the more admirable motive we can perhaps think of as more tolerable, the ego's struggle between self-justification and a genuine appreciation of what we think is good poetry. In either case his path was not the same as a Han Shan who gave his personal life over to esoteric methods of spiritual cultivation and to write from the various dimensions of that way of experiencing life, although there is some evidence that he still suffered with envy.

So, at this point in time Western poetry may have more to gain from a more participatory involvement in Chinese culture. Yeats and Pound had tangential interests in Asian culture. Neither worked at fluency in the Chinese language and neither seriously pursued the practices of inner cultivation in Buddhist or Daoist methodologies. However, there are more Westerners these days who do participate in these ways. We can now look to the effect of this even as we go beyond Ginsberg and the Beat generation's American style fascination with Zen and like matters. This fascination emerges from America's crisis of faith in its material reality, the thingliness of things—to borrow from the New Critics for a second—has become the weightiness of weight. The machine that produced this wealth is now threatening to consume the entire world, certainly America, if we do not feed this *maker of things*. New Criticism and its child, the American creative writing workshop, have produced a giant of a child that is too self-indulgent to be embraced in the public.

Contemporary Chinese poets emerge from centuries of poetry, much of it attuned to the art of living, of observing human and natural circumstance with a singular concision in the language, of bringing eons of meaning to a single lift of a tea cup to the lips. Some still do write traditional verse, but the greater majority write in and to this material world of ours that grows more material with every passing second, as we weigh the planet by converting it into things, as the increasing weight is the planet's annoyance, which is our own annoyance. Maybe that is now a more important reason for poets to scribble, to remind ourselves and thus the world that we are not beings apart from this great host of ours. But I am only one poet, and many would not agree. Still I think the tradition of Chinese poetry is such a strong force, even in contemporary manifestations, such a strong force that it can help American poets navigate the great divide we have created in our own selves. In this way we poets might see the opportunities that wait for us in deeper levels of acceptance.

Conversely, Chinese poets may see the dangers that await them as the material world moves over them in the absence of restraint. Contemporary Chinese poets do not have the same celebrated place in the society as did their forbears in that long and glorious tradition. This is thus a more grievous relative anonymity that could make the Chinese tradition seem less relevant to contemporary Chinese poets and obscure the ways in which transcendence might embellish the poetic life. American poetry has only the stepchild's claim to the English tradition from its former colonizer.

These two spaces now live in the same time in history, the centuries-old tradition emerging from its engagement with various forms of modernism, and this American tradition that is only a few hundred years into its making and is having to define itself as it goes. The Chinese entry into the overdetermination of materialism's carnival and America's dizzied stumbling about in its aftermath are an intriguing place for poets and the poetry they are yet to write. If indeed deeper acceptance says Western abandon is equivalent to Chinese methods for transcendence, the question to each might be, "What is the value of the sublime?" So even if Eliot and Stevens were never to know the experience of spiritual cultivation that Han Shan knew and practiced, we cannot take their achievements away from them. But we can allow ourselves to wonder what their work would have been like had they known the meaning of making the mind so strong that it does not shake in a world that is always shaking, a stillness fashioned against adversity such as the way modern poets are ignored. If they had known that, then American poetry would perhaps not be the self-indulgent child that it is.

Yeats felt the difficult realization that transcendence is yet another several universes away from us. So he would later write about this deeper distance in "Among School Children" where he wonders in the last line about knowing the difference between "the dancer and the dance."

The heart itself is a gift as is this soldier above it, this reasoning or essaying toward a larger truth. The heart is a delicate cornucopia of precious experience, feelings, and emotions that amount to a poet's sensitivity in life, the tendency to perceive and respond to things that go unnoticed by others; although the poet is no more or less human than any other person for this sensitivity, he or she is nonetheless challenged with an awareness of the same. In other words, if we did not know that we do not know, we might perhaps more blissfully waddle along, but that is not the nature of sensitivity or the struggle for more than waddling, such as is the mission of the blues, the acquisition of a treaty with the heart. Yeats's rag and bone shop of the heart becomes the tired fingers of a turpentine worker in the American south finding his way through his emotional web through a song, the blues as lyric.

Eastern and Western ways differ in their attitude toward a natural harmony, and this difference makes for different ways of seeing art and suffering. In Buddhism it is said that to live is to know suffering. Poets know that to be born a poet is to serve as witness to suffering as well as joy. Some would say happiness comes with acceptance. Perhaps, but one thing is certain. Suffering does shake and shape the world.

The world indeed shakes and has a complex rhythm, which is why I watched anxiously as Chinese poets from all over the Diaspora came to The Fenway to share and discuss their own work and their own selves at this significant point in time as we approach this shifting in world power with all its accoutrements, the changing of the faces of the young, the daily opening of Pandora-like boxes of discovery, the simultaneous enlarging and shrinking of the world and much more. It is a world where our current lingua franca, English, is like Costco's, the behemoth of a large volume shopping venue. Here all sold in bulk and largeness enables mass consumption so that tasting is impossible. One can only gulp and gape. As English gulps and gapes, its obesity flows into the primary art of the language where poets struggle as sentries. Chinese potentially holds so much for all of us, even as Chinese poets wonder what it means to be Chinese. This is not just the heritage of handling matters of emotions and feelings—if we can take lyricism as being that—but also one of the world's most beautiful systems of writing, a system that has had much to do with the culture's continuity and one's sense of being Chinese. This is where we American poets can come and listen, and that remains my hope as I think of what it is to bring Chinese poets, members of one of the world's largest literary communities to convene in a place where a slow and lazy river winds and where a flock of geese adorned in nonchalance tip at the edge of the river and over into the park with its autumnal pavilions of multicolored light.

Light is the poet's lyric, and this is why we sing. Some of us cling to the singing and do not hope for release, while others cannot bear the sound and so hope for a sweeter silence in words that are tempered in nature's harmony. Whatever our course, there is always the moon and its dance, where the song is played in a blues kind of rendering of the lyric.

The moon and its dance live in a place where egos dare not go.

Afaa Michael Weaver
b. Michael S. Weaver
蔚雅風
和南寺
花連, 台灣
5/17/05

About the Contributors

John Balcom (Ph.D. Washington University, St. Louis) is Associate Professor in and Chinese Program Head of the Graduate School of Translation and Interpretation at the Monterey Institute of International Studies. His translations and cotranslations include an abridged version of Li Qiao's epic novel *Wintry Night* (2001, Columbia University Press), *Indigenous Writers of Taiwan* (2005, Columbia University Press) and Luo Fu's *Driftwood* (2007, Zephyr).

John A. Crespi (Ph.D. University of Chicago) is Henry R. Luce Assistant Professor of Chinese at Colgate University in Hamilton, New York, and is currently researching voice and social context of performed poetry in modern China.

Michael Day (Ph.D. Leiden University) is Assistant Professor of Chinese Language and Studies at National University in San Diego. He is the poetry contributor to the Digital Archive for Chinese Studies <http://www.sino.uni-heidelberg.de/dachs/>. His doctoral thesis on avant-garde Chinese poetry is downloadable at <http://leiden.dachs-archive.org/poetry/md.html>.

Yibing Huang (Ph.D. Beijing University and Ph.D. UCLA) is Associate Professor of Chinese at Connecticut College. He has written (under the penname Mai Mang) two poetry collections: *Stone Turtle: Poems 1987–2000* (2005, Godavaya) and *Approaching Blindness* (2005, Writers Publishing House, Beijing). He is also the author of *Contemporary Chinese Literature: From the Cultural Revolution to the Future* (2007, Palgrave Macmillan).

Nick Kaldis (Ph.D. The Ohio State University) is Associate Professor of Chinese at Binghamton University and has published essays on modern and contemporary Chinese literature and film and numerous translations. He has completed a manuscript on Lu Xun's *Yecao* and is cotranslating a collection of nature writing essays by Liu Kexiang.

Dian Li (Ph.D. University of Michigan) is Associate Professor of East Asian Studies at the University of Arizona, Tucson. His numerous publications on modern and contemporary Chinese poetry include

The Chinese Poetry of Bei Dao, 1978–2000: Resistance and Exile (2006, Edwin Mellen).

Andrea Lingenfelter (Ph.D. University of Washington) is an independent scholar. In addition to her Chinese poetry scholarship, she has translated Chinese poetry (*Chicago Review, Frontier Taiwan,* and *Full Tilt*) and fiction, such as *Farewell My Concubine* (1994, Harper Perennial) and *Candy* (2003, Bay Back).

Christopher Lupke (Ph.D. Cornell University) is Associate Professor of Chinese at Washington State University in Pullman and has edited a book on the Chinese notion of *Ming* (fate, command, life's allotment) (2005, Hawai'i). He has translated Ye Shitao's *A History of Taiwan Literature* (UCSB Center for Taiwanese Studies) and is finishing a book on filmmaker Hou Hsiao-hsien (University of Illinois Press).

Paul Manfredi (Ph.D. Indiana University) is Associate Professor of Chinese at Pacific Lutheran University in Tacoma, Washington, and has been the recipient of grants from the National Endowment of Humanities and Chiang Ching-kuo Foundation. His articles have appeared in *Modern Chinese Literature and Culture* and the *Journal of Modern Literature in Chinese.* His current work is on contemporary Chinese poetry and visual art.

Steven L. Riep (Ph.D. UCLA) is Assistant Professor of Chinese at Brigham Young University in Provo, Utah, where he teaches modern and contemporary literature, film, and culture. He is currently working on religion and woman's emancipation in the work of Xu Dishan, environmental themes in the essays of Yang Mu, and disability in transnational Chinese cinema.

Afaa Michael Weaver (M.F.A. Brown University) is the Alumnae Professor of English at Simmons College in Boston and founder and Director of the Zora Neale Hurston Literary Center. His tenth collection of poetry, *The Plum Flower Dance/poems 1985 to 2005* is forthcoming (University of Pittsburgh Press). He has convened an international symposium on contemporary Chinese poetry; this volume represents the scholarly fruits of that symposium.

Michelle Yeh (Ph.D. University of Southern California) is Professor of Chinese at the University of California, Davis. Her prolific scholarship on modern Chinese poetry from mainland China, Taiwan, Hong Kong, and the Chinese Diaspora has met with international acclaim. Most recently, she has coedited the anthology *Sailing to Formosa: A Poetic Companion to Taiwan* (2006, University of Washington Press).

Chapter One

Introduction:
Toward a Chinese Lyrical
Modernity

Christopher Lupke

In the storied tradition of Chinese literature, poetry occupies a hallowed position. The scholarship on traditional Chinese poetry fills entire archives. But while modern Chinese literature has now established itself as a thriving field of inquiry, most of the critical writing on it is directed toward narrative. What has happened to poetry in the contemporary period? The development of modern Chinese poetry and contemporary Chinese poetry has had an uneasy history. In addition to the upheavals that have affected all Chinese over the past 150 years, the pressures put on Chinese poetry and poets have been especially heavy. The political tumult in China has often made it difficult to create. But this alone cannot account for the attitude toward modern poetry. Poetry in the modern era has undergone a vast transformation and now bears little resemblance to its illustrious forebears. For the sake of convenience, this volume refers to "contemporary" Chinese poetry. By that we simply mean poetry written after the midcentury war period. All the papers except Michelle Yeh's, which sets the stage for the rest, focus on the postwar period. But even in the poetry of the postwar period, the development in writing Chinese poetry cannot be understood in neat rubrics. First, with the bitter end to the civil war, many poet intellectuals ended up in Hong Kong and Taiwan. Their development bears little in common with that of mainland China, where political repression and propaganda pervaded all realms, including literary creation. Whereas contemporary poetry in Hong Kong and Taiwan evolved in a manner reasonably clear of unwanted political attention, in mainland China poetry was pressed into the service of the state. Thus, despite the division of this book into two major sections, one representing contemporary poetry of Taiwan and the other that of mainland China, the time periods and time spans are still quite different. That no one has devoted a chapter to the study of Hong Kong poets is a regrettable result not of our desire not to do so, but of the severe constraints put on the length of this pithy volume.

The book emerges from a large conference called "The Simmons International Chinese Poetry Conference," featuring scholars and poets of contemporary China and Chinese studies, that took place on the campus of Simmons College in the fall of 2004. The organizer and inspiration behind the conference was Afaa Weaver, director of the Zora Neale Hurston Literary Center at Simmons and himself a well-known African American poet who has learned Chinese and is interested in promoting interaction between Chinese and American poets. What began as a wonderful idea to bring a few poets and scholars together ended up being a vast gathering of about seventy-five poets and scholars of modern Chinese literature from all over the world. This volume brings together some of the essays that grew out of the conference with a few additions. That it exists in the first place, and that this conference, which will reprise at Simmons College in fall 2008, is due to the vision and charisma of Afaa Weaver.

In his preface to our book, Professor Weaver investigates *shi* 詩, the ancient character for poetry, by comparing its structure to aspects of the geography of the Fens area in Boston where the conference took place. *Shi*'s composition of the scholar radical over the heart resembles the structure of the poetry award Professor Weaver gave at the conference, a glass decanter with a heart's shape. Immediately outside the window of Simmons's newly renovated third-floor conference center where the events took place wanders the Muddy River, so named due to the fact that the area was once marshland. Nowadays, a number of interesting birds inhabit the area, most notably a flock of Canada geese, who made it their project to occupy the street on the final day of the conference, a sunny Sunday afternoon when they felt the need to be oblivious to the world. Among other aspects of this comparison, Weaver likens the juxtaposition of the geese over the river to the victory of the mind over the heart in Zen poetry, specifically that of Han Shan.

Michelle Yeh's chapter examines what exactly is modern about Chinese poetry and why that is good. Her chapter spans the twentieth century in its scope. It seeks to go beyond the long-standing dichotomy of tradition and modernity that underscored major debates and controversies throughout the past century. Addressing the issues of form and content, language, the new conceptualization of poetry, and relations with indigenous and foreign traditions, Yeh problematizes the continuing concern with Chineseness over modernity.

Contemporary Poets of Taiwan

The political trajectory of modern China brought with it profound implications for Chinese poetry, for the emergence of the Maoist brand of Communism in mainland China meant that after 1949 free expression in verse was a near impossibility. On the island of Taiwan, by contrast, poetry flourished during the 1950s in spite of the repressive nature of the Guomindang (GMD) regime under Chiang Kai-shek. Whereas Mao took a proprietary interest in poetic production, Chiang was indifferent to verse, as long as it did not tread too closely to taboo political subject matter. Under these circumstances, fine Chinese poetry from Taiwan developed naturally. One of the most beloved poets to come on the scene in Taiwan in the 1950s was Zheng Chouyu.

In chapter 3, I investigate Zheng's ability to recover the lyrical, the melodious, and the musical from traditional Chinese poetry for use in the creation of contemporary poetry. For Zheng Chouyu, the meaning of lyrical is found in the indeterminacy of imagery to establish a sustained and fixed notion in the mind of the reader of a concrete notion in space. Zheng's imagery bespeaks a feeling of alienation and exile and, consequently, of nostalgia. For Zheng Chouyu, the lyric emerged as the only possible mode of articulation precisely when narrative was ineffective for conveying this sense of alienation. As far as Zheng is concerned, only the lyric—with its elliptical qualities of half music, half referential language, part discourse and part object of art—was suitable for the traumatic reality of the political predicament of China in mid-century. Zheng's lyrics flowed freely and vividly and became an immediate and lasting sensation in Taiwan and elsewhere. Submerged in the laconic stanzas of Zheng's short poetry there is a strong element of political upheaval and historical tumult.

Throughout the 1950s and 1960s, the threat of imminent war hung over the island of Taiwan under Chiang Kai-shek's rule. Having endured the trauma of two wars, soldiers and civilian refugees from China found themselves living under martial law, an experience they shared with the native population of Taiwanese, Hakka, and aboriginal peoples, who had themselves endured the Sino-Japanese War as colonial subjects of the Japanese and then suffered the predations of the Nationalist military. During the two decades that followed the

Nationalist retreat to Taiwan in the late-1940s, although explicit and implicit censorship existed, creative writers including several poets serving actively in the Nationalist navy wrote works that through their critique of war engaged their government's military policies. Ya Xian, the subject of Steven Riep's chapter, wrote eloquently of the impact of battle on soldiers and civilians in an age when the government called for patriotic, anticommunist propaganda. Ya Xian's masterful use of irony, his haunting imagery and his experiments with terminal and circular structures set him apart as an antiwar poet par excellence. This chapter examines Ya's war poems, which Riep argues, should also be read as a critique of war.

Another poet deeply affected by the specter of war was Luo Fu. In his chapter on Luo, John Balcom illustrates how Luo's first major creative breakthrough as a poet came in 1958 when, as the shells rained down overhead, he began writing inside a bomb shelter. His poetry can be described as a vast canvas upon which the great themes of life, death, love, and war are painted. Luo Fu's reflections on the nature of human existence and man's fate in the modern world are expressed through a complex array of personal symbols to create a stunning and hermetic poetry of rich texture. His most recent collection entitled *Driftwood* is actually a 240-page epic poem, and Balcom has translated it in its entirety.

In his chapter, Nick Kaldis ponders what he sees as an inherent contradiction in nature writing in Taiwan. In his theoretical reflection on this genre, he notes that the moment we convert an experience of nature into discourse—poetic or otherwise—everything that is not reducible to that discourse disappears from the original experience. That is, the impenetrable otherness of nature cannot be made to appear in written form, and even the noblest literary attempt to convey the moment of a person's immersion in that otherness risks colonizing nature as a reductive concept within a rational-discursive format. Treating Taiwan nature poetry as just another literary genre, therefore, betrays the very thing the scholar is ostensibly venerating. Kaldis explores the ways in which the contradictions inherent in the study of nature writing have manifested themselves in academic experience, and he suggests some ways of mediating these contradictions.

The final chapter in this section of the book, an examination of two major contemporary Chinese women poets—Xia Yu from Taiwan and Zhai Yongming from Sichuan—provides a corrective to the perception the volume may have given thus far that most Chinese poets are men. It also forms a convenient bridge between the first set of five chapters and the second set, for unlike all other chapters, this one straddles the

Taiwan Strait. Andrea Lingenfelter's discussion of these two important woman poets who are only a year apart in age raises an interesting question: Is it necessarily the case that poetry written by women feature themes of women? While it may not be possible to provide a conclusive answer to that question, Lingenfelter shows through a discussion of an array of poems by Xia and Zhai how issues of sexuality, marriage, and social acceptance are important themes that weigh in their respective consciousnesses. She also demonstrates how to one extent or another each poet engages her past, incorporating into her own creative work both cultural and discursive elements of traditional Chinese society with respect to women, in some cases creating an internal polemic and in others appropriating the mythic imagery of ancient China as a way of revivifying Chinese language in the present.

Contemporary Poets of Mainland China

The second portion of the book focuses on PRC poets and developments related to them in the most recent times in China. Yibing Huang observes in his chapter that Gu Cheng's position in contemporary Chinese poetry constitutes an ultimate mystery. Despite his early recognition and success, somehow Gu Cheng has never been accepted as a fully mature poet. He was labeled as a "poet of fairy-tales," which seemed a curse instead of a blessing. While in his early lyric poetry Gu Cheng yearns to "walk over the world," in his late poetry he longs to return to the "city,"—a "city" to which he was native and a "city" that serves as his last mental refuge. Eventually, this "child" is anything but "innocent" and the "nature" is anything but "natural"; and what was born is neither a poetry of "innocence" nor a poetry of "experience," but a "ghost" poetry. This transformation or metamorphosis from "willful child" to "wandering ghost" and the return from "nature" to "city" forms the essence of Huang's treatment of Gu Cheng's poetry.

Reading Yan Li's recent poetry, including in particular his "Polyhedral Mirror," Paul Manfredi's chapter depicts the shifts in Yan Li's nature imagery over the past fifteen years. He situates this evolution in terms of Yan's own locale, namely residence in major urban centers in the United States, (greater) China, and Australia over the same period of time. He concludes that the increasing consciousness of a degraded natural global environment held by people worldwide is working its way into the otherwise rather unevironmentally conscious world of Yan Li's poetic and artistic work. Yan's growing environmental consciousness does not, however, demonstrate alarmist or didactic inclinations, but rather the seamless reformulations of how the thriving of the man-made world and the continuance if not flourishing of the natural world might be less of the zero-sum game that it has become.

In his chapter, John Crespi explores the role of memory in contemporary Chinese poetry, focusing on two series of poems, Yu Jian's "Two or Three Things from the Past" and Sun Wenbo's "1960s Bicycle." He asks what characterizes this lyrical turn in the literary memory of the Cultural Revolution. How does the construction of past events and emotions in these poems extend, supplement, or subvert existing narrative accounts? What does the presence of these poems portend for the evolving historical memory of the Cultural Revolution years? What he finds is that memories of the trauma of the Cultural Revolution, for example, are encoded in poetry not as past experiences but as fragments in the present, thus offering an alternative to the conventional memoirs of this period that tend to dominate the attention of foreign audiences.

Dian Li's chapter outlines a now infamous debate that occurred around 1999–2002 between "intellectual" poets, who tend to gravitate toward major cities such as Beijing and Shanghai and are associated with major academic centers, on the one hand, and "popular" or *minjian* 民間 poets, as Li prefers to call them, who are more at home in the provinces and have less access to the typical avenues of symbolic capital in China, on the other. His chapter focuses on several of the main players in this heated debate, including Xi Chuan, Wang Jiaxin, Cheng Guangwei, and Zang Di, representing the "intellectuals," and Yu Jian, Yi Sha, Yang Ke, and Xu Jiang in the *"minjian"* camp. In the conclusion to his chapter, Li interestingly dwells on the actual issue of naming itself, citing another renowned contemporary Chinese poet, Wang Xiaoni, who argues that poetry is always "antinaming." In so doing, Li throws open the question of whether such debates as the one he surveys in his article are fruitful ways of attempting to characterize the contemporary poetry scene in China.

Michael Day does a great service for those of us still not accustomed to getting our poetic fix over the cyber waves. Day derives this survey of current trends in online poetry from his freshly minted dissertation on the topic. An interesting question one could ask is: Does the medium of inscription affect the form and content of the poetry itself? It would seem so to some extent at least, as Day shows through a broad discussion of a number of Web sites how the grittiness of contemporary reality and less-than-sublime, if you will, subject matter have crept into the creative palette of this new generation of poets. In addition, he examines the egalitarian benefits of Internet poetry— there are Web sites where aspiring poets who otherwise would have little hope cracking the establishment channels to publication can freely post their work in a wide variety of venues for a number of different reading constituencies. That his chapter caps the volume is testament to the fact that this slim work, which does not promise to be exhaustive or definitive, nevertheless makes strides toward filling some of the gaps in scholarship on contemporary Chinese poetry, a field that is still growing and continues to offer fertile ground for scholars of Chinese literature.

This volume would not have been possible without the hard work of the contributors and without all the energy generated by a number of people at the Simmons Conference. On behalf of the contributors, I also would like to thank Julia Cohen, Farideh Koohi-Kamali, Katie Fahey and the others at Palgrave Macmillan who have lent their support to this work, as well as Maran Elancheran and the people at Newgen Imaging Systems. I add a word of appreciation to the anonymous referees, whose constructive comments have improved the outcome of this project. I also am grateful to Yan Li for permission to use an image from his "poetry gum" series to grace the book cover. A grant from the College of Liberal Arts at Washington State University helped enable me to complete this project. My gratitude to John Kicza, former Associate Dean, for facilitating that. A few words on practical matters: Hanyu pinyin romanization is used throughout for the sake of convenience in reading; traditional or simplified characters are used depending on the original source; and all translations are those of each chapter's author, unless otherwise noted.

Chapter Two

"There Are no Camels in the Koran": What Is Modern about Modern Chinese Poetry?

Michelle Yeh

In 1951, in response to the criticism from fellow Argentines that his work lacked local color, Jorge Luis Borges wrote an essay titled "The Argentine Writer and Tradition." Referring to the Islamic prophet Mohammed, the writer observed that "in the Arab book par excellence, the Koran, there are no camels," for "[Mohammed] knew he could be an Arab without camels." "What is truly native can and often does dispense with local color" (1999: 423).

The issue Borges addressed more than half a century ago sounds all too familiar to students of non-Western literature. In the case of Chinese literature, debates throughout the history of Modern Chinese Poetry have almost always revolved around cultural identity or "Chineseness." In other genres such as fiction, visual art, and film, we have witnessed a similar tension between being native and being international, between being national and being modern. The crux of the issue is representation. When literature is interpreted primarily, if not exclusively, as an index to, and mapping of, the culture or nation of its origin, it is only logical for readers to measure it by how well it represents; hence, the expectation of "local color," the demand for "authenticity."

A comparable situation obtains in the current interest in and market for "ethnic writers" in the United States. Rarely do we find a non-white American writer who is not primarily identified by his or her ethnicity, such as Asian American, African American, or Native American. Although some writers consider such labeling limiting, they accept it with little protest, as ethnicity has become a common organizing principle for the publishing industry, college curricula, conferences, even literary awards, readings, and festivals. Each ethnic category has become a "niche," a selling point in the literary market.

I use the word "market" broadly to include the academy as well. For the insistence on literature as representation resonates with a popular trend in literary studies in American academia today, which privileges the local over the global, the ethnic over the universal, difference over commonality. The irony is that, when literature is treated as representation of a culture or ethnic group, it is often found wanting for being either "too much" or "too little": too little, if a literary work does not sufficiently "reflect" the culture or ethnic group it supposedly represents; too much, if it overemphasizes a certain aspect at the expense of other aspects of a culture or ethnic group. Paradoxically, although these two perceptions seem contrary to each other, they lead to the same conclusion that the writer or artist "panders" to foreign readers or audiences. Filmmakers such as Ang Lee and Zhang Yimou and fiction writers such as Ha Jin and Gao Xingjian have all been criticized in one way or another for catering to Western voyeurism, the West's appetite for exotic China, or the taste of Western readers, especially the Swedish Academy's Committee on the Nobel Prize in Literature!

This kind of criticism finds explicit expression in an article published in *China Daily* on July 24, 2000, by Li Rui, the renowned Chinese fiction writer. Li aims his rebuke at the avant-garde Chinese writers of the 1980s, who "pandered to the Western literary establishment." "None of their works were truly original; none expressed the true spirit of the Chinese people. But the Western academy loved them." He then urges his fellow writers to reject Western values as the sole yardstick for literature and to "reflect the spiritual world of the Chinese people and China's unique culture" (Li Rui 2000).

Li's passionate appeal to Chineseness reveals two contradictions. One is a contradiction between antiuniversalism and universalism. While he rejects Western taste as the universal standard for evaluating literatures from different parts of the world, he nevertheless resorts to "Chinese culture," "Chinese people," or "the Chinese spirit" as a universal category. When he calls upon his fellow writers to adhere to "Chinese characteristics," we must ask: what are they exactly? Who decides what is characteristic and what is not, and which of the countless "lives and experiences of the Chinese people" should a writer portray to represent "the soul of our culture"?

Returning briefly to Borges's essay, we see the irony of which Li Rui seems unaware, that the insistence that "a literature . . . must define itself in terms of its national traits is a relatively new . . . and arbitrary concept," a fairly "recent European cult" (Borges 1999: 423). Elsewhere I have called such preconceived notions of what

Chineseness should mean, how it should be represented, and who should represent it as constituting the "myth of authenticity" or "cult of purism" (Yeh 2000b).

The other contradiction underlying Li Rui's argument is that, while he disparages the imperialistic West as monopolizing the role as the arbiter of world literature, he nevertheless continues to validate it by acknowledging the serious consequence of *not* being taken seriously by the West. "Under the [dominance of the Western literary] establishment," he says, "Chinese literature is being looked down on in the international arena, which means that Chinese people might begin to lose their self-respect and their artistic independence" (Li 2000). But if what Li says were true, then Chinese writers could never get out of the quandary of self-representation. For if they won the approval of the West, they would be called "sellouts"; but if they failed to matter to the West, they would lose self-respect!

In my view, any insistence on defining and judging Chinese literature by Chineseness, in contradistinction from its counterparts from the rest of the world, is problematic. To reify Chineseness is to put the cart before the horse: if readers have acquired a sense of Chinese literature, it should derive from the numerous individual works that they have read over time, not from some a priori notion of Chineseness that they are told to look for in works.

The irony of Li Rui's criticism of the "Western literary establishment" is that he sounds exactly like the academy in North America: the critique of Western hegemony, the resistance from the non-West, the embrace of cultural particularism, the demand for equal representation and recognition based on ethnicity, nation, gender, and other categories. Neil Larsen uses the term "inverted Eurocentrisms" to characterize a similar phenomenon in Latin America: "[T]he dominant, Eurocentrist culturalism of the center is matched by the contestatory culturalisms of the periphery" (Larsen 1995: 134).

In her book, *The Protestant Ethnic and the Spirit of Capitalism*, Rey Chow calls mimeticism "the central problematic in cross-ethnic representation in the postcolonial world" (Chow 2002: 103). She further divides it into three levels, with the third being the most evolved and complex, where "the original that is supposed to be replicated is no longer the white man or his culture but rather an image, a stereotyped view of the ethnic," such as "Asianness," "Africanness," "Arabness," and the like (107). Under the subheading "I Protest, Therefore I Am: The Ethnic in the Age of Global Capital," Chow argues that ethnic representation and self-representation are "firmly inscribed within the economic and ideological workings of capitalism, replete with their mechanisms of callings, opportunities, and rewards" (48).

By questioning literature as representation, I am not denying it provides an invaluable window on a culture, society, or time period; in fact, in undergraduate courses we often use literature that way. But, in teaching literature as a means of introducing students to China, we also teach—or should teach—them how to appreciate Chinese literature as art. When some of them decide to further their study of Chinese literature, be it a particular writer, genre, period, or theme, they do so not so much out of a desire to gain more knowledge about China— because that goal may as well be served by other fields of study—as out of a desire to experience again and again the pleasure and power of imaginative writing. After all, literature is a special kind of discourse distinct in fundamental ways from other discourses. To treat it as if it is no different from any other discourse is to be not only extremely reductive but to also implicitly and effectively acquiesce to other disciplines the legitimacy and value of literary study.

The obsession with Chineseness is particularly pervasive in Modern Chinese Poetry.[1] Associations with foreign—especially Western—influences have always been cause for disdain and dismissal, and the concern with the cultural identity of Modern Chinese Poetry, or the lack thereof, has underscored many debates and controversies throughout the twentieth century. Between 1910 and 1930, critics of New Poetry 新詩 or Vernacular Poetry 白話詩—the earliest names of Modern Chinese Poetry—regarded it a mere imitation of the avant-garde in the West; quite a few mistakenly attributed its emergence to the influence of Imagism, a mistake perpetuated by later critics both in and outside China. In Taiwan in the early 1970s, during the Modern Poetry Debate 現代詩論戰, modernist poetry was condemned as "colonial," "narcissistic," and "decadent" for having drawn inspirations from Anglo-European modernism, including surrealism, existentialism, and psychoanalysis (Xi 1998b). In mainland China in the late 1970s and early 1980s, the revival of poetry that departed from the PRC norm of the political lyric puzzled and angered the cultural establishment. The unfamiliarity of the new poetry immediately made it look "Westernized" and earned it the derogatory name Misty Poetry (*menglongshi* 朦朧詩) (Yeh 1992). In the early 1990s, the veteran poet and literary scholar Zheng Min 鄭敏 (b. 1920) lambasted Modern Poetry *in toto* for its Westernized character and urged poets to return to the Chinese tradition (Yeh 1991b). Finally, in mainland China in 1999–2000, the prolonged debate between the People's Poets and the Intellectual Poets revolved around the issue of language—a language used by the masses in everyday life as opposed to a language that was allegedly overly Westernized and elitist (Van Crevel 2007).

Why is there this recurrent anxiety about the lack of Chineseness in Modern Chinese Poetry? Why does the linguistic register alone—that is, the fact that the poetry is written in Chinese—fail to convince critics of its Chineseness? To offer an answer, we must understand the historical positioning and the new orientation of Modern Poetry—in short, the "modernity" of Modern Chinese Poetry.

Central to the modernity of Modern Chinese Poetry is a paradox resulting from specific historical circumstances. In advocating the use of the modern vernacular as the poetic medium, Modern Poetry was part of China's nation-building project that had begun in the late Qing, which sought to raise the level of literacy and train new "citizens" by promoting the vernacular. With Mandarin institutionalized as the National Language by the early 1920s and effectively integrated into the modern educational system, Modern Poetry gained legitimacy in a relatively short period of time. Although poetry written in traditional forms has continued to be written, at least until recently it is predominantly Modern Poetry that is the requisite form for poetry prizes and appears in most newspapers, literary journals, and poetry anthologies.

If Modern Poetry is legitimized in institutional terms, its validity and value in the cultural sphere has been questioned since its inception in 1916–17. Elsewhere, I have discussed the marginalization of poetry in the twentieth century (Yeh 1994). When Modern Poetry arose to challenge Classical Poetry, it was not unlike David taking on Goliath. Beginning with Confucius and through later institutionalization of Confucianism, poetry had always enjoyed a special place in traditional China. First of the "three sister arts" (along with calligraphy and painting), poetry was highly esteemed as the most elegant art and one of the most prestigious forms of writing. To this day, Chinese people take pride in their glorious heritage of Classical Poetry and refer to China as a "nation of poetry" 詩的民族. Moreover, poetry was important not only for its cultural form but also for its moral, educational, and sociopolitical role in traditional China. Although quantitatively speaking, Classical Poetry was primarily written by and for members of the literati, it occupied a central position in culture and society.

Into the twentieth century, the role of poetry underwent dramatic transformation due to the adoption of a Western-styled education system, the compartmentalization of modern learning, the abolition of the civil service examination system, and the rise of the modern media and publishing system, among other factors. Poetry is no longer the privileged form of writing that it once was, nor does it serve the public and institutional functions that it once served. In short, Modern Poetry has lost the stature and functionality that its traditional counterpart enjoyed for centuries. Compared with Classical Poetry, it is marginalized.

If poetry can never regain the multifarious role it once played in a premodern, pre–Media Age society, Modern Chinese Poetry faces another difficulty that does not necessarily exist in other literary traditions. As a new way of writing, Modern Poetry is both challenging and challenged because, in form and content, in language and aesthetic orientation, it is *not* Classical Poetry. This is where "modernity" clashes with "Chineseness." Developed over a period of more than two thousand years, Classical Poetry has perfected an aesthetic paradigm with regard to language (formal or informal, elegant or folksy, archaic or colloquial), imagery and other figures of speech (e.g., allusion, symbol, etc.), form (subgenres of *shi* 詩, song lyric, aria, etc., each with a prescribed prosody), and content (occasional, public, private, etc.). Although there is always room for individual variations and innovations, they usually take place within a well-defined framework of predecessors as models to be emulated. The paradigmatic Classical Poetry is super-stable and has remained pretty much the same over the past millennium. For Modern Poetry to challenge this paradigm is to challenge Chinese readers' notion of poetry in a fundamental way. It is no wonder that to many Chinese readers, Modern Poetry seems decidedly "unpoetic." The reason is because Modern Poetry, as a new aesthetic paradigm, does not meet their expectations of "poetry" and those expectations are almost solely based on, and derived from, Classical Poetry.

Moreover, Classical Poetry has not only played multiple roles and enjoyed high prestige in traditional society and culture, but it has also been integrated into and is deeply embedded in the Chinese language itself over the centuries. It is virtually impossible for the educated to speak and write Chinese without using the phrases, images, proverbs, and direct quotes from numerous immortalized verses from the past. Classical Poetry is thus inseparable from the cultural identity of China. My own experience in interacting with Chinese audiences at lectures suggests that the more educated Chinese readers are, the more they tend to adhere to the classical paradigm and resist Modern Poetry. The adulation by Ezra Pound and other American Imagists in the early twentieth century only reaffirms the enduring beauty and value of Classical Poetry as China's unique contribution to the world.

In contrast, Modern Poetry may seem "impure" and "un-Chinese." Born in the Literary Revolution 文學革命 in 1917, Modern Poetry is such a radical departure from Classical Poetry that it looks "foreign" to many Chinese readers even today. Historically, the origin of Modern Poetry was embedded in foreign settings and poets drew on foreign resources freely and eclectically. Hu Shi 胡適 (1891–1962), the architect of the Literary Revolution, developed his theory of Modern Poetry while he was studying in the United States in 1910–17, especially 1916–17. As a student at Cornell and Columbia Universities, he was widely exposed to Anglo-American poetry, such as Shakespeare, Tennyson, Robert Browning, Longfellow, Thomas Campbell, and Sara Teasdale. Hu's situation was not unique. Many modern poets in the 1920s–1940s studied abroad and quite a few wrote their representative works there: for example, Zhou Zuoren 周作人 (1885–1967) and Guo Moruo 郭沫若 (1892–1978) in Japan; Wen Yiduo 聞一多 (1899–1946), Bing Xin 冰心 (1900–99), Mu Dan 穆旦 (1918–77), and Zheng Min 鄭敏 (b. 1920) in the United States; Xu Zhimo 徐志摩 (1896–1931) in England; Zong Baihua 宗白華 (1897–1986) and Feng Zhi 馮至 (1905–93) in Germany; Wang Duqing 王獨清 (1898–1940), Li Jinfa 李金髮 (1900–76), Liang Zongdai 梁宗岱 (1903–83), Dai Wangshu 戴望舒 (1905–50), Luo Dagang 羅大岡 (1909–98), and Ai Qing 艾青 (1910–96) in France. This has become a common phenomenon in Modern Chinese Poetry, with the exception of mainland China in 1949–1979 due to the political situation in that country. Today, a fair number of Chinese poets have settled permanently in North America, Europe, or Australia and continue to write and publish in Chinese.

Also significant is the fact that many poets translate world poetry into Chinese, a distinct feature of Modern Poetry not found in Classical Poetry. Regardless of their educational background, the majority of Chinese poets are avid readers of world poetry in translation.[2] Broad exposure to world literature also means that non-Chinese images, symbols, myths, allusions, and the like find their way into Modern Poetry, clearly distinguishing it from its traditional counterpart. The cross-fertilization between native and foreign, original and translated literatures is inevitable and profound. We may say that, from its very beginning, Modern Poetry has been a "hybrid" of Chinese and non-Chinese elements.

In itself, cultural hybridity should not be cause for concern. After all, Westernization of material culture—housing, clothing, transportation, and other elements of daily life—is not only taken for granted but actively sought after in China. Even when we look at "intangible culture," debates over Chineseness in modern fiction and drama are few and far in between. But because Classical Poetry is inextricable from and emblematic of China, Modern Poetry is perceived by many Chinese readers as a challenge to the very cultural identity of China. Here lies another dimension to the paradox of Modern Chinese Poetry: it is both "legitimate"—as the representative form of poetry in modern China—and "illegitimate"—as the inferior successor or, worse still, the "unfilial son," of Classical Poetry. In comparison with the quintessential Chinese poetry, the modern hybrid pales.

Once we understand the fetishization of Classical Poetry as a superior embodiment of cultural identity and national pride, the question of Chineseness seems misplaced, even irrelevant, and the obsession with Chineseness stands as a barrier to a full appreciation of Modern Poetry. After all, we do not question the "Americanness" of American poetry or the "Frenchness" of French poetry. Moreover, we do not question their identity just because they have been influenced by literary traditions other than their own. Therefore, instead of asking "What is Chinese about Modern Chinese Poetry?" a more meaningful and constructive question is: What is modern about Modern Chinese Poetry?

The above discussion has highlighted two important aspects of the modernity of Modern Chinese Poetry: first, its international and hybrid nature, and, second, its iconoclastic and experimental spirit. The first suggests a new model for self-renewal. Traditionally, poets usually looked to an earlier master, school, or style to emulate. While periodically there were reactions against this neoclassicist or revivalist model by emphasizing individuality and spontaneity, for example, the dominant trend from the Song to the late Qing was to turn to the indigenous past for resources. The second characteristic of Modern Poetry is manifest in both form and content, both aesthetic orientation and artistic experimentation. As I have discussed elsewhere (Yeh 1991b), the rethinking of the ontology of poetry in Modern Chinese Poetry is crystallized in these questions: what is poetry? whom is poetry for? and why poetry?

If one had to choose one word to describe Modern Chinese Poetry, it would be "revolution." The first time the word "revolution" was used in connection with poetry was in 1898, when the young intellectual Liang Qichao declared a *revolution* in the Poetry Domain 詩界革命. The goals of the revolution, according to Liang, were to introduce "new diction" 新詞語 and "new perspectives" 新意境 and to revive "ancient styles" 古風格 in poetry. As a result of the first two goals, new words such as "parliament" and "telegram" and new concepts such as the revolution of Earth and time zones were incorporated into poetry. These innovations reflected the influx of new knowledge and the rapidly changing culture as a result of China's extensive contact, voluntary or involuntary, with the rest of the world, particularly Japan, Europe, and the United States. Part of a tripartite program that also included fiction and prose, Liang's poetry revolution was inseparable from his vision of political and social reform at the time. However, despite the new diction and new concepts, it did not challenge the classical paradigm of poetry. In fact, it was very much a continuation of the Confucian tradition, which viewed poetry as a significant educational tool and sociopolitical vehicle.

Thus, the Revolution in the Poetry Domain advocated by Liang Qichao at the turn of the twentieth century had little success for two reasons. First, by advocating "ancient styles," it did not go beyond the neoclassicist or revivalist model in Classical Poetry, where change was to be effected by reviving a certain school or style in a past era, and still operated exclusively within the traditional frame of reference. The second, and more important, reason is that the new poetry that Liang envisioned was constrained by traditional forms, with prescribed structures, prosody, and tonal patterns. The Poetry Revolution turned out to be an ephemeral event, remembered more for its historic significance than for memorable poetry.

A true revolution in poetry would have to wait until 1917. Discontent with the earlier attempt to revolutionize the genre, Hu Shi called for the use of the modern vernacular as the poetic medium, on the one hand, and a "great emancipation of the poetic form" 詩體大解放, on the other. In practice, the modernity of Modern Chinese Poetry is manifest first and foremost in two things: language and form.

Since the late nineteenth century, there had been a continuing movement to promote the modern vernacular as the written medium, and progressive newspapers and journals had begun using the vernacular alongside Classical Chinese. What was new about Hu Shi's Literary Revolution is the constructed binary opposition between Classical and Vernacular Chinese. From a historical point of view, it was obviously a gross exaggeration to call Classical Chinese a "dead" language, but such construction aided Hu's agenda of nationalizing the vernacular and promoting New Poetry. In truth, the language of Modern Poetry is a hybrid or polyglot; it contains Classical Chinese, premodern vernacular, modern vernacular, Japanese and European loan words, neologism, various Chinese regionalisms, translated words and phrases, Europeanized syntax, and modern Western punctuation. Sometimes, even foreign words are directly incorporated into a poem. The eclectic elements offer modern poets new resources not necessarily available in Classical Poetry and also partly accounts for the difficulty that readers encounter in Modern Poetry.

Modern poets have at their disposal a greatly enlarged repertoire of linguistic devices that, coupled with freedom in form and a treasure trove of images and ideas both indigenous and imported, enable them to engage in robust experimentation. A modern poem may be as condensed as a classical poem; it can also be purposely prosaic and syntactically complex. A modern poem may be an imagist "ideogram"; it can also be highly abstract. It is no wonder that a number of poets, such as Luo Zhicheng 羅智成 (b. 1955), Zheng Chouyu 鄭愁予 (b. 1933), and Yu Jian 于堅 (b. 1954) speak of poetry as "wizardry."

To illustrate some of the new possibilities in syntax, semantics, tone, and cadence that the hybrid modern Chinese brings, I would like to look at two early examples of Modern Poetry. The first is Wang Duqing's "I Come Out of a Café" 我從Café中出來, written in the 1920s:

I come out of a café,	我從Café中出來,
my body	身上添了
fatigued	中酒的
from inebriation,	疲乏,
I have no idea	我不知道
which way I am going, to find	向那一處走去, 纔是我底
a temporary home	暫時的住家 . . . .
oh, streets cold and quiet,	啊, 冷靜的街衢,
twilight, fine rain!	黃昏, 細雨！
I come out of a café,	我從Café中出來,
sodden	在帶著醉
speechless	無言地
walking alone,	獨走,
in my heart,	我地心內,
I feel the sadness of a drifter, who's	感著一種, 要失了故國的
about to lose his homeland	浪人底哀愁 . . . . . .
oh, streets cold and quiet,	啊, 冷靜的街衢,
twilight, fine rain!	黃昏, 細雨！

(Wang 1974)

Several immediately noticeable registers distinguish the poem from Classical Poetry: the sentences each begin with the first personal pronoun (often omitted in Classical Chinese); the number of words vary irregularly in each line; the use of modern punctuation; the typography; and the French word in the title and the text of the poem. Combined, these registers create a rhythm that is also clearly modern despite the structural regularity in the two stanzas and the use of end rhymes in the last two lines of each stanza that may be reminiscent of Classical Poetry.

The use of line breaks in the poem conveys a sense of halting, physical as well as emotional. The breaks are especially dramatic in the shortest lines in each stanza: surrounded by disproportionately large blank spaces, these fragments suggest a sense of isolation and desolation. It may be said that for the first time in Chinese poetry, typography (which hardly exists in Classical Poetry), including blank spaces, becomes a semantically significant component. Similarly, the seemingly superfluous commas in lines 5–6 in each stanza, which depart from standard grammar, create pauses in the word flow. Modern punctuation (based on Western punctuation) was adopted in China in 1918–20. Here we see how it also can serve poetic purposes. Besides the commas, the ellipses indicating an unfinished or unspeakable thought in line 7 and the exclamatory mark in the last line in each stanza are important; they help to intensify the feeling of uncertainty and dejection that the poem tries to convey. Finally, all of the above devices slow down the tempo of the whole piece and intimate the speaker's state of mind. The slow tempo allows readers to fully appreciate the word "lengjing" 冷靜 in the penultimate line in each stanza. If "lengjing" is a common word meaning calm or composed, here the two characters that make up the word, *leng-jing*, function independently to suggest the scene: for the solitary wanderer, the streets in the dark are both "cold" and "quiet."

If Wang draws on several "foreign" resources in the above, the next poem illustrates how classical resources can be equally effective in Modern Poetry. Written in March 1937, Dai Wangshu's "I Think" 我思想 reads:

I think, therefore I am a butterfly	我思想, 故我是蝴蝶。
Ten millennia from now a tiny	萬年後小花的輕呼
flower's gentle call	透過無夢無醒的雲霧,
Will penetrate the clouds of no	來振撼我斑斕的彩翼。
dreams and no awakenings	
To flutter my splendid	
colored wings	

(Dai 1989: 126)

Numerous critics have noted the Zhuangzi allusion in the image of the butterfly. Many also have identified the reference to René Descartes. Most notable is how Dai uses the syntax of the Descartes maxim but surprises us with the insertion of an equally famous image from an ancient Daoist text. In the original *Zhuangzi* allegory, the butterfly evokes endless transformation of Being and the interchangeability of all forms (e.g., "dream" and "reality," "Self" and "Other"). Here, Dai uses transcendence in a wholly different context. Structurally, the first line is a complete sentence consisting of eight characters; with the copula "shi" it is a static sentence designating a state of being. In contrast, the other three lines of the poem also form a complete sentence, but three times as long and full of movement. "Call," "penetrate," "flutter"—these transitive verbs are not only dynamic rather than static, they convey interaction between the subject and the object of the sentence. The transition from the first line to the next three lines, from a pithy epigrammatic line to a long dynamic sentence seems to open up an internal vista; we are taken on a fantastic journey by the butterfly. Paradoxically, the frailty and impermanence of beauty usually associated with the winged butterfly is reversed. The butterfly flies through the infinite Space of eternal Time in response to the gentle call of a flower. Undeterred by thick "clouds of no dreams and no awakenings," the butterfly transcends Time and Space.[3]

Zhuangzi's notion of interchangeability and transcendence takes on new meaning in Dai Wangshu's quatrain. In the image of the butterfly, the binary oppositions of transience and eternity, frailty and immortality, are resolved. The interaction between the butterfly and the tiny flower is symbolic of the relationship between imagination and the world. No matter how insignificant or easily overlooked a thing of beauty may be, the poetic imagination never fails to perceive and respond to it. Contained in a miniature form, Dai's conviction of the power of the imagination, the power of poetry, is itself embodied in the butterfly—frail yet indestructible, short-lived yet eternal. For Dai, and many other poets who were physically destroyed in the turbulent times of modern China, the poem may well be read as a testimonial to the lasting beauty of their poetry.

Modern Poetry could not explore the new medium without new form. Although Hu Shi is usually credited with the revolution of poetic language, his absolute separation of Modern Chinese and Classical Chinese was misleading. In my view, Hu's greatest accomplishment lies in the revolution in form. Without freedom from traditional forms with their rigid rules, the potentials of the modern vernacular as the poetic medium could not be realized.

The formal revolution clearly illustrates the experimental spirit of Modern Chinese Poetry to "make it new." The first collection of Modern Poetry, by Hu Shi, published in 1920, is appropriately titled *Experiments* 嘗試集. In the May Fourth period, it was poetry more than any other genre that played the role of the avant-garde on the cultural scene. In postwar Taiwan, poetry spearheaded the modernist movement with the founding of the Modernist School 現代派 by Ji Xian 紀弦 (b. 1913) in February 1956. The Modern Poetry Debate in Taiwan in 1972–74 was an immediate precursor to the Nativist Literature Movement 鄉土文學運動 in 1977–79, which changed the course of Taiwan literature for decades to come. In the late 1970s and early 1980s, it was underground poetry and Misty Poetry that ushered in a renaissance in post-Mao China and heralded the Root-Seeking Movement in the mid-1980s.

With complete freedom in form, modern poets have engaged in theoretical discussions about the relation between form and content. What is the rationale for using, say, the quatrain instead of the couplet? Why divide a poem into stanzas at all? What about the ever-vexing question of prose poetry? Is it poetry or prose? In the early 1920s to the late 1930s, a variety of foreign forms was introduced into China. Lu Zhiwei 陸志韋 (1894–1970) and Zhu Xiang 朱湘 (1904–33) were among the pioneers to experiment with them. Wen Yiduo advanced the ideal of "tailoring the clothes to the body" 相體裁衣, meaning to give a poem a clear sense of structure while simultaneously relating it organically to the content. Besides the Crescent School 新月派 of which Wen was a leader, other poets such as Wu Xinghua 吳興華 (1921–66) and Bian Zhilin 卞之琳 (1910–2000) also experimented with regular forms of their own making. Finally, in the mid-1950s, the Modernist School in Taiwan advocated the notion that "content determines form."

With the old rules governing rhyme, tones, the number of lines in a poem, and the number of characters in a line abandoned, poets could begin to explore the modern vernacular to its fullest potential as the new medium. Although free verse has been the most common form from 1917 onward, Modern Chinese Poetry employs a wide range of forms, from various regular forms to prose poetry and concrete poetry. The regular forms are either borrowed from other literary traditions, such as the sonnet, or from modified traditional Chinese forms, such as the modern "quatrain" 絕句. Although the sonnet from the West is no less restrictive than traditional Chinese forms, it is rather freely adapted by Chinese poets. Prose poetry and concrete poetry are distinctly modern forms. The first has established a minor tradition of its own in Modern Chinese Poetry, from Lu Xun 魯迅 to Shang Qin 商禽 (b. 1930), Su Shaolian 蘇紹連 (b. 1949), and Liu Kexiang 劉克襄 (b. 1957) (Yeh 2000b). The first concrete poem in Chinese was probably "The Second Obituary of the World" 第二次世界訃聞 by the Hong Kong poet Ou Wai'ou 鷗外鷗 (1911–95). The first six lines of the poem read, in English:

WAR!
WAR!
WAR!
WAR!
WAR!
WAR! WAR!

(Ou 1998)

By making the word much larger in lines 4–6 and repeating it twice in line 6, the poet created the visual effect of the approaching war as well as an oral simulation of the newspaper boy hawking the special issue on the street. Written in early 1937, the poem presaged the coming of the full-blown War of Resistance against Japan.

A more recent example of concrete poetry is Chen Li's 陳黎 (b. 1954) "War Symphony" 戰爭交響曲, written in July 1995:

兵兵兵兵兵兵兵兵兵兵兵兵兵兵兵兵兵兵兵兵兵兵
兵兵兵兵兵兵兵兵兵兵兵兵兵兵兵兵兵兵兵兵兵兵
兵兵兵兵兵兵兵兵兵兵兵兵兵兵兵兵兵兵兵兵兵兵
兵兵兵兵兵兵兵兵兵兵兵兵兵兵兵兵兵兵兵兵兵兵
兵兵兵兵兵兵兵兵兵兵兵兵兵兵兵兵兵兵兵兵兵兵
兵兵兵兵兵兵兵兵兵兵兵兵兵兵兵兵兵兵兵兵兵兵
兵兵兵兵兵兵兵兵兵兵兵兵兵兵兵兵兵兵兵兵兵兵
兵兵兵兵兵兵兵兵兵兵兵兵兵兵兵兵兵兵兵兵兵兵
兵兵兵兵兵兵兵兵兵兵兵兵兵兵兵兵兵兵兵兵兵兵
兵兵兵兵兵兵兵兵兵兵兵兵兵兵兵兵兵兵兵兵兵兵
兵兵兵兵兵兵兵兵兵兵兵兵兵兵兵兵兵兵兵兵兵兵
兵兵兵兵兵兵兵兵兵兵兵兵兵兵兵兵兵兵兵兵兵兵
兵兵兵兵兵兵兵兵兵兵兵兵兵兵兵兵兵兵兵兵兵兵
兵兵兵兵兵兵兵兵兵兵兵兵兵兵兵兵兵兵兵兵兵兵
兵兵兵兵兵兵兵兵兵兵兵兵兵兵兵兵兵兵兵兵兵兵
兵兵兵兵兵兵兵兵兵兵兵兵兵兵兵兵兵兵兵兵兵兵

兵兵兵兵兵兵兵乒乒乓乓兵兵乒乓兵兵兵乒乒兵
兵兵兵乒兵兵乒乒乓乒乓兵乒乒兵兵乓兵兵乒乓兵
兵乒乒兵兵乒乓乒乓乒乓乓乒乒乒乒乓兵乒乒乓兵
兵乒乒乒乒乒乓乒兵兵乒乓乓乒乓乒乓乒乒乒兵兵

兵兵兵兵兵兵兵兵兵兵兵兵兵兵兵兵兵兵兵兵兵兵兵兵
兵兵兵兵兵兵兵兵兵兵兵兵兵兵兵兵兵兵兵兵兵兵兵兵
兵兵兵兵兵兵兵兵兵兵兵兵兵兵兵兵兵兵兵兵兵兵兵兵
兵兵兵兵兵兵兵兵兵兵兵兵兵兵兵兵兵兵兵兵兵兵兵兵
兵兵兵兵兵兵兵兵兵兵兵兵兵兵兵兵兵兵兵兵兵兵兵兵
兵兵兵兵兵兵兵兵兵兵兵兵兵兵兵兵兵兵　兵兵兵　兵
兵兵　兵兵兵兵　兵　兵　　兵兵　　兵兵　　兵兵
兵兵　　兵兵　兵　兵　兵　兵　兵兵兵　　兵　兵
　兵兵　兵　兵兵　兵　　兵　兵　兵　兵　　　兵
兵　　　兵兵　　　　兵　　　　兵　　兵　兵
　兵　　兵　　　兵　　　　兵　　　　兵
　　兵　　　　　兵　　　　　　兵

丘丘丘丘丘丘丘丘丘丘丘丘丘丘丘丘丘丘丘丘丘丘丘丘
丘丘丘丘丘丘丘丘丘丘丘丘丘丘丘丘丘丘丘丘丘丘丘丘
丘丘丘丘丘丘丘丘丘丘丘丘丘丘丘丘丘丘丘丘丘丘丘丘
丘丘丘丘丘丘丘丘丘丘丘丘丘丘丘丘丘丘丘丘丘丘丘丘
丘丘丘丘丘丘丘丘丘丘丘丘丘丘丘丘丘丘丘丘丘丘丘丘
丘丘丘丘丘丘丘丘丘丘丘丘丘丘丘丘丘丘丘丘丘丘丘丘
丘丘丘丘丘丘丘丘丘丘丘丘丘丘丘丘丘丘丘丘丘丘丘丘
丘丘丘丘丘丘丘丘丘丘丘丘丘丘丘丘丘丘丘丘丘丘丘丘
丘丘丘丘丘丘丘丘丘丘丘丘丘丘丘丘丘丘丘丘丘丘丘丘
丘丘丘丘丘丘丘丘丘丘丘丘丘丘丘丘丘丘丘丘丘丘丘丘
丘丘丘丘丘丘丘丘丘丘丘丘丘丘丘丘丘丘丘丘丘丘丘丘
丘丘丘丘丘丘丘丘丘丘丘丘丘丘丘丘丘丘丘丘丘丘丘丘
丘丘丘丘丘丘丘丘丘丘丘丘丘丘丘丘丘丘丘丘丘丘丘丘
丘丘丘丘丘丘丘丘丘丘丘丘丘丘丘丘丘丘丘丘丘丘丘丘
丘丘丘丘丘丘丘丘丘丘丘丘丘丘丘丘丘丘丘丘丘丘丘丘
丘丘丘丘丘丘丘丘丘丘丘丘丘丘丘丘丘丘丘丘丘丘丘丘

(Chen 2003: 102–04)

In accordance with the typical structure of a symphony, the poem is divided into three stanzas of identical size (24 × 16 = 384 spaces). The first stanza is composed of 384 *bing*'s 兵 ("soldiers"). The perfect rectangle evokes the magnificence of a military formation. The second stanza introduces irregularities embodied by two new characters *ping* 乒 and *pong* 乓. Two onomatopoeic words suggesting gunshots, the characters differ from *bing* only in that they have one stroke less. The missing stroke in the lower part of *bing* makes *ping* and *pong* look like soldiers with missing limbs. The blank spaces where the *bing*'s are in the first stanza evoke the disappearance of some soldiers. The splendid formation that we saw in the first stanza is now broken up, and as the battle goes on, more and more soldiers are missing. The last stanza returns to perfect regularity. Now all the *bing*'s in the first stanza are replaced by *qiu*'s 丘

("mound"). A pictograph, the character *qiu* evokes graves to which all the soldiers belong in the end.

What distinguishes this poem from most concrete poems is the ingenious combination and mutual reinforcement of visual and aural effects. Not only do the characters *bing*, *ping-pong*, and *qiu* give a visual representation of the loss of lives in war, but their sounds also contribute to the structure and meaning of the poem. In the first stanza, the 384 *bing*'s create a bright and uplifting, yet at the same time hard and intimidating, string of sounds. It conjures up the picture of soldiers marching off bravely. In the second stanza, the gunshots become fewer and fewer, farther and farther apart as we move down the lines, which literally captures the diminishing of fighting soldiers and the winding down of the battle. All three characters—*bing*, *ping*, *pong*—are open sounds. In contrast, *qiu* in the last stanza is a closed, aspirated sound; pronouncing it literally takes longer than the open sounds in the first two stanzas. While the pictograph *qiu* visually resembles a mound, it is also a homonym of "autumn" 秋, the season of decline that is associated, in traditional Chinese culture, with change and impermanence, and the concomitant sense of sadness. On Chen Li's CD, when he reads the last stanza of the poem, he slows down considerably and, in protracting the sound *qiu*, imitates the whistling wind. Thus, the last stanza not only visually represents row after row of graves but also aurally suggests the wind blowing across the graveyard. Progressing from marching soldiers to wounded soldiers to soldiers in their wind-blown graves, "War Symphony" makes a powerful statement against war.

Modern Poetry embodies a new paradigm that is radically different from the revered paradigm of Classical Poetry. The modernity of Modern Poetry derives from interrelated intrinsic and extrinsic factors. Externally, the transformation of Chinese society and culture since the early twentieth century has resulted in the marginalization of poetry. Having lost the broader social and cultural import that Classical Poetry enjoyed for centuries, Modern Poetry is, above all, an individual creative act. Rather than writing for other members of a sophisticated literary community with similar training and shared tastes, the Modern Poet is a creator of original works that, through the modern publishing mechanism, are read by unknown readers from diverse backgrounds. This condition perhaps accounts for the new convention of the Modern Poet invoking the Goddess of Poetry 詩神 or the Muse 繆斯, an invocation that did not exist in Classical Poetry and is clearly a borrowing from the West.

Born in the Literary Revolution of 1917, Modern Poetry was the culmination of discontent with the status quo of Classical Poetry and attempts to reform it that had begun in the late nineteenth century. Going beyond previous efforts, Modern Poetry as theorized by Hu Shi sought to revolutionize the language as well as the form. But I hope even the few examples that we have seen above make it clear that, as a conscious break with Classical Poetry, Modern Poetry does not dismiss Tradition as a significant resource, just as it draws freely on other literary traditions of the world. In practice, Modern Poets do not write *against* Tradition but *through* Tradition; they reappropriate Tradition in imaginative ways, finding new meanings and bringing forth new insights from therein. In a sense, it is not even a choice whether or not to engage in a dialogue with Tradition because the modern vernacular is always already fused with classical Chinese. One cannot fully appreciate the beauty and ingenuity of Modern Poetry without a deep understanding of Classical Poetry, as the two are mutually defined.

Why do I enjoy reading Modern Poetry? A simple answer would be: because it is not Classical Poetry. This by no means suggests that I do not enjoy reading Classical Poetry just as much; however, we should "give to Caesar what belongs to Caesar, and to God what belongs to God." To compare Classical and Modern Poetry is, as the saying goes, to compare apples and oranges. One does not read Modern Poetry to find a Li Bo or Du Fu because there can never be a Li Bo or Du Fu in the twenty-first century, just as one cannot find a Dai Wangshu or Chen Li in Tang poetry. The difficulty for many readers of Modern Poetry derives from the fact that they bring to it long-established expectations inherited from Classical Poetry, with which they are far more familiar, such as rhyme, parallelism, formal symmetry, condensed imagery, recurrent themes and moods. For many Chinese readers, the process of acculturation into Modern Poetry is far from complete. However, as Modern Poetry gets more and more integrated into the curriculum in the Chinese education system, as it exerts a greater influence, through its best works, on the Chinese language, and as it becomes more and more available in multimedia, including the Internet, we can be reasonably optimistic about the future of Modern Poetry.

From a historical perspective, Modern Poetry has established itself as a new branch of Chinese poetry that is parallel to, not in competition with, various branches of Classical Poetry. Classical Poetry, especially in the *shi* and *ci* 詞 modes, continues to be written in modern times. In recent years, poetry clubs and journals devoted to the writing of Classical Poetry have mushroomed in mainland China. Some Modern poets and critics are worried that the trend may further marginalize Modern Poetry. As a longtime student of Modern Poetry, I do not share their concern. Rather, I agree with Hu Shi who declared some eighty years ago: every age has its own literature. With its inexhaustible ability to express, in contemporary language and unlimited forms, human experience in all its richness, Modern Poetry is the "living literature" of our time.

Notes

1. I use "Modern Poetry" or "Modern Chinese Poetry" to refer to poetry written in modern vernacular Chinese in nontraditional forms and I use "Classical Poetry" to refer to poetry written in classical Chinese in traditional forms. These terms designate the genres rather than periods of time, as Classical Poetry has been written throughout the twentieth century and is still being written in the twenty-first century.
2. Interest in translated literature is not limited to Chinese poets, of course; it has been prevalent in China throughout the twentieth century. To this day, translation is a standard feature in Chinese journals and literary supplements to newspapers. In sharp contrast to North America or Europe, translations make up a significant percentage of literary works and often top the bestseller lists in the Chinese-speaking world, whether mainland China, Hong Kong, or Taiwan.
3. It is interesting to note that in ancient Greece the human soul is represented as a butterfly. It cannot be ruled out that Dai Wangshu fused the Daoist and Ancient Greek meanings of the image here.

Part I

Contemporary Poetry of Taiwan

Chapter Three

Zheng Chouyu and the Search for Voice in Contemporary Chinese Lyric Poetry

Christopher Lupke

Despite the paucity of scholarship on him in English, Zheng Chouyu 鄭愁予 (b. 1933; penname of Zheng Wentao 鄭文韜) is a poet of considerable renown in Chinese-speaking communities. In Taiwan, for example, Zheng's broad popularity is second to none. His was ranked first by far in a poll of "classic" contemporary poetic works conducted by the *United Daily News* 聯合報 in the late 1990s (Chen Yizhi 1999: 507). Considering that many of his best-known poems were written forty to fifty years ago, this survey exhibits impressive longevity. The poet and critic Jiao Tong 焦桐 adds that the well-known selection of Zheng's poems *Zheng Chouyu Shiji* 鄭愁予詩集 "is the most pervasive, best selling, and by far most influential collection of modern poetry in Taiwan" (Jiao 1999: 286). Originally published by Hongfan in 1979, the book has seen over sixty reprints. Another selection, several individual poetry collections, and a second volume to the Hongfan publication compete with each other, but all sell well. His verse is anthologized in textbooks, and musicians such as Li Taixiang 李太祥 have set it to music. In mainland China, Zheng enjoys some popular appeal as well and is known by most educated people. The scholarship in Taiwan on Zheng is voluminous. Mainland scholarship is considerably less, as one would imagine, but serious attention there has nonetheless been devoted to his work.

What is the source of this magnetism? While the average reader may not be conscious of this fact in the historical development of modern Chinese verse, Zheng Chouyu occupies a pivotal position as someone who is traditional and conservative and yet at the same time radical and innovative. The poet-scholar Yang Mu 楊牧 (C.H. Wang), arguing that Zheng is "the most Chinese of Chinese poets," identifies Zheng's ability to forge a poetic style that is both modern (a term virtually synonymous with "Western") and Chinese, a feat, he contends in the introduction to a collection of Zheng's, that was unprecedented before Zheng emerged on the poetry scene (Yang 1974: 11). Few would try to make the case that his poetry is not unique and none can gainsay his crucial place in Chinese literary history. The sustained attraction that his work holds can be attributed to the fact that his verse, particularly of the early period, represents a return to the vivid imagery reminiscent of traditional Chinese poetry combined with an adherence to the internal rhyme schemes of modern Western free verse, tightly crafted yet unregimented prosodic structure. Zheng is among a distinguished coterie of émigré poets who emerged in Taiwan in the decade after the War of Resistance, certainly one of its most important exponents precisely for his enchanting ability to rescue the lyrical, the melodious, and the musical for modern Chinese verse:

Error

 I'm coming over from the
  Yangtze Valley
  That seasonable countenance-
  like lotus blossoms ready
  to fall
 No east wind, the willow catkins
  aren't flying
 Your heart is like a tiny,
  lonely town
 Just like the cobblestone street
  approaching evening
 Muted footsteps, March's
  spring blinds aren't opening
 Your heart is a tiny, tightly
  closed shutter

 The clickety clack of my
  horse's hooves is a lovely error
 I'm not returning, I'm a
  passerby

錯誤

 我打江南走過
  那等在季節裏的容顏如蓮花的開落
東風不來, 三月的柳絮不飛
你底心如小小的寂寞的城
恰若青石的街道向晚
跫音不響, 三月的春帷不揭
你底心是小小的窗扉緊掩

我達達的馬蹄是美麗的錯誤
我不是歸人, 是個過客。。。。。。

(Zheng [1954] 2003: 8)

Although "Error," so famous it is said to be "seared on everyone's lips" 膾炙人口 (Jiao 1999: 289; He 1981: 257), is written neither according to the regulated idiom of traditional Chinese prosody nor to established conventions from the Western tradition such as iambic pentameter with systematic end rhyme as practiced by many poets of the Republican Era, it nevertheless is mellifluous and resonant. Its audible merit rests in the poet's effort to forge a new style of verse for modern Chinese poetry, a style that eschews the strictures of traditional Chinese poetry while not steadfastly resorting to those of Western verse—in short, a style that retains both rhythms and rhymes and yet shuns fixed structures: free verse. The reader can detect rhythmic echoes in lines one and four of the middle stanza through the double repetition of one word: *bu—bulai* and *buxiang*; *bufei* and *bujie*, as well as the repetition of *sanyue* and the particle *de*. In key elements of the two lines, the vocabulary is varied slightly so as to minutely vary the meaning: *dongfeng* with *qiongyin*, *liuxu* with *chunwei* and *fei* with *jie*. Even in these instances there is syllabic parallel. The result is verse without a rigid rhyme scheme or meter, something that splits the difference between straightforward narrative and highly structured poetry, something that works for the Chinese language without being procrustean—an easy commerce, as Eliot would call it, between the old and the new. The second and fifth lines also provide an audible parallel that solidifies the sense of a unified rhythm: *nidixin* and *xiaoxiaode* are both repeated, and in the first half of the lines, these phrases would be completely repetitive if it were not for the substitution of *ru* "to resemble" with *shi* "to be." The final four syllables of each are completely different although the imagery, as I will discuss in a moment, is complementary. As Julia Lin has stated: "this lyric abounds in harmonious vowels (both mute and open), rhythmic parallels, repetition of key sounds of words—verbal plays that Cheng customarily employs to obtain an echoing effect that further enhances the haunting musicality of the lines" (Lin 1985b: 4–5).

This leaves us with line three, the pivotal line between the first two and the final two, which are parallel. This middle line serves as a stanzaic caesura (what Julie Chiu calls a "'swing' line" 2005: 210), a break in the rhythm, as it is neither paralleled elsewhere in the poem nor does it remotely resemble the rhythm of the other four lines of this stanza. *Qiaruo qingshi de jiedao xiang wan* "Just like the cobblestone street approaching evening" is short, simple, direct, and assonant. It is a conceit that underscores the wistful tone of the poem even as it refers back to the literal imagery of the traveler entering the village. It is nightfall and it is best not to be out on the streets but rather at home or at least looking for a place to sleep. For the traveler, however, the spring curtains will not open and the shutters are tightly shut, creating an unwelcoming atmosphere, setting a tone of isolation, loneliness and, by extension, exile. But all is not lost, for there is yearning, and with yearning hope remains. The yearning is found in the perspective of the speaker who is addressing some unknown second person.

The central stanza in the poem is framed by a couplet before and one after it. The interaction of these two framing couplets with the central stanza offers a touch of irony and pathos and compels us to think beyond the physical setting described in the central stanza. The crux of the poem hinges on the reversal of expectation brought about in the last two lines. The poem seems to develop the voice of a returning speaker addressing his (presumably a male) feelings toward his lover. The final couplet, however, reveals that the speaker is just a passerby, not the one who is returning. This reversal of expectation is thrust upon the one presumed to be waiting, an erroneous belief that is encapsulated in perhaps the most famous oxymoron in modern Chinese poetry: "a lovely error" *meili de cuowu*. The error has been concretized in both image and sound not by describing the reaction of the person waiting, but by projecting it outward into the objective correlative of what she sees and hears: "the clickety-clack of my horse's hooves" *wo dada de mati*. Why would this error be lovely? There are two reasons for this, one literal and one allegorical: first, the case of mistaken identity was based on a yearning for the one who is absent and is thus an indication of the separation of two lovers; second, the error therefore is also emblematic of the fracture of Chinese society, of the diaspora in which the author finds himself, away from home and unable to return, even though his thoughts for home endure. This persistence is articulated through the allegory of a man returning home from war or from traveling business, the sort of image one finds, for example, in the "Nineteen Ancient Poems" 古詩十九首. The notion of alienation or exile is also manifested in the use of the verb "*da*" 打 in the first line—我打江南走過—meaning "from." The disconcerting element here is that "*da*" is a colloquialism usually used in northern China, yet here it pertains to a place in the south—an instance of regional catachresis. That there is an abrupt shift in subject between the two framing couplets and the central stanza, the subject in the framing couplets being first person while in the central stanza it is second person, accentuates the disorienting feeling of mistaken identity and the sense of deracination. The perplexing image of the "lovely error" conjures notions of the political disjuncture of China after the Communist Liberation as well as of the cultural discontinuity between traditional Chinese literature and modern, notably with respect to poetry. The articulation of this discontinuity in an innovative style of verse signifies a new age of poetry in the Chinese language, a new mode of expression even as the content of this expression spells exile.

Zheng Chouyu's poetry is often described as being lyrical. But what does it mean to be "lyrical"? Lyrical, from the word lyre, denotes musical. As noted above, Zheng has been instrumental in injecting a sense of the musical into modern Chinese literature. "'[L]yric,'" as David Lindley argues, "is held to apply to poems employing a first-person speaker, and, by extension, to indicate a preoccupation with the expression of individual feeling or emotion" (Lindley 1985: 2). Lyrical poetry, like much of Zheng Chouyu's own corpus, tends to be succinct. Helen Vendler has argued that the unitary subject of the lyric is so powerful and so crisply worded that one is tempted to read the lyric poem over and over until the reader virtually assumes the voice of the speaker in the poem. Thus, in the lyric, the reader is no longer a reader "but an utterer" (Vendler 1995: xi). Fredric Jameson's reinter-pretation of Baudelaire's poetry as emblematic of a new phase in capitalism, and thus as a new notion of the sublime, affords us some useful tools in connecting the highly aestheticized and near eremitic atmosphere of Zheng Chouyu's lyricism with a profound sense of the political and historical (Jameson 1985: 247–263). For Zheng Chouyu, the economistic reading that Jameson applies to Baudelaire may not be so relevant, but surely submerged in the suggestive stanzas of Zheng's laconic poetry lurks a strong element of political upheaval, of histori-cal tumult. This tumult has called into question the very integrity of the Chinese nation state in the middle of the twentieth century. But even as his poetry articulates in repressed and oblique ways the upheaval of multiple wars and an exodus from mainland Chinese to the impermanent island asylum of Taiwan, it also is the historical product of a new dispensation. Hardly without its own brand of polit-ical repression, this new dispensation nevertheless afforded select intellectuals in Taiwan in the early 1950s, preoccupied with neither upholding nor challenging this nascent cold war ideology, a carefully proscribed space within which to stretch their stylistic wings and carve out a totally new arena for "pure" literature. With a freshly brewing war in Korea, a "surrogate" war between the United States and the PRC, Taiwan became an indispensable geopolitical pawn in this cold war. Within Taiwan, the Chiang Kai-shek regime was afforded relative carte blanche to place a lock on political power. Within this framework, however, there was room for experimentation of a literary nature. Thus, in Taiwan, the time was ripe for the practitioners of a mature Modernism—the sort that eventually was exhibited by Zheng Chouyu and others such as Luo Fu and Ya Xian (also represented in this volume)—to take the fully digested components of the previous half century's formalistic trials and experiments and begin creating sophisticated verse in various ways, depending on the style of each. Zheng Chouyu was at least one of the people for whom it may be said—he was the right person in the right place at the right time. Part of this is certainly some sort of innate poetic gift that only a few possess—access to a muse, if you will. Part of it was another sort of access: access to high quality education (as the son of a prominent educator in the military) (Zhang Meifang 2001: 257). And part of it was the historical milieu that allowed for relative peace at the center of a global storm that still raged, a storm that gave those in power the confidence that Washington DC would turn a blind eye to the excesses of political repression deemed necessary in the ultimate name of the "Free World." But while others preferred to serve as the collective mouthpiece for this sort of worldview, most of the Modernist poets (in various camps) elected to ply their own literary trade. It would be naive to assume there was no political tincture to their work. One must remember that poetry is a medium nicely suited to understatement. The romance and beauty of the exile motif in Zheng's verse, for example, is never without its melancholy edge, and this melancholia had to have its source. In the poets' views, exile in Taiwan in the 1950s was nothing to crow about. Thus, while the critics tend to focus on the important formal innovations that Zheng's lyrical style has come to epitomize, it is not likely that his poetry could have manifested itself without the unique set of historical circumstances in which it did.

In the past twenty-five years, the conception of the lyric has undergone considerable scrutiny and reevaluation in contemporary American, mainly poststructuralist, criticism. The lyric—given its reliance on the performative capacity of language over and above, to some extent, its referential capacity, its relative density and terseness, and its invitation to close textual reading—has been one of the favorite sons of Modernism and, by extension, of analysis informed by the epistemological stance of New Criticism. The modern Western lyric virtually dictates that one dissect it with careful attention to form and formal considerations. In an article written in the 1980s surveying poststructural methods of parsing the lyric, Jonathan Culler, at the time something of a postmodern gadfly in U.S. academic circles, contends that the modern lyric goes far beyond the bounds of its formal density, threatening, in fact, to undo itself even as it is in the process of constructing itself. The lure of the lyric to compel the reader into close analysis is a sort of trap, for, as Culler states,

> Our inclinations [are to] to use notions of unity and thematic coherence to exclude possibilities that are manifestly awakened by the language and that pose a problem. (Culler 1985: 54)

It is in the realm of these problems posed by the lyric where the difficulty of their structure as a literary unit and the challenges to interpretation manifest themselves. It is not that the lyric is uniquely suited to this sort of analysis, which would be the New Critical position, or that such interpretation is completely anathema or unsustainable, but that it precisely subverts what in the first place it entices us to do. Moreover, within the conundrums, the impasses into which verse leads us, the lyric's true worth is finally apprehended. Others, such as Barbara Johnson, have argued that the modern French lyric, beginning in the latter half of the nineteenth century, privileged a new incarnation of intertextual relations between the poets of the time, considered quite radical, and the oppressiveness of their literary forebears. Paul de Man, reading the lyrics of Rilke, focuses our attention on the fact that the lyric in a very basic sense can simply be babble—"poetry wagering all on the mastery of sound" (Johnson 1985: 46). While this assertion may seem sophomoric, de Man is in fact being quite sincere in his argument, for what the resistance to referentiality fosters in the reading experience is, in fact, a sort of receding mirage of endless imperfect interpretations that never deliver us to the ultimate interpretation. And it is in this deferring of the ultimate meaning of the work that the essence of the lyric may be discovered. From the accumulated re-reading of the theory of the lyric, we can distil several trends in contemporary accounts of it: the idea that lyrics create riddles that beg to be resolved but ultimately defy resolution; the fact that this paradoxical tendency results from a combination of the performativity of lyrical language and the intertextuality of its semantic side; that this radical intertexuality ironically then leads to a profound self-referentiality; and that one can therefore not understand the poem from the point of view of simply symbol but must instead trace the complex lines of allegory at work both in individual lyrics and in the lyrical network that some poets establish through groups of poems whether they are closely associated or whether their association is looser and more a matter of the reader connecting the dots.

For Zheng Chouyu, the significance of the lyric is found in the indeterminacy of imagery that undermines the reader's ability to establish a sustained and fixed notion in the mind of a fully concrete location in space. Zheng's imagery evokes alienation and exile and, by extension, nostalgia. The lyrical is what conveys that sense of living outside the nation. In the aftermath of war and in the midst of political division, the lyric emerged for Zheng Chouyu as the only salvageable mode of articulation precisely when narrative became an impractical alternative for communicating the historical and political situation of modern China and Taiwan. The 1950s fiction in Taiwan was largely ideological or romantic in nature, with larger forces of the age overwhelming realistic description. Only the lyric—with its elliptical qualities of half music, half referential language, part discursive construct and part aesthetic object—was suitable for the terrifying reality of the political predicament of writers of the Chinese diaspora in the mid-century. With cold war–ideology tending to dictate narrative modes of representation, Zheng Chouyu's lyrics flowed freely and vividly and became an immediate and lasting sensation in Taiwan.

The sensational, or more precisely, sublime sentiment that Zheng's lyricism elicited stems from the underspecified yet unmistakably present anxiety over political exile. As a northerner, Zheng Chouyu is twice exiled both from mainland China and eventually, at least spiritually, from Taiwan or any Chinese cultural milieu. His poem "In Dreamland" 夢土上 crystallizes this sentiment of geographical displacement through its discordant mixture of images and an aura of hopeless relationships:

The forest is already at my feet,
  my cottage is still ahead,
The fence is in sight, but with a
  turn it's obscured again.
Someone should be at the
  door waiting for me,
Waiting for me to bring new
  books, and the repaired zither,
But all I've brought is a
  jug of wine,
Because the person waiting
  for me has long since left.

Clouds are in my road,
  and on my clothes,
I reside in an indistinct thought,
A high elevation without
  birdsongs, and no blossoms,
I reside in a cold, cold
  dreamland . . .
The forest is already at my
  feet, my cottage is still ahead,
The fence is in sight, but with
  a turn it's obscured again.

森林已在我腳下了, 我底小屋仍在上頭,
那籬笆已見到, 轉彎卻又隱去了。
該有一個人倚門等我,
等我帶來的新書, 和修理好了的琴,
而我只帶來一壺酒,
因等我的人已離去。

雲在我的路上, 在我底衣上,
我在一個隱隱的思念上,
高處沒有鳥喉, 沒有花蕊,
我在一片冷冷的夢土上。。。
森林已在我腳下了, 我底小屋仍在上頭,
那籬笆已見到, 轉彎卻又隱去了。

(Zheng [1954] 2003: 10)

Missed opportunities, ships passing in the night, often comprise the imagery of Zheng Chouyu's lyrical verse. In this case, the bizarre quality of this bucolic setting is that it affords no sense of comfort or refuge from the city, as might be expected, but rather indicates a difference in expectation between the speaker and the other figure mentioned in the poem. There is also a problem with causation and therefore with the logic of the action as well, as, on the one hand, the speaker states that the person who *should* be leaning against the door, waiting for this bearer of new books and repaired zither, has already gone. On the other hand, though, he then cites the reason for bringing the jug of wine instead of the books and zither as the person's departure. How is it that the person waiting for him to bring these items has already left, yet prior to this the speaker has decided to bring back wine instead *because* this person is no longer waiting? The illogic lends itself to the dreamlike quality of the poem first signaled in its title. Also like a dream, the intermittent indistinct quality of the fence, indicating the border of the home, first appears in sight and then not: 那籬笆已見到, 轉彎卻又隱去了. Fences and walls in Chinese culture signify the border of one's home; it is highly unlikely for a home to not have one if economics is not an obstacle. And if we can extrapolate and think of the interpretation of this poem in relation to the Chinese nation-state for a moment, we will note that the character for nation 國 is a walled-in undefined area with the inside element of the character 或 meaning chaos. It is the circumscription of *huo* that transforms chaos into the nation. I will return to this point.

The entire setting for this poem is ethereal—the speaker finds himself enshrouded in mist: 雲在我底路上, 在我底衣上. The natural setting does not afford a sense of the bucolic, for there are no sounds from birds, no idyllic imagery. The scene is not inviting but mystifying. The choice of classical diction, such as "blossom" 花蕾, evokes a wistful nostalgia for a bygone elegance, but this invocation of bygone elegance ironically accentuates the fact that it cannot be recovered. Another logical reversal is the speaker's statement that "I occupy an indistinct thought" 我在一個隱隱的思念上. This again appears to test the bounds of logic, as the speaker should be the one dreaming, yet from this line it seems that he is actually the object of someone else's thoughts and dreams. It is one of those reversals where one first imagines oneself as the focus only to realize afterward that one is playing a supporting role. Indeed, it is a cold, cold dreamland in which the speaker dwells.

Zheng Chouyu will not be undone by the sort of melancholy that pervades "In Dreamland" and many other such poems in his corpus,

for one can also find playful and even joyous poems that are set in the
cold and dank confines of a water well in the winter. Wells in Chinese
discourse recur with great consistency and are associated with society,
as a community cannot exist without water. Water, traditionally,
comes from a well. In addition to the natural connection to sustenance, however, the well also conjures images of social oppression.
It often has been the chosen venue for exploited young women to
commit suicide, thus ending their own lives and literally poisoning the
well in the process. As we shall see after reading this next poem, the
well has another connotation in Chinese philosophy, one that is toyed
with in this jocund verse:

Skylight   天窗

Each night, the stars all   每夜, 星子們都來我的屋瓦上汲水
  come to my roof tiles to tap water   我在井底仰臥着, 好深的井啊
I'm flat on my back in the bottom
  of a well, a very deep well.   自從有了天窗
                                            就像親手揭開覆身的冰雪
Ever since I've had a skylight   - - - - - - 我是北地忍不住的春天
  It's like I scraped off the frozen
    snow cover myself   星子們都美麗, 分佔了循環著的七個夜,
  - - - - - - I'm the unstoppable   而那南方的藍色的小星呢?
    spring in the north   源自春泉的水已在四壁間蕩着
                                          那叮叮有聲的陶瓶還未垂下來。
The stars are all lovely, taking   啊, 星子們都美麗
  turns occupying the seven nights,   而在夢中也響著的, 祇有一個名字
And as for that southern, that   那名字, 自在得如流水。。。
  blue, that tiny star?
Harking from the spring brook,
  the water's lapping the walls
That clanging earthen
  urn hasn't been lowered yet.
Ah, the stars are all lovely
And echoing in my dreams,
  is just one name
That name, is carefree
  as the flowing water . . .

                                          (Zheng [1957] 2003: 120–121)

The operating cultural allusion in this poem is to the Daoist
philosopher Zhuangzi's metaphor of the "frog in a well" 井底之蛙
involving a frog who, because he lives in a well, can only see a cylinder of the sky. He then takes this cylinder to be the whole sky, thus
illustrating the narrow-mindedness of one who assumes that his individual frame of reference is universal. But in this modern use of frog in

a well, the speaker becomes the well denizen and the reference shifts to a different image in the Daoist palette, that of someone "carefree" 自在. This carefree tone (a laudable ideal by Daoist standards but not to be confused with Zhuangzi's frog metaphor) of embracing life and lingering in the luminescence of the star-filled night is an example of how vivid Zheng's imagination can be. But the memory of the well frog always lurks in the background of the learned reader's mind; thus, there is a sense of irony in the delusions of grandeur that the speaker exhibits as s/he boasts her/his power against the northern forces of nature. In contrast to "In Dreamland," the speaker in "Skylight," when faced with the freezing snow and water poured upon him, literally brushes it aside, equating himself with the more temperate weather of the spring that will soon return to defeat the cold of winter.

A more social and less contemplative poem is Zheng's "Uncouth Bar" 野店, which depicts the general state of rootlessness in an ironic and poignant manner. Julia Lin comments on the "nomadic" sensibility in this poem, suggesting it may be rooted in the transient conditions that Zheng, and many of his generation, had to endure while growing up in war-torn China (Lin 1985b: 2). Whether beneficial or not, early in his life, Zheng Chouyu was subjected to the trying experience of being forced to move with little notice and never being able to develop, much less maintain, a sense of home on either an individual/familial or a national level. This began with frequent relocations in mainland China, extended to his late teen years in Taiwan (a place he is inextricably associated with yet does not consider his home), and has ended with his immigration to the United States. But the nomadic lifestyle to which Lin refers, which Yang Mu (Yang 1974: 44) feels is more forcefully verbalized in Zheng's poetry than in any of the others of his age (unusual, since most of his peers shared this rootless upbringing), cannot simply be attributed to his own or his peers' personal experiences during the war years in China and subsequent retreat to Taiwan. Even though that may have provided the necessary foundation for this sensibility, the poem itself firmly places the burden on the shoulders of the poet in a rather perceptive prosopoetic query that sets the tone for the entire lyric:

Who is it that bequeathed the poet's trade	是誰傳下這詩人的行業
Hanging a lantern in the dusk	黃昏裏挂起一盞燈
Ah, they're here - - - - - -	啊，來了- - - - - -
Camels with fate dangling from the necks	有命運垂在頸間的駱駝
	有寂寞含在眼裏的旅客
	是誰挂起的這盞燈啊

Travelers with loneliness
  brimming in their eyes
Who is it hanging this lantern?
On the vast uncouth plane,
  a misty home
Smiling . . .
    A place with the low song
    of pine fire
    A place with warming wine
    and lamb meat
With people swapping their
  itinerant directions

曠野上，一個矇矓的家
微笑著。。。。。
　有松火低歌的地方啊
　有燒酒羊肉的地方啊
　有人交換著流浪的方向

(Zheng [1951] 2003: 22–23)

We should be impressed, as Shen Qi 沈奇 was (Shen 1995: 256–257), when we take into account that this poem was written before the poet finished college. The rhythmic and sonic qualities, which we will get to in a moment, are stunning enough. Equally astonishing is Zheng's brief meditation, at the beginning, on the career of the poet himself. Wondering who it is that bequeaths the poet's trade *chuanxia zhe shiren de hangye*, Zheng likens it to hanging a lantern in the dusk. The act of hanging a lantern in the coming evening is a futile one: one lantern cannot illuminate the night. Yet it is a deliberate act. The poet seeks to brighten the night while acknowledging the futility of it. And he continues to do it, as is underscored by the repetition of the line midway through the poem. This reiteration reinforces the lyrical quality of the poem, but it also implies that the deed is done again and again. The poet, in other words, is not discouraged by the futility of his actions. He repeats them regularly, just as he continues to boldly ply his trade as a poet in the face of the hopelessness of the world and human existence.

The repetition of key sounds creates balance in the poem and evokes a sense of rhythm, even though the poem follows no rigid prosodic rules. The poem is free verse, but in spite of that, it is actually highly symmetrical. Julie Chiu, in her structuralist analysis of Zheng's poetic lines, remarks on the poem's "metrical harmony" (Chiu 2005: 198). It is not solely the line lengths that create this harmony; the choice of diction is as integral to the uniformity as the lines. In my translation, for example, I attempt to replicate some of the rhythmic repetition of words such as *you* 有 by using the word "with" in the five places where *you* occurs in the original. The image of "swapping" in the final line contains two connotations: the sense of the meaninglessness of a particular direction, and by extension, the futility of human existence in general; and also the sense of conviviality, as in sharing stories over a campfire. Echoing the aforementioned discussion of the poet's trade, this depiction of the vagabonds swapping their directions is the kernel of Zheng's bittersweet cogitations over the vagaries of life (Cf. Wong 1979: 274–275). Zheng has moved beyond the specific personal trajectory of his own life, and beyond even the historical reality of Chinese society in the twentieth century, to opine upon the nature of the human condition in all its frailties. We are all vagabonds, Zheng would argue, in the sojourn of life. This point is accentuated by the bizarre image of the camels with "fate" hanging from their necks and the tearful loneliness of the travelers riding them. Why would the image be so somber if not for the uncultured, infirm and, perhaps, hostile territory in which our lonely lives are thrown? But Zheng is not despondent. He appeals to the rustic yet convivial image of the vagabonds cooking around a campfire, eating and drinking together in a makeshift attempt to create the semblance of home out in the wild, "uncouth" 野 terrain in which the poem is set.

The last poem under discussion was written slightly later than the previous four. This poem, entitled "Borderline Bar" 邊界酒店, extends to a degree themes from the previous poems. The previous poem refers to a bar. Drinking is clearly a favorite theme of Zheng's. That poem takes place in a remote, wild, or, as I have worded it, "uncouth" venue. "Borderline Bar," while not containing the conviviality of the former, nevertheless does feature drink and song. Yet the poem is even more solitary than early poems of Zheng that I have discussed, such as "Error." In "Error," there is evidence of at least a potential relationship between the speaker and an unknown "you," articulated in the form of an apostrophe. In this poem, however, there is no indication whatsoever of any kind of communion, be it between supposed lovers or between drinking companions. The poem is instead preoccupied with the issue of borders and border crossing. In traditional Chinese culture and thinking, borders are viewed as unsafe places. Political or State borders are naturally dangerous in that they can represent the delineation between two political entities that are antagonistic to one other. Even in friendly situations, the border nevertheless denotes the difference between one's territory and another's. Even if two such entities were on the best of terms, there must be some need for such a delimitation, and this international delimitation is generally dealt with cautiously. But more deeply than this, borders of all sorts exist on many different levels and are consistently treated with the utmost care in the Chinese reckoning, not just in the political sense. They represent not just concrete delineations, but transitional spaces that can be spiritual as well. For example, a typical home in northern China will have a wall around it. At the front door, there might be an inset wall so that nothing can proceed directly into the home. The area around the front doorway is dealt with in a very cautious and ritualistic manner. The reason for this is that the protected space within the home is relatively *yang* 陽 in contrast to the polluted *yin* 陰 of the exterior world. Anything could be creeping around out there. One must be not only physically on one's guard for what may enter, but spiritually as well. As China began thinking of itself as something larger than a patchwork of individual states, in the post-feudal Qin and early Han dynasties, it began to view itself as a large home and, therefore, took measures to consolidate a huge wall around itself, the Great Wall, for the same reasons that walls are built around houses. But walls themselves elicit an element of curiosity on the part of restless spirits such as Zheng Chouyu: the wayfarer who still pines for his homeland, as Yang Mu describes him (Yang 1974: 4–45):

The frontier earth in autumn halved
  under a common failing sun
On these abutting lands stand
  chrysanthemums, silent and sallow
And he came a long way to
  soberly down his drink
Beyond the window is alien land

What he wouldn't give to cross
  over, merely a step and he'd
  be longing
That lovely longing for home,
  only a glance of the hand away

Maybe he should just get drunk,
  that would be good enough
(He gladly lets the taxman
  take his due)

Or, maybe, he should belt
  out a tune
And not just stand there like
  those funereal mums
Just verging on the borderline,
  standing

秋天的疆土, 分界在同一個夕下
接壤處, 默立些黃菊花
而他打遠道來, 清醒著喝酒
窗外是異國

多想跨出去, 一步即鄉愁
那美麗的鄉愁, 伸手可觸及

或者, 就飲醉了也好
(他是熱心的納稅人)

或者, 將歌聲吐出
便不祇是立着像那雛菊
祇憑邊界立著

(Zheng [1965] 2003: 198–199)

Jiao Tong observes that the poem, while exposing the desire on the speaker's part for the nomadic existence, indicates that he "lacks the real power to become a drifter" (Jiao 1999: 290). The crux of the poem resides in the subject's ambivalence toward leaving his homeland, a venture that offers excitement and fresh opportunities but at the same time inevitably entails feelings of homesickness. There is tension in the imagery between stasis, as represented by the chrysanthemums (a flower associated with funerals), and action as shown by the fact that the subject has traveled a long way to get to this border crossing. There also is tension between the competing emotions behind "what he wouldn't give to . . ." 多想 and "longing [for home]" 鄉愁. That he turns to drink—itself an action of sorts, even if an action that allows one to attempt to escape from the realities one faces—underscores his ambivalence. To "soberly down his drink" 清醒著喝酒 is a pivotal oxymoron and indicates the complexity of the subject's emotions. Common sense dictates that one drinks precisely to leave a sober state, to blur one's perception and blunt one's senses. But in this case, the subject is clear-headed and wide awake. The subject cannot put aside what has gotten him this far or what the road ahead may entail. Of course, we know that he is a habitual drinker, as he is a willing taxpayer. Since alcohol at the time of writing was taxed onerously, this figure of speech became synonymous with heavy drinkers. The subject upbraids himself for not taking action, for not embarking on this new and perilous trip across the border. He entertains the idea that, like the lovely yet stationery chrysanthemums, he may hanker after adventure but drink or sing instead. The use of the chrysanthemums here is a wonderful pathetic fallacy as they "merely verge on the borderline, standing" 祇憑邊界立著. The image of the same sun being split 分界 highlights the fact that nature itself knows no such borders. It is humans that construct these artificial demarcations. The characteristic rhythmic quality of Zheng's is felt through the repetition, for example, of *huozhe* 或者 meaning "perhaps" or "or." Singing, like drinking, is an action, but not one that will garner concrete results. But just as we already know the subject enjoys his drink, we can assume by the poem itself that he loves the role of the bard, a minstrel of sorts. But singing is still an action of some kind, a creative action that is placed on par not just with drinking but with roaming as well. Looking back at the image of the chrysanthemums, we see that they not only just stand there, and in that sense come to symbolize the stationary, but they are silent as well. So there is some room for maneuver in contrast to complete stasis on the one hand and plunging forth across the border on the other. And it is in this space that the drinking and singing might occur.

Wai-leung Wong mentions this poem in an article that illustrates Zheng's intertextual relationship with traditional Chinese poetry, in particular Song *ci* 宋辭, illustrating the delicateness of Zheng's imagery and his ability to create modern images that retain an indebtedness to the poetic tradition (Wong 1979: 276–277). The "traditional" dimension to Zheng's poetry has been remarked upon by nearly all critics of Zheng's verse. But what Wong does better than most is, first, to isolate in a detailed way exactly how he is traditional, or how his poetry is related to the tradition; second, to establish a specific body of texts to which Zheng is particularly indebted, the Song lyric (though not to the exclusion of other traditional Chinese poetry); and, third, to articulate the subtle manner in which Zheng is beholden to his forebears. This last element of the argument is crucial, for Zheng must be beholden in such a way as not to replicate the forms or semantic properties of traditional poetry in a wholesale fashion, or he would not be a modern poet. Rather, what Zheng expresses in his own work are the sort of "patterns of rhetoric" to which Cynthia Chase refers in her discussion of intertextuality in the work of John Keats, the "viewless wings of poesy" on which the new forges forward while still utilizing the old (Chase 1985: 208–225). This intertextuality takes the form not so much of specified literal references to past poets as it does particular rhetorical styles of poetic structuring. In Keat's case, Chase argues, these are prosopopoeia and apostrophe (215–216 and passim). Wong is careful to convey how the "vocabulary and syntax" of Zheng's poetry "are unmistakably modern" (Wong 1979: 276), and that, although imagery may be derived in raw form from the ancients (a point also made by Yang Mu, see especially Yang 1974: 11, 15, 22–23, and 36–37), he shows how they are reworked in a modern mode.[1] In so doing, Wong demonstrates how Zheng was both traditional and radical at the same time, displaying a maturity of language that few Chinese poets up until mid-century had done. In other words, one way to understand Zheng's poetic oeuvre is by examining it as an extended straddling of the border between the traditional and the modern. It could be averred, therefore, that the relationship between tradition and modernity is another tempting but still risky border. Modern Chinese poetry was vociferously reviled in the first half of the twentieth century, and its practitioners tended to be the most culturally revolutionary intellectuals. (Hu Shi, for example, a doyen of the May Fourth movement, was the first to extensively propound vernacular poetry that assiduously avoided the trappings of traditional poetry.)

By the time of Zheng Chouyu, whose maturation coincided with the end of the civil war and the retreat of the Nationalists to Taiwan, modern poetry was ready for those who wished to venture back into the tradition without abandoning the vernacular quality of poetry that took a half century to establish. But the issue of the agony of influence from such a hallowed tradition necessitated a very gingerly approach to the employment of allusion. Such a border criss-crossing, if you will, which Zheng Chouyu has traveled upon, could easily have spoiled the effect of Zheng's tender imagery and his deftly wrought assonance, aspects that require not only the nostalgia that the tradition can provide but also the fluidity possible only in the contemporary vernacular. By the time "Borderline Bar" was written, Zheng had been engaging in this tightrope act for over fifteen years. Thus, on an allegorical, perhaps speculative, level, the poet may also be mulling this figurative breach. It would make sense that he would broach the issue of the relationship between modern and traditional poetry in his own work only in the most muted and implicit of ways. What one finds in Zheng's path-breaking lyricism, then, in his apostrophes to unknown ears and monologues on the life of the drifter, is another type of communication—a subterranean dialogue of sorts between the poet and his tradition. This dialogue lives in every line of verse and saturates all the diction. It simultaneously communicates and conceals the layers of tradition and the history that the poet has experienced, either personally or intellectually through acculturation, and situates him within the constellation of Chinese poets both ancient and modern.

What one discovers in the poetry of Zheng Chouyu, therefore, and what accounts for his lasting allure, is beauty in the sounds and visual imagery of his verse, verse that is not set to predictable end rhyme or rigid meter but follows the conventions of free verse—somewhere between the structured conventions of old and the limpid vernacular prose of the present. There is a sort of babble quality or resistance to precise interpretation that de Man spoke of, and yet one can almost read over the shoulder of the poet so that, with repeated readings, which poetry invites us to conduct, the reader becomes almost one with the voice of the poem or an "utterer," to use Helen Vendler's terms, of it. We note the sotto voce dialogue with the ancients that Cynthia Chase shows is common in the lyric and Wai-leung Wong demonstrates. In addition, we cannot forget the historical and overdetermined specificities that first provided the fertile ground on which Zheng has sewn his lyrical seed. Consistencies between Zheng's poems can be seen across a wide spectrum of his work, and each of the five poems examined in this chapter points to a kind of "dislocation," as the Chinese critic Shen Qi has termed it (Shen 1995: 247–249), that comes from the double diaspora in which the poet lives. Reading allegorically through his work does not ultimately unlock the door to the definitive meaning of each line, which still functions like a receding horizon before the road of interpretation, but it does help us understand the overall sentiment conveyed by his remarkable body of work.

Note

1. Yang notes in many cases how Zheng actually violates the rules of syntax by inverting word order (Yang 1974: 24) and of semantics by, for example, changing nouns into verbs, pressing adjectives into the service of verbs, and employing catachresis—insights that are supported by Julia Lin (Lin 1985: 5), Shen Qi (Shen 1995: 252), among others.

Chapter Four

The View from the Buckwheat Field: Capturing War in the Poetry of Ya Xian

Steven L. Riep

During the mid-to late-1950s, the Republic of China on Taiwan (ROC) under Chiang Kai-shek and the Nationalist Party (GMD) faced an increased threat of war with the People's Republic of China (PRC). Having lost a civil war to the PRC and now in island exile on Taiwan, the ROC found itself in a difficult military position. Skirmishes over the disputed offshore islands, Jinmen and Mazu, took place in 1954 and again in 1958. The Nationalists sought to retake lost territory on mainland China but lacked the forces to do so.

While poets such as Luo Fu 落夫 (b. 1928), Yu Guangzhong 余光中 (b. 1928), and Shang Qin 商禽 (b. 1931) wrote works that took the impact of war as their themes, Ya Xian (Ya Hsien) 瘂弦 (b. 1932) created arguably the most significant, well-crafted, and poignant treatments of combat and its impacts in post-1949 Taiwan literature. Some of his best works reveal the physical and emotional costs of war with a candor unique to the period. That Ya not only looks back to such key events in recent and remote Chinese history as the War of Resistance and ancient wars of the Shang dynasty for allusions in his work but also expands his treatment beyond the scope of Nationalist and even Chinese history to treat the topic of war in more universal terms that embrace war-torn Naples as well as Luoyang during World War II attests to the comprehensiveness of his vision. He thus produces a general critique on the institution of war, a critique that is inclusive of non-Chinese cultures. Since Ya's career as a poet lasted little more than a decade and a half, these poems made up a significant portion of his total creative output. Given the importance of military spending, combat readiness, and the continued goal of national reunification in Taiwan in the 1950s and early 1960s, Ya's antiwar works written between 1957 and 1962 offer a timely commentary on contemporary events and a subtle attack on government policy.

Ya Xian belongs to an anomalous group of creative writers that existed in post-1949 Taiwan: military officers or soldiers who also wrote trend-setting modernist poetry (Winckler 1994: 40). Luo Fu, Shang Qin, Zhang Mo 張默 (b. 1931), Xin Yu 辛鬱 (b. 1933), Chu Ge 楚戈 (b. 1932), Guan Guan 管管 (b. 1930), as well as Ya, all members of the Epoch Poetry Club 創世紀詩社, had military connections from serving in the armed forces on the mainland or after arriving in Taiwan (Xi 1998a). Some had come to Taiwan as part of the Nationalist troops that accompanied Chiang Kai-shek in his retreat to island exile. These poets largely ignored calls for patriotic anticommunist literature and chose to experiment with modernist aesthetics to create new poetry outside of the narrow bounds prescribed by the government and by semiofficial literary institutions. Previous or current service in the military, graduation from military-sponsored schools or programs, and postings in military or civilian government offices or installations gave these men the prestige, honor, and authority that allowed them to experiment with a variety of styles, forms, and themes free from censorship. The heightened subjectivity and idiosyncratic tendencies common to the Epoch group's creative writing made their poems more difficult for others to read and thus gave them what Ross Chambers terms "room for maneuver," which allowed them to conceal critiques of government and society in their works. By publishing their poems in unofficial journals such as *Epoch Poetry* 創世紀詩刊, their work appeared in literary venues outside the government-affiliated periodicals that prevailed in the mid-1950s publishing scene.

Ya Xian[1] has enjoyed a long career as a poet, literary historian, editor, and teacher. Born Wang Qinglin 王慶麟 in Nanyang, Henan, Ya joined the GMD Army in August 1949 in Hunan and soon after came with them to Taiwan. A graduate in film and dramatic arts from the Political Cadre Academy in 1953, he rose to the rank of lieutenant commander in the ROC Navy before his retirement in 1966. He had early on adopted the penname of Ya Xian and joined fellow military poets Zhang Mo and Luo Fu in founding the Epoch Poetry Club in 1954 and starting the poetry journal *Epoch Poetry* later that year. This journal would provide a key venue for publishing experimental verse and for introducing both modernist poets from the prewar period and major Western poets and movements, most notably surrealism, to readers in Taiwan from the late 1950s through the 1960s. Ya first went abroad in 1966 and spent two years studying in the International Writing Program at the University of Iowa. He later returned to the

United States to study at the University of Wisconsin and earned a master's degree in East Asian Studies in 1977. Ya returned to Taiwan where he taught Chinese literature part-time at Furen Catholic University.

From the 1960s onward Ya Xian became one of the leading figures in the development of literature and literary institutions in Taiwan. His editorial career began in 1969 when he became head of the China Young Writers Association 中國青年寫作協會, a government-affiliated organ for promoting young creative writers, and helped lead the organization away from anticommunist literary policies and toward the creation of literature for literature's sake. In 1977, Ya Xian became the editor of the literary supplement of the *United Daily News* 聯合報, advancing to become the associate chief editor of the paper. He was instrumental in promoting through contests the writing of new works of literature by emerging artists, the results of which he edited and published. He founded and served as head of *Unitas* 聯合文學, what would become one of the most respected journals of modern and contemporary literary studies published in Taiwan. In 1999, he retired from his editorial posts; he now divides his time between Taiwan and Vancouver, Canada.

No discussion of Ya Xian's literary endeavors would be complete without mention of his role as literary historian. From the early 1950s through the lifting of martial law in 1987, the government banned the publication of works by almost all prewar Chinese writers, particularly those who had not followed the GMD to Taiwan. In 1966, in the pages of *Epoch Poetry*, Ya wrote essays discussing the lives and work of the poets Fei Ming 廢名 (1910–1967), Zhu Xiang 朱湘 (1904–1933), and Wang Duqing 王獨清 (1898–1940). In this first series of essays, Ya specifically chose poets whose artistic and political stances did not go against GMD policies. Beginning in 1972, Ya wrote a series of short essays introducing poets such as Xin Di 辛笛 (b. 1912), Li Jinfa 李金髮 (1900–1976), Liu Dabai 劉大白 (1880–1932) and longer analytical essays on Dai Wangshu 戴望舒 (1905–1950), Liu Bannong 劉半農 (1891–1934), and Kang Baiqing 康白情 (1896–1945), which included selections of their poetry. The longer essays on Dai and Liu became the introductions for book-length collections of each authors' works that Ya published in 1977 and 1982. In the preface to his landmark *Studies in Modern Chinese Poetry* 中國新詩研究, which collects all of his essays on pre-1949 poetry, Ya notes that he began writing these articles so that younger writers in Taiwan would have access to the lives, thought, and some of the works of pioneer Chinese poets of the first half of the twentieth century (see Ya 1981a: i).

Although an influential editor and literary historian, Ya Xian's greatest influence has been through his poetry. This may seem surprising given the shortness of his career, which lasted only eleven years. Yet between 1954 and 1965, he produced some ninety works. His output reached a peak in the years 1957 and 1958 when he completed and published twenty-nine and nineteen poems respectively. While not as prolific as many of his peers, he developed a unique structure and style that has set his poems apart from those of his contemporaries, influenced several generations of younger poets from throughout the Sinophone world, and made him one of the most frequently anthologized Chinese poets alive today. Written almost exclusively in free verse, Ya Xian's poems range in length from two lines ("Sunning Books" 曬書, found in his "Collection of Short Songs" 短歌集, written in 1957) to his ninety-eight-line masterpiece "The Abyss" 深淵, completed near the height of his career in 1959.

Ya Xian draws upon a wide variety of images from history, nature, literature, and modern life to construct his verse. Inspired by surrealism, he frequently juxtaposes disparate images: the Asian and the Western, the ancient and the modern, as well as the timeless and significant against the quotidian and the meaningless, leaving the reader to draw connections between ideas and conclusions as to his meaning. He is well-read in Chinese and Western literature and has read and been influenced by He Qifang 何其芳 (1912–1977), Dai Wangshu, Rainer Maria Rilke, Jean-Paul Sartre, W. H. Auden, Emile Verharen, and Charles Baudelaire.

Though his poems vary considerably in theme, Ya Xian has written most often about the search for meaning in a modern world. His oeuvre encompasses not only reminiscences from youth and occasional poetry, but also carefully wrought portraits of people—real and fictional—which he grouped in his collected works under the heading "Profiles" 側面 (see Ya 1981b: 4–5). Another cycle of poems entitled the "Broken Pillars Collection" 斷柱集 offers glimpses of great cultures and their cities both ancient (Babylonia, Arabia, Greece, Rome, and Jerusalem) and modern (Paris, London, and Chicago) with a trajectory leading toward modernizing and industrializing societies as described in the poem "Chicago" 芝加哥. They embrace what may be the most common theme in all of Ya Xian's work: assessing the costs that progress and industrialization have wrought. To this end, Ya turns repeatedly to religion and existentialism, often pitting the latter against the former. The poet headed his longest poem, "The Abyss," with a quotation from Jean Paul Sartre that reads, "I want to exist—this and nothing more. Yet at the same time I have also discovered its unhappiness" (Ya 1981b: 239). Ya's work frequently references Christian religious symbolism including Jesus Christ, angels, ministers, crosses, and other Christian imagery—that appear powerless in a world devoid of faith and human feeling, in which meaning seems to derive more from the mundane realities of everyday life than from transcendent beliefs.

Given his military background, his interest in recent history, and his search for meaning in a mechanized and depersonalized world, Ya Xian's interest in war is not surprising. As noted at the outset, the years from 1954 to 1965, during which Ya Xian wrote most of his work, were marked by the possibility of imminent war with China due to the Nationalist government's aim of retaking mainland China and the ongoing disputes with the PRC over offshore island territories. References to war occur throughout Ya's work. One of the section headings in his collected poems is entitled "In Time of War" 戰時, named after a poem he penned in 1962 by the same name. Of the eighty-eight poems in the collection, at least six take war as their theme and another twelve make at least passing reference to war. Thus, nearly one-fifth of his works touch on war directly or indirectly.[2]

Images of War

Perhaps the best way to appreciate the depiction of war in Ya Xian's poetry is through close readings of five of his best-known war poems. I will demonstrate how Ya focuses on the victims of war, particularly civilians, and the absence of the enemy in his works. His ironic and understated use of the beautiful to represent the horrific amplifies the trauma he finds characteristic of battle. He stresses the transnational nature of war and its universal impact through his use of imagery, settings, and allusions to Asian as well as Western culture. I will examine the significance of the buckwheat field as a site of war and symbol of death. Finally, I will explore how Ya tends to trivialize rather than glorify war, most often by focusing on the quotidian and ordinary rather than on the heroic and the extraordinary.

Ya Xian's war poetry eschews the image of the courageous soldier in favor of the suffering civilian. In "The God of War" 戰神 he offers a bleak look at the tragedy wrought by battle:

Only death, black victory
this is a year of famine. Many
  mothers cry for souls

只有死, 黑色的勝利
這是荒年。很多母親在喊魂
孩子們的夭亡, 十五歲的小白楊

the early deaths of children,
  young fifteen-year-old poplars
yesterday's skirt cannot be worn today

Broken wineskins, the piercing
  of the sword of Damascus
the bugles have fallen silent, the
  torches have gone dark
someone is lying on a carved
  shield now broken through
the sobbing of wives, infants
  wrapped in tattered banners

昨天的裙子今天不能再穿

破酒囊, 大馬士革刀的刺穿
號角沉默, 火把沉默
有人躺在擊裂的雕盾上
婦人們的呻吟, 殘旗包裹着嬰兒

(Ya 1981b: 48–49)

The impact of war on the civilian populace, represented by women and children, is traced out in the reference to famine and the deaths of children symbolized by the fifteen-year-old poplars in lines 6 through 8 and the flag-wrapped infants in line 12. The battlefield scenes of broken wineskins, silent bugles, and fallen men shown in the third stanza are registered in the grieving of their wives. The only victor appears to be the God of War himself, shown later in line 16 "polishing his boots" oblivious to the human toll he has exacted.

"Naples" 那不勒斯, completed on May 10, 1958 and subtitled "what was seen in 1943," opens by describing statues of women buried in rubble from bombings. The smiles on the statues seem ironic in light of the destruction that they signify. Ya Xian moves from physical damage to human suffering in the fourth stanza with the images of children playing on streets after bombings:

Children, many
nameless
play on the streets after bombings
like a tea-pear tree
growing beneath the Blessed
  Virgin's throne
and sends forth shoots, and blooms
  what appear to be
    flowers of suffering
      But for whom were they planted?

孩子餓們, 很多
沒有姓氏
嬉戲於轟炸後的街道上
似一株茶梨樹
在聖瑪麗亞的椅子下面生長
也發芽, 也開看起來
  很苦的花
    但不知道為誰種植

(Ya 1981b: 126–127)

The namelessness of the children suggests that they have lost their parents, families, and pasts and have become orphans. Most likely they are the illegitimate children of the invading soldiers, who in the sixth stanza are described as "possible fathers . . . who suddenly lose their country's proper dignity" 孩子們可能的父親 . . . (忽然失去了他們底國家應有的英名) from their dalliances with local women (Ya 1981b: 127). The image of the pear tree sending forth shoots becomes an allegory for the children, as the identity of the planter of the tree, like that of the fathers of the children, is unknown. The children themselves can be read as the "flowers of bitterness" or "flowers of suffering," the innocent by-product of war seen in the inclusion of the reference to Mary, the "Blessed Virgin," as a symbol of compassion.

When Ya Xian does show combatants, they appear as victims of war and injury. Completed on August 26, 1960, "The Colonel" 上校 belongs to a series of short poetic portraits of people from different walks of life grouped under the title "Profiles." Like "Naples," "The Colonel" was included in Ya's own small anthology of English poems compiled while studying at the University of Iowa. Ten brief lines in length, it captures the trauma of war and suffering from the point of view of a retired military officer. Rather than recounting heroic battle scenes, Ya focuses instead on how the poetic subject lost his leg in one of the greatest battles in 1943 during the War of Resistance. The solemnity of this summary of the colonel's personal battle history, during what was for him the greatest battle of the war, is undercut by the focus on the disabling injury and the mock-comic tone of the poet when he notes that the leg "bid farewell" or "said goodbye" 訣別 to him. While "The Colonel" ostensibly profiles an individual, it makes reference in the first stanza to a wider body of people who allow one retired and disabled officer to stand metonymically for an army of his fellow combatants and perhaps the entire Nationalist military. In line 3 we read that "In the buckwheat field *they* 他們 encountered their greatest battle"—clear reference to a wider group than just one soldier as "they" do the fighting. Ya Xian's reading of history, couched in terms of a single individual, actually represents a commentary of a much broader nature than we might originally have expected.

The poet makes concrete the magnitude of war and the suffering it causes in arresting scenes that ironically mingle the beautiful with the horrific. In "The Colonel," he opens with an image of beauty, a rose formed or "born" of flames, that the reader quickly discovers signifies the explosion in which the poetic subject loses his leg. The poet substitutes beauty for pain and suffering, thus leaving the reader to imagine the trauma and unspoken horror the colonel experienced when his leg was blown off. "Wartime" (戰時, 1962), subtitled "Luoyang 1942" 洛陽一九四二年, opens by describing the very personal impact that war has had on the poetic subject, who reveals in line 5 that his mother was killed in battle. We do not see the mother or her corpse, but instead see a chair burnt by an incendiary bomb, a chair in which she may have frequently sat, on which the poetic subject sees her "set smile" 硬的微笑, a reference to her death, until it passes into his memory. Here the poet uses the unexpected image of a fan, which normally connotes refinement, delicacy, and beauty, to describe the violent explosion that rips up the street and kills the mother. The irony of the fan image, like the rose in "The Colonel," heightens the horror of the explosion.[3] That a chair, a piece of furniture, comes to represent the mother indicates the depersonalizing and dehumanizing effects wrought by war and its carnage. In "Naples," Ya Xian describes an incendiary bomb using nature imagery as a "tree of flame" 火焰樹 (Ya 1981b: 126 and 351–352). In each case, the irony of the beautiful standing for the horrific creates memorable images that the reader will not soon forget.

Ya Xian's war poems make little or no reference to enemy combatants. We do not know who caused the suffering experienced by the women and children in "God of War" and "Naples," nor does Ya inform us who blew off the colonel's leg. Ultimately this does not matter, for neither individuals nor even countries are culpable. Instead the institution of battle, represented by the heartless God of War, who calmly and coldly wipes the blood of his victims from his boots, is to blame.

The absence of combatants also suggests Ya's desire to universalize the impact of war, rather than reading it as a specific conflict between a few nations. His frequent use of both Asian and Western imagery amplifies this. "God of War" opens as follows:

In the evening	在夜晚
an evening of many black crosses	很多黑十字架的夜晚
in the sick clock tower, two sisters die:	病鐘樓裏, 死了的兩姐妹:
the minute hand and hour hand	時針和分針
their frozen arms paint a final V	僵冷的臂膀, 畫着最後的V
	(Ya 1981b: 48)

The crosses that appear in line 2, and the clock tower, with its prominent hour and minute hands both bespeak Western rather than Chinese or other Asian traditions, as do the wineskins and perhaps even the God of War himself that appear later. That the poet describes the crosses as black, a color with reference to death in Western culture, reinforces the connection. Ya indicates the scale of death by referring in line 2 to "an evening of many crosses," a suggestion of the great magnitude of war (48). The absence of names on the crosses indicates that they mark the graves of unknown combatants or civilians, reminding us of the impersonality of war, whereas the "many black crosses" referred to in line 17 suggest numerous corpses and hence underscore the massive scale and impact of war (49). In "Naples," Ya Xian draws exclusively upon Italian artistic and religious culture in his reference to the ruined plaster statues of women and the Catholic imagery of Mary, the Blessed Virgin, as well as St. Nicholas's Market, evening prayers, God, and angels. War thus becomes an international and hence universal phenomenon.

In "The Buckwheat Field" (蕎麥田, 1957), the poet integrates stanza-long descriptions of Japan, France, and the United States into a poem with a refrain referring to the Chinese city of Luoyang:

The cuckoo sings in the grove	布穀在林子裏唱着
sings in a haiku-like style	俳句般的唱着
that year spring was in Asakusa	那年春天在淺草
geishas, samisens, folding fans	藝伎哪, 三絃哪, 摺扇哪
such a joyous spring	多麼快樂的春天哪
(She waited for me in Luoyang	(伊在洛陽等着我
waited for me in a buckwheat field)	在蕎麥田裏等着我)
sings in a haiku-like style	俳句般的唱着
the cuckoo in the grove	林子裏的布穀
The jasmine blooms in the park	茉莉在公園中開着
blooms in a pointillist way	點畫派般的開着
that year spring was in Paris	那年春天在巴黎
the Seine, old bookstalls, Hugo	塞納河哪, 舊書攤哪, 雨果哪
such a beautiful spring	多麼美麗的春天哪
(She waited for me in Luoyang	(伊在洛陽等着我
waited for me in a buckwheat field)	在蕎麥田裏等着我)
it blooms in a pointillist way	點畫派般的開着
the jasmine in the park	公園中的茉莉
The raven perches on the cross	烏鴉在十字架上棲着
perches in an Edgar Allen	愛倫‧坡般的棲着
Poe–esque sort of way	春天我在肯塔基
at springtime I was in Kentucky	紅土壤哪, 驛馬車哪, 亡魂谷哪
red loam, stagecoaches, the	多麼悲哀的春天哪
Valley of the Dead	(伊在洛陽等着我
such a mournful spring	在蕎麥田裏等着我)
(She waited for me in Luoyang	愛倫‧坡般的
waited for me in a buckwheat field)	棲着
it perches in an Edgar Allen Poe–esque	十字架上的烏鴉
sort of way	
the raven on the cross	

(Ya 1981b: 297–299)

At first glance, the poem appears to have little to do with war. Ya Xian employs a common structure in all three stanzas that focuses first on a specific image, the cuckoo, the jasmine, and the raven; then makes a seasonal reference to spring; provides scenes from a locale unique to each area (the Asakusa district of Tokyo, Paris, and Kentucky), a second reference to spring that includes a description of mood or tone, a two-line refrain referring to the Chinese city of Luoyang, and then repetitions of the second and then the first line of each stanza. The tone in the first two stanzas is upbeat, with spring described at first as "joyous" and then as "beautiful." The images Ya focuses on, the cuckoo and the jasmine, have positive connotations in nature, just as the haiku and pointillism used to describe them are artistic in nature, one a literary form and the other an art movement. In the third stanza, the poet opens with the image of a raven and references to Edgar Allen Poe, suggesting a bleak setting and a somber tone, as is revealed in the reference to spring being "mournful" in line 23. The poet refers to Kentucky and images associated with the nineteenth century American West. Why does the poet suddenly shift the tone in the final stanza? What does the recurring reference to Luoyang mean? How does war play a role here?

Several of the images Ya has chosen are recurrent. The image of the cross in the final stanza is used in a similar fashion in "The God of War" where it symbolizes casualties of war. The presence of a cross with a raven perching upon it suggests a cemetery in which cruciform headstones mark a grave, most likely the graves of soldiers who died in battle. The mournful tone evoked by the ominous references to the color black, the raven, the Valley of the Dead, and the mournful spring season support this reading. The city of Luoyang was also referred to in the subtitle to "Wartime," which reads "Luoyang 1942," thus establishing the time and place in which the events described in the poem occur. The allusion to "Wartime" thus links "The Buckwheat Field" to war, specifically World War II. All four countries mentioned in the poem—Japan, France, the United States, and China—fought in the war and suffered military and civilian casualties. But what of the buckwheat field referred to in the title? Does it confirm a reading of the work as an example of Ya Xian's war poetry?

Images of buckwheat flowers or buckwheat fields occur in many of Ya's war poems. In an interview with Ya conducted at the University of California, Davis, on May 29, 2002, he revealed that he chose buckwheat specifically because its flowers bloom white, the color of death in Chinese traditional color symbolism (Ya 2002). This suggests that the flowers symbolize death and the buckwheat fields become the site of death, representing battlefields or villages torn by war. We find this in "The God of War," where in line 13, the poet writes: "trampling through many fields, the withering of the buckwheat flowers/at Waterloo" 踩過很多田野, 蕎麥花的枯萎/在滑鐵盧. Given the description of battle scenes in the third stanza and the mention of Waterloo in line 14, the setting for the buckwheat flowers is most likely a battlefield. Thus the subject of line 13, the person or persons who trample the fields and cause the buckwheat to wither, refers to soldiers at war. Buckwheat therefore represents the site of war and the crosses signify those who die in the fighting. Similar images are found in both "Wartime" and "The Colonel." In the former, we find the phrase "frightening a field of buckwheat" 驚駭一田蕎麥 ("Or startle a field of buckwheat," Ya 1981b: 67; Yip 1970: 53). This last image refers to a battlefield since the most likely source of fear would be military conflict and this would make the site of terror a place where battles occur. In "The Colonel," Ya specifies that "they encountered the greatest battle of the war in a buckwheat field / and his leg bid him farewell in 1943" (Ya 1981b: 145). The colonel suffers his disabling injury in the midst of combat in a buckwheat field—a battlefield.

Now the meaning of the repeated parenthetic comment, "She waited for me in Luoyang / waited for me in a buckwheat field," becomes clear. In "The God of War," "Wartime," and "The Colonel," Ya Xian consistently employs buckwheat fields or buckwheat flowers as references to battlefields, which by extension are sites of human suffering. The references to Luoyang, like those found in "Wartime," refer to one particular location plagued by fighting. The title of the poem focuses the reader's interest on the image of the buckwheat field, and thus on battle and death.

Finally, Ya Xian tends to trivialize the suffering and trauma of war, at once an ironic heightening of war's significance and a critique of war as an institution. This is best illustrated in "The Colonel," where Ya Xian uses satire to attack war in three different ways. First, he underplays the incident in which the poetic subject loses his leg. What would have been a moment of great trauma and pain is described in comic tones in the phrasing in line 4, in which one of his legs literally "bids farewell" or "parts" from him. The reader is not only prevented from feeling sympathy for the victim and the physical and emotional suffering he experiences, she is also blocked from reading the scene as heroic—as might have been the case in a patriotic poem.

The second stanza, a single line in length, is the core of the poem: "He has heard history and laughter" (Ya 1981b: 145/Yeh and

Malmqvist 2001: 207). Bridging the historical significance of the first
stanza and the quotidian issues raised in the third, it problematizes the
nature of history. The line literally reads, "He has previously heard of
history and laughter," with history and laughter being the object of
what the colonel has heard. We may be sorely tempted to misread the
stanza as "He has previously heard of history and, as a result,
laughed," substituting the conjunction *er* 而 for *he* 和 (and), but the
original clearly places equal emphasis on both objects, not subordi-
nating one to the other as suggested by the misreading. Yet the elision
of history and laughter as common objects of the verb *ting* 聽 (to
listen) causes us to question the relation of the two objects and consider the seriousness, the sacred quality, and the very reliability of
history. The first stanza forces the reader to listen, like the colonel, to
both history in terms of his wartime experience *and* laughter as
defined in the ironic description of the historical event. The poem thus
desanctifies war and its history.

Ya emotionally distances the reader from the poetic subject again in
the third stanza, which begins with the question, "What is immortality?"
(Ya 1981b: 145/Yeh and Malmqvist 2001: 207). The poet invites the
reader to ponder a question that the poet has already answered himself.
His use of parataxis leads us to conclude that immortality resides in
"Cough syrup, razor blades, last month's rent, and so on and so forth,"
or in other words, the quotidian detail of life (Ya 1981b: 146/Yeh and
Malmqvist 2001: 207). This answer also suggests that what immortality cannot be equated with is history and that history therefore is not
immortal. Like laughter, history is ephemeral, passing, and evanescent.
The colonel, the user of the cough syrup and razor blades, the one who
pays the rent, faces only one threat: the sun. The colonel's enemy has
become time, the passage of which the sun marks in daily, weekly,
seasonal, and yearly cycles. Far from being an immortal hero, an individual whose significance rests in his ties to great historical events, the
poetic subject is now most closely identified with the ephemeral, the
transitory, and the conditional that comes from the quotidian. The poet
has drained all heroism from war in his portrait of a disabled veteran
confronting time in a battle he will inevitably lose.

Like the use of beauty to describe the horrific discussed earlier,
trivialization becomes an unexpected and ironic substitute for physical
suffering in Ya Xian's war poems. The repeated nature of death, Ya
suggests in "Wartime," makes it all the more familiar and hence dis-
pensable. In the second stanza, the poet remarks in lines 7 and 8 that
his mother was "half-drowned in the many / Dove-gray deaths last
year" 半掩於去年/很多鴿灰色的死的中間, an indication that so many

have died that her death has become insignificant and may, in fact, eventually be forgotten. The image of drowning reminds us that his mother in essence dies twice: once in the explosion and again when she is forgotten.

Terminality and Circularity: Experiments in Theme and Form

Reflecting on the foregoing discussion of Ya Xian's work, we find that the poet resists any promilitary position in his thoroughgoing critique of war. On the thematic level, he adopts a terminal perspective by using imagery and symbolism that focus on death and destruction and convey a sense of pessimism and hopelessness. On the structural level, he experiments with circular forms that prevent the possibility of forward movement and halt the flow of time and action.

Terminality views the future as doomed, chaotic, and often apocalyptic. It frequently invokes images of death and depersonalizes or dehumanizes its subject. Fraught with pain and suffering, the terminal world is characterized by feelings of hopelessness and despair where attempts to alter the future prove futile because death and destruction are seen as inevitable. In this mode of description, one "thinks of . . . war in terms of its casualties" (Booth 1996: 110). The poem "Wartime" focuses on death and dying from beginning to end. It opens with the death of the poetic subject's mother, which we learn in the second stanza is forgotten amidst the many deaths that occurred in the same period. The poem concludes with images of death in the final stanza:

But all these things are already completed
The people were too tired to wait
  and expect and after all
   you had to participate
In the making of grass amid
  the buzzing of death;
And even—
Angels were no longer necessary.

不過這些都已完成了
人民已倦於守望。而無論早晚
  你必得參與
草之建設。在死的營營聲中
甚至——
已無需天使

(Ya 1981b: 67)

What has been "completed" is the devastation and death of war, which has destroyed any sense of optimism or hope as people are now "too tired to wait and expect." The concluding lines amplify the sense of hopelessness by noting that angels have no power or function in this war-ravaged world, thus signifying that help from a higher source is unlikely.

"Naples," which contains numerous descriptions of the destruction wrought by war, can be read as a companion piece to "Wartime." The poem opens by describing statues of women buried in rubble from bombings. The smiles on the statues seem ironic in light of the destruction that they signify. The theme of destruction continues with a mixing of natural imagery including ivy "losing its last defenses" 失去最後的防衛 and an incendiary bomb described as a "tree of flame" (Ya 1981b: 126 and 351–352). Ya Xian moves from physical damage to human suffering in the fourth stanza with the images of orphaned children playing on streets after bombings. References in the fifth stanza to nameless children, who are described as flowers of unknown origin, support this reading. The poem concludes with images of death seen in closing references to the cross scratched with a bayonet and the view of Naples's future as "worse than the poisonous rose" 比毒玫瑰更壞的 (Ya 1981b: 128 and 350).

The concluding stanza of "The Buckwheat Field" likewise captures the hopelessness brought by war. The references to the raven and Poe echo the mood of a "mournful spring." The images of crosses and the allusion to the Valley of the Dead symbolize death, which extends also to the references to the buckwheat field in Luoyang that appear as a refrain in each stanza. The poem's shift from the beauty and joy discussed in the first two stanzas to sadness in the last underscores the movement toward death that lays concealed in the battlefield reference in the refrain. Terminality takes a different twist in "The Colonel" where we see an example of the future made trivial by the quotidian. The poem moves from the past and its historical meaning to a present in which only day-to-day events and objects hold significance and the only challenge comes from the passage of time and the inevitable approach of death.

The views of war and the future expressed in the poems of Ya Xian either offer a catalog of negative images—death, destruction, suffering—or focus on their utter meaninglessness. Ya's poetry either drains war of any positive meaning or, as in the case of "The Colonel," drains it of all meaning and significance. Read in the context of the late-1950s and early-1960s, a period when the Nationalist military establishment wielded considerable power in a society under martial law and during which the Nationalist government still called for reunification by armed force, these poems fly in the face of the anticommunist literature promoted by the government and take poetry in a new direction.

Ya's critique of war also functions on a structural level as seen in his attempts to halt the flow of time in his poetry. In the preface to *The Collected Poetry of Ya Xian*, the poet writes: "Human life is like the morning dew, and art lasts a thousand years. For me, the only thing on earth that can resist time is probably poetry" (Ya 1981b: ii). He later states that he hopes to "ascend against the current of the flow of time" (Ya 1981b: ii). While Ya's comments refer to his ambitions for his poetry as a whole, this sensitivity to countering time also appears in many of his war poems including "The God of War." In the first and last stanzas, he uses the image of a broken tower clock whose arms have jammed in an upward position forming the letter "V," which ironically stand for victory:

In the evening
an evening of many black crosses
in the sick clock tower, two sisters die:
   the minute hand and hour hand
their frozen arms paint a final V

. . . .

Many black crosses, without names
cold feast for corpse-eating birds,
   desolate tapping
in the sick clock tower, the pair
   of dead sisters'
frozen arms paint a final V

在夜晚
很多黑十字架的夜晚
病鐘樓裏, 死了的兩姐妹:
   時針和分針
僵冷的臂膀, 畫着最後的V

很多黑十字架, 沒有名字
食屍鳥的冷宴, 淒涼的剝啄
病鐘樓, 死了的姐兒倆
僵冷的臂膀, 畫着最後的V

(Ya 1981b: 48–50)

Time has become frozen because the clock has stopped, and the hands are "frozen" in a V-shaped position. The result is a painfully ironic symbol of the hollow victory that comes from war. By stopping time, the poet has subverted closure and thus prevented any possible resolution or alternative reading to the bleak portrait of war he depicts.

This stoppage of time occurs frequently in European literature during and after World War I. Allyson Booth observes that "The clocks of modernism seem . . . to cease ticking altogether" (Booth 1996: 117). She illustrates this with a quote from Virginia Woolf's *Orlando*: "'As a cloud crosses the sun', the narrator reports, 'silence falls on London; and falls on the mind. Effort ceases. Time flaps on the mast. There we stop; there we stand'" (117). Booth traces this tendency toward the freezing of time to the impact of new trends in warfare on those writing during and immediately after World War I. In *Postcards from the Trenches*, Booth contends that the literature of World War I captures the conflict between the notion of progress that predominated in the Victorian age and the immobility of fighting that characterized the battles of the Great War. Citing historians Modris Ecksteins, John Keegan, and Asa Briggs, she contends that during the nineteenth century the concept of linear time that came from a view of personal and natural progress held sway. This was the age of Darwin and Marx, the Industrial Revolution, the growth of industries and markets, and the expansion of colonial empires. The concept of progress influenced the ways in which people viewed war as well; Booth makes reference to Keegan in her discussion of Edward Creasy's notion of "decisive battles." Rather than seeing war as evil, a violation of "Christian formulations of justice" that derailed progress, Creasy concluded that war actually played a key role in shaping the world (105). Thus for most people in Britain and France, according to Ecksteins, "the war . . . was a stage in the march of civilization, in the continuation of progress" (105).

The unfolding of the military campaigns of World War I did not fit within this conceptual framework of progress brought about by decisive battles. Rather than lightning battles and advancing movement, fighting in Europe quickly devolved into trench warfare exemplified by immobility and attrition. Despite the high cost in human life, the war grew static with little progress to report. The impact of these trends on literature came, in Booth's view, in moves away from plotting war as a story and seeing it more as a condition (12). She notes: "Attrition takes the story out of war by reconstituting its action. War's plot is no longer geared toward battle but rather spreads itself thin over the maintenance of routine" (108). She argues that war derails the sense of narrative sequence of beginning, middle, and end by substituting a condition that, "because static, forces narrative to circle around either a single moment or a series of moments that overlap and repeat themselves" (108). With the collapse of plot comes the fading of climax and of resolution as both of these require story development. The nature of literature during and after World War I changed with the breakdown of narrative and the tendency to depict static conditions rather than vectors of action moving forward.

Half a world away and some forty years later, Ya Xian found himself in a similar situation as the modernist writers in Britain. A climate of war persisted in Taiwan during the late-1950s and early-1960s as the country remained under martial law and the government actively promulgated calls for anticommunism and the recovery of mainland

China. However, the GMD-led military neither made gains in taking territory nor made good on its pledge to retake China, such that the war climate became one of waiting and watching rather than of conquering—a static situation analogous to the one Booth describes. At the same time, Nationalist government rhetoric called for progress that was translated into projects for national reconstruction framed as a series of large-scale, multiyear national industrial development plans. Planning, resources, and effort gradually shifted from an offensive military posture to a defensive one accompanied by an aggressive economic development strategy. Like the situation in Europe during 1910–1920, war in Taiwan became a static condition that continued with no end in sight.

In this environment, Ya Xian's poetry takes on new meaning. In light of the prolongation of war and calls for progress on the economic front, we can read his desire to stop the flow of time as a response to the static nature of the war milieu and the forward motion of economic progress. Turning again to "The God of War," let us recall the parallel opening and closing stanzas of the poem: the image of the frozen clock hands that opens the poem appears again at the conclusion, causing the poem to circle back on itself, ending where in fact it had begun. This reminds us of Allyson Booth's observation that literature tends "to circle around either a single moment or a series of moments that overlap and repeat themselves" (108). Why does the author use this particular structure? What does this circling imply?

In *Modern Chinese Poetry: Theory and Practice Since 1917*, Michelle Yeh devotes a chapter to the use of circular structure in the works of twentieth-century Chinese poets. She defines circularity as follows:

> By circular structure I am referring to poems in which the beginning and ending contain the same image or motif, which appears nowhere else. The circular structure describes a pattern of return or a configuration of symmetry. (Yeh 1991a: 91)

This structure was used by a number of earlier poets including Kang Baiqing, Liu Dabai, He Qifang, Sun Dayu 孫大雨 (1905–1997), and Dai Wangshu, whose works Ya Xian had read and on which he had written a series of articles that appeared in *Epoch Poetry*, as noted earlier. Yeh persuasively argues that circularity offered a radical way of closing a poem by first frustrating any "sense of finality" by returning to the beginning of the poem and by transgressing the linear nature of the poetic art by turning it back upon itself (92). She suggests in her survey of pre-1949 modern poetry that writers used circularity to, among other things, describe closed states of mind and convey feelings of frustration or futility that came as they subverted closure. In later poetry, particularly in the work of Shang Qin, we find "circularity at its most negative" when Shang uses the technique to convey fragmentation, disruption, fear, and the inescapability of death (105).

The emotions Yeh links to the use of circularity correspond with the view of war found in our earlier analysis of the terminal qualities of Ya Xian's poetry. The inescapability of suffering and death as well as the disruption of everyday life and routine found in his war poems parallel the disruption brought to the lives of war's victims, both children and adults, and to combatants and civilians alike. Just as the image of the frozen clock hands stop time, the presence of this same image at both the opening and closing of "The God of War" reminds us that we cannot escape from war. The cloud of fear that hung over Taiwan when Ya Xian wrote these works hangs over his poetry as well, brought on the thematic level by terminality and on the structural level by circularity. Ya's treatment of war looks beyond the strictly Chinese historical context and treats the impact of combat on human civilization in general. Less lyrical and more detached than other poets, Ya's commentary avoids excessive moralizing or Sinocentric patriotism and frames its observations of society in more universal terms.

Notes

1. While the poet spells his name Ya Xian, he prefers to pronounce it Ya Xuan, which means a mute string or strings (Palandri 1972: 144).
2. War is used in making reference to time (as in "prewar" [戰前, Ya 1981a: 217] or "postwar" [戰後, 200]); military paraphernalia (armor [甲冑, 56], scabbards [鞘, 102], shields [盾牌, 56], bugles [兵營裏的喇叭, 147], banners [龍旗, 56], bayonets [刺刀, 164], atomic weapons ["the bomb" in English, 212–213] and more general references to cavalry horses [55 and 102]); people impacted by war (blind prisoners of war 盲目的戰俘 [100], soldiers [100 and 216], and White Russian officers 白俄軍官 [150]); historical references to past wars (Chi You 蚩尤 [96], Athenian War 雅典戰 [158]), and even the terms "war" (戰爭, 212) and "revolution" (革命, 70) themselves.
3. This use of the beautiful to describe the horrors of war recalls Wen Yiduo's landmark poem "Dead Water" (Sishui), in which Wen elevates the ordinary or ugly to the sublime in order to reveal the beauty of the quotidian and to problematize conventional notions of the beautiful (see Yeh 1992: 17).

Chapter Five

To the Heart of Exile:
The Poetic Odyssey of Luo Fu

John Balcom

Luo Fu (Lo Fu) 洛夫 is the penname of Mo Luofu 莫洛夫, born in Hunan Province in 1928. He started writing poetry in mainland China in the mid-1940s. He joined the military during the war and was part of the Guomindang (GMD) exodus to Taiwan in 1949, a move that would have a profound impact on his life and writing. He cofounded the Epoch Poetry Society 創世紀詩社 with Zhang Mo 張默 (b. 1931) and Ya Xian 瘂弦 (b. 1932) in 1954 and served as editor of the association's *Epoch Poetry Quarterly* 創世紀 for more than a decade. A controversial figure in many literary debates that shaped the evolution of modern Chinese poetry, immensely influential in Taiwan and China, Luo is the author of twelve volumes of poetry; an equal number of personal anthologies published in Taiwan, Hong Kong, and mainland China; five collections of essays; five volumes of literary criticism; and eight book-length translations.

Luo Fu's ability to remake himself and his poetry over the years has earned him the nickname of Poet-Magus. In reading Luo Fu's oeuvre, what emerges in retrospect is a kind of Chinese literary odyssey—a mythic journey through time over which the history of modern China and Taiwan stands as a guiding presence. The shadow of China's and Taiwan's recent history establishes the broader ethos within which the quest is enacted. The progression of the quest can be divided into several stages that are manifest in the stylistic developments in his work where change finds itself inscribed in literary form. His writing is always on the pulse of the times, articulating the tragedy of the twentieth century. Throughout his career, Luo Fu has engaged the nature of the self and expressed its troubled relationship with the Chinese milieu. This engagement has been a search for the self and China, and what it means to be Chinese; but as counterpoint to this, Luo Fu has sought freedom, an ontological freedom from historicity.

The poems in Luo Fu's first book, *River of the Soul* 靈河 (1957), are unexceptional and typical of the sort of poetry written then. The lyrics in the collection tend to deal with dichotomies: freedom versus imprisonment, real world experience versus an imaginary paradise of love. "Chimney" 烟囱 is a good example:

Standing alone under a pale setting sun
Black hair lifted by the wind,
  but a slender shadow stands still
It is a little cool below the
  city wall, a little lonely
I am a chimney longing to fly

Head lowered, I gaze at the
  long moat
The water brimming, meandering
  for thousands of years
Who has had me imprisoned?
Every afternoon I gaze up
At the white clouds' footprints
  in the sky

I yearn to travel afar; Oh! that
  long river, those blue mountains
If I could be a wild crane
  chasing the clouds
Or even a fine speck of dust
But I'm just a shadow cast
  below the city wall
--yielding loneliness to others

矗立於漠漠的斜陽裏
風撩起黑髮, 而瘦長的投影靜止
那城牆下便有點寂寞, 有點蒼涼
我是一隻想飛的煙囱

俯首望著那條長長的護城河
河水盈盈, 流著千年前的那種蜿蜒
誰使我禁錮,
每天下午我都在仰望
白雲在天空留下的腳印

我想遠遊, 哦!那長長的河, 青青的山
如能化為一隻逐雲的野鶴
甚至一粒微塵
但我只是城牆下一片投影
-----讓人寂寞

(Luo 1957: 40–41)

The fixed and immobile chimney stands in stark contrast to its lively surroundings, the flowing water and the drifting clouds. The chimney is powerless to break free from its physical imprisonment; it longs to have the freedom of motion possessed by the wild crane, or even the passive freedom of a speck of dust blown about on the wind. In addition to the freedom inherent in nature, from which the chimney, as a manmade object, is barred, there exists a second kind of freedom: spiritual or existential freedom. Although the chimney lacks the freedom of physical mobility, it possesses freedom of thought and imagination; the chimney can imagine its own freedom. Yet the consciousness of the chimney remains imprisoned in its material form.

Paradoxically, in the last stanza, the chimney is apparently freed from its imprisoning form: it has shifted from the solid form to the immaterial shadow. Material restrictions gone, the chimney is a shadow of itself but remains equally unfree. The shadow is ultimately determined by the interaction or synthesis of the spiritual (sunlight) and the material (chimney). The poet seems to imply that it is in the pursuit of the ideal that man can change himself and his surroundings, his fate, and history. Though complete freedom from the contingencies of a painful reality may elude the personae of Luo Fu's lyric poems, they can find its temporary approximation in love. Love is an ideal that enables man to transcend the limitations placed on him by circumstance. Lover and beloved in Luo Fu's early lyric poems enter their own private world, providing release from the world, even if only temporarily.

Yet Luo Fu, like many other poets in Taiwan in the 1950s and 1960s, was growing dissatisfied with such poetry, finding that it was inadequate to capture the times in which he lived. Something new was needed. His first major creative breakthrough as a poet came in 1958 when he was stationed on Quemoy during the PRC bombardment of the island. One day, as the shells rained down overhead, he began writing inside a bomb shelter. The work would grow into a sequence of sixty-four poems that took five years to complete. The sequence was published in 1965 as his second book of poetry titled *Death of a Stone Cell* 石室之死亡. The sequence is one of the most representative works of high Modernist poetry written in Taiwan during the 1960s.

Along with nearly two million people in 1949, Luo Fu fled a country devastated by years of war for an island province with an unsure future. To ensure political control over the island, the GMD government had earlier declared martial law and suspended the constitution. In the early 1950s, the government also began to crackdown on local intellectuals with leftist views, executing and imprisoning many during the White Terror. Seen more as rulers from outside than as compatriots, the mainland émigrés found themselves to be strangers in a strange land. The government also insisted that their sojourn on the island was temporary. Together, these factors gave rise to an "exile" mentality, an intense feeling of rootlessness and alienation, which would have a profound impact on literature in Taiwan.

The direction literature was to take in Taiwan was also determined in large part by government policy. To maintain ideological hegemony, the government proscribed most modern Chinese literature and the use of Japanese, which had been in use on the island for fifty years. This policy effectively eliminated the social-realist and nativist traditions in modern literature, silenced most of the local poets who could write only in Japanese, and reduced the aesthetic options to anticommunist propaganda or a Romanticism modelled on the works of Xu Zhimo and others from the 1930s. Luo Fu, like many émigré poets, while believing in the GMD cause, never really took poetry-as-propaganda seriously; instead, he opted for Romanticism.

However, they soon found the romantic idiom inadequate for expressing the anxieties they experienced living in uncertain times, cut off from a sense of place and tradition. Modernism, a multifaceted movement, emerged to fill the void. The movement grew out of the émigré experience; the debates and theory that shaped the movement were initiated and controlled by mainlanders.

The poets in the various camps—the Moderns, the Blue Stars, and the Epoch poets—collectively termed Modernists, wrote out of their own subjectivity, producing the period's poetry of interiority and individualistic styles. The physical and ideological realities of China had been negated; and this attenuation of reality served to undermine their sense of self. The fragmentation of China was embodied on an individual level by many Modernist writers and internalized as the tissue of experience. This sense of fragmentation eventually came to operate as the organizing principle for Modernist works. With no consistent worldview, their own fragmentary experience and an equally eclectic blend of ideas drawn from the West formed the basis for an aesthetic that explained their own life situation.

Modernism quickly became the dominant form of poetic discourse on the island, eclipsing anticommunist propaganda and Romanticism. The Modernists were primarily concerned with the primacy of art and eschewed political engagement. Thus they never met government opposition as did the social-realists and nativists poets. For nearly two decades, from the 1950s through the 1970s, the movement's authority was unchallenged. But in the early 1970s, a new generation of poets emerged. Stung by Taiwan's declining political fortunes in the West, they rejected Modernism and all elitism in art, advocating a new realism. Facing such popular opposition, Modernism went into decline. Luo Fu gradually abandoned his avant-garde position for writing increasingly steeped in tradition.

Death of a Stone Cell can be described as a vast canvas upon which the great themes of life, death, love, and war are painted. Luo Fu described the poem as "a portrait of man's uncertainty and anxiety in modern life; a lonely outcry wrung from between life and death, love and hate, gain and loss" (Luo 1974: 3). (The stone cell forms a symbol of modern man's alienated condition or his existence in a man-made reality that does not correspond to the intentions of his activities or dreams.) Luo Fu's reflections on the nature of human existence and man's fate in the modern world are expressed through a complex array of personal symbols to create a stunning and hermetic poetry of rich texture. He has noted the influence of Rilke; however, stylistically, the book owes something to Surrealism, and philosophically to Existentialism. The publication of the collection heralded a major new talent.

Stylistically, nothing could be further removed from Luo Fu's earlier poetry. The book received immediate attention and comment from poets and critics alike, eventually contributing to and culminating in the Modernist debates of the 1960s and early 1970s. The poet Ya Xian called the sequence a modern epic (Ya 1981a: 23). However, unlike a conventional epic, which obeys certain literary principles in the treatment of a culture's great historic events and which functions as a repository of cultural memory, Luo Fu's sequence offers a far more individualistic and idiosyncratic vision of history. The material for Luo Fu's "epic" is drawn from his own immediate life experience. The first poem, the frame poem for the sequence, is representative:

Simply by chance I raised my
  eyes toward the neighbouring
  tunnel; / I was stunned
At dawn, that man rebelled
  against death with his
  naked body
Allowed a black tributary to
  roar through his veins
I was stunned, my eyes swept
  over the stone wall
Gouging out two channels of
  blood on its surface

My face spreads like a tree, a
  tree grown in fire
All is still, behind eyelids
  only the pupils move
Move in a direction most
  people fear to mention
And I am a bitter pear tree,
  cut down
On my annual rings you can
  still hear wind and cicadas

祇偶然昂首向鄰居的甬道, 我便怔住
在清晨, 那人以裸體去背叛死
任一條黑色支流咆哮橫過他的脈管
我便怔住, 我以目光掃過那座石壁
上面即鑿成兩道血槽

我的面容展開如一株樹, 樹在火中成長
一切靜止, 唯眸子在眼瞼後面移動
移向許多人都怕談及的方向
而我確是那株被鋸斷的苦梨
在年輪上, 你仍可聽清楚風聲, 蟬聲

(Luo 1975: 39–40)

The frame poem begins with an oblique reference to the bombardment of Quemoy, the nearness of death, and the genesis of the poem.

Although it had its origins in the experience of war, the poem does not pretend to describe reality, representing instead an inner landscape that is externalized by way of symbolic images. The first two lines set the scene but also immediately present a rift of rupture in the speaker's normal experience; by chance he happens to look up from some ordinary activity and sees something that shatters his complacency. Stunned, he sees a man fight against death at dawn, the start of a new day. A human being's naked confrontation with death provides the epiphany that changes the speaker's awareness. The man has no weapons to fight an implacable and invincible enemy, and defeat would seem inevitable. The third verse tells us as much: Death is already inside him in the form of a black tributary flowing through his veins. Death is thus characterized for two reasons: first, each individual's death represents a small stream flowing into a larger sea of death; second, each life is lived in tribute to Death. Observing all this, the speaker's reaction is one of shock and dismay. He turns his eyes away from the scene and looks at the stone walls around him. As his eyes sweep over the lifeless stone, blood begins to flow from the wall. The imagery is stunning, but what is the reader to make of it?

The most problematic image in the first quintet is the bleeding stone wall. This image is also related to the paradoxical title of the sequence, *Death of a Stone Cell*. How can stone bleed and die? In the sequence, the image functions on two levels. Blood flows from the stone just as the black stream of death flows in the veins of a living man; life flows invisibly in what is apparently lifeless, the way death flows undetected inside what lives. Life and death are complementary, two parts of a larger whole; to ignore one is to diminish the whole.

On another level, the image of the lifeless but bleeding stone wall must be examined in light of the fact that the wall is a man-made object. The wall can also be read as a symbol of modern man's alienated condition in that although it exists in fact, he did not necessarily construct it himself. Marxist and existentialist philosophers hold that the fate of man can be characterized by alienation. For Marx, alienation consists of a system of relations that have become autonomous against the very individuals who participated in creating it. In other words, alienation consists in man creating a reality that does not correspond to the intentions of his activities or his wishes and dreams (Bottomore 1983: 9–11). In the modern world, the sum of man's historical conditioning—his fate—has become an inert lifeless mass that stands against him like a stone wall.

Living under the constant threat of death on Quemoy certainly influenced Luo Fu's perception and understanding of life and destiny.

In his early poems, Luo Fu sought to transcend the painful historical reality he encountered in Taiwan. On Quemoy, the regular shellings had a catalyzing effect on Luo Fu's art. An acute awareness of death led Luo Fu to an awareness of his own alienated condition, which he shared with all the people of China, if not with the entire modern world. The immediate threat of death threw Luo Fu's own alienated condition into high relief. History for Luo Fu had become an "atrocity exhibition at which he was an unwilling spectator" (Ballard 1970: 15).

According to Sartre, man attempts to overcome his alienated condition through a dialectical process by internalizing his objective circumstances and then externalizing them through action, in an attempt to change them. By this free act of consciousness, he takes what is outside and makes of it a structure of his inner life. But he must objectify himself through his own acts in the outside world. Through creation, man realizes himself and detaches himself from things as he inscribes his work on them (Sartre 1968: 150). This dialectical process is what is expressed symbolically in the first quintet of the frame poem. The speaker internalizes the external—his stunned reaction to the naked man battling death and the black stream roaring through his veins—and then externalizes what he has internalized—his eyes make the stone wall bleed. In this way, modern man's creative activities become a form of revenge on his cruel fate. Luo Fu observes: "What we see reflected in the mirror is not the image of modern man, but their cruel destinies against which writing poetry is a form of revenge" (Luo 1965: 1).

But exactly what form will this revenge take in Luo Fu's case? The second quintet provides the answer. In the opening lines, the speaker compares himself to a tree, but one grown in fire. The life of such a tree is symbolic of the lives of the Chinese people and China. Luo Fu grew up during the war with Japan and the subsequent civil war and division of China. On Quemoy, violence continued. It is the violence, the uncertainties, and ultimately death that most people prefer to ignore. In the last two lines, the speaker again compares himself to a tree—in this case a bitter pear tree that has been chopped down, its annual rings exposed to the light of day.

A tree's annual rings are a record of its life; they are the tree's inner record of its life experience. Luo Fu is again speaking in symbols— what the speaker is offering the reader is a record of his own inner life. Luo Fu will have his revenge on history by banishing it and in its place substituting his own authentic or existential history—what Heidegger called *Geschichte* (Heidegger 1962: 236–311). His poetry, as he says in the introduction to the collection, is a means of revenge against modern man's merciless destiny. Modern man can transcend the limitations of a specific time and place by returning to the immediacy of experience. As Luo Fu says in "The Poet's Mirror," the introduction to the sequence,

> For the Surrealist poet, logic and reason are nooses on a gallows; if he puts his head in, it's all over. According to Breton, spiritual freedom can only be realized by entering the world of subjectivity, which is far more real than the world of logic. The Surrealist slogan of "more self-consciousness" is the only means by which humankind can realize pure existence. (Luo 1975: 239)

The remaining sixty-three poems can be read as a record of such experience. He would incorporate significant events from his life, such as the birth of his daughter and the death of a friend. But his poem is much more than just a record of his personal experiences; it expresses the existential drama of a generation of Chinese writers. Luo Fu sought to transcend his historical situation by revealing and determining his own situation, transcending it by objectifying himself through his poetry. His words have the authenticity of wind and cicada; they cut through alienation and lead to freedom.

A third collection titled *Poems from Beyond* 外外集 was published in 1967 with simpler and more concise expressions of his philosophical outlook. Luo Fu returns with greater clarity to the conflict between his desire for transcendence and the demands of reality. He begins to discard his surrealist position and abandons the style of regular stanza lengths. Most of the poems in the collection involve a conceit based on the word "beyond." Poems such as "Beyond the Fog" 霧之外 are less dense than previous ones:

An egret	一隻鷺鷥
Reads *Les Nourritures Terrestes* in a rice paddy	在水田中讀著 "地糧"
It circles a certain point, swirling like fog	且繞著某一定點, 旋走如霧
Lowering its head by chance	偶然垂首
It snaps up a cloud on the water's surface	便啣住水面的一片雲
Contemplation is nothing more than	沉思. 不外乎想那些
Pondering whether or not the sun is a nihilist	太陽是不是虛無主義者之類的問題
Lifting its left leg, it wonders	左腳剛一提起, 整個身子
If its body should swing into the fog	就不知該擺在霧裡
Or beyond the fog	或霧外
	一展翅, 宇宙隨之浮升
	清晨是一支閃爍的歌
	在霧中自燃

It spreads its wings and the
  universe follows, drifting upward
Dawn is a song, short and bright
Igniting itself in the fog
If the horizon line rises to bind you
  It can only bind your wings,
    not your flight

如果地平線拋起將你繫住
繫住羽翼呵繫不住飛翔

(Luo 1967: 18–19)

In the first stanza, we meet a fashionable egret that reads turn-of-the-century French novels. Luo Fu's mention of Gide's novel actually functions well in the poem. It creates an interesting dichotomy of imagery within the text: the heavy, earthy quality of the book's title contrasts sharply with the fleeting, ephemeral qualities of both the egret's mental processes as well as the fog and reflections of its physical environment. This produces a tension between earthbound limitations and free mental flight.

The contrast between body and mind continues in the second stanza as well and achieves resolution in the final stanza. The egret takes flight, leaving the world behind for a realm of freedom. We learn in the last two lines that even if its wings were tied, its freedom would not be diminished. The poem expresses the age-old truth that iron bars do not a prison make.

In 1970, Luo Fu published a collection titled *River Without Banks* 無岸之河, the most significant portion of which was a small group of eleven poems titled "Saigon Poems" 西貢詩抄 derived from Luo Fu's experience in Vietnam. The poems effectively combine a Surrealist poetics with the tighter structure and more succinct language of his third collection, such as in "Fish" 魚:

Anyway, only a petal of the
  setting sun remains in his eyes
There'll still be time tomorrow
  to break the mirror
He stands reverently at H-town
A poplar flies around him
Casually looking up, he sees
Bone ashes drifting from a chimney
Or is it butterflies?

He wrings his hands and ponders
As the whiteness beyond the
  window becomes a myriad of colors
He is the sole hero of a thousand tales
Washing his hands may only
  create another woe

反正他眼中只剩下那麼一朵夕陽
明天摔掉還不太遲
那漢子仍肅然而立, 在H-鎮上
一株白楊繞著他飛
偶然仰首
從煙囪中飄出來的是骨灰
抑是蝴蝶?

然後想著心事搓著手
當窗戶自成許多顏色的時候
他是千個故事中僅有的主角
洗手可能洗出另一種悲哀
翻過雙掌, 你看!
有鱗而無鰭的
算條什麼魚!

Turning his palms up . . . Look!
Scales but no fins
What kind of fish are they?

Later, squatting under the eaves
He eats a fruit called the moon
Spitting the crushed seeds into
 the sky; they become stars
On the ice-cold tip of his tongue
Is the pure scent of burnt snow
Later he kicks a stone, waltzes
Along the wall, around the mouth
 of a dried-up well
And looking down
He no longer sees his own face

然後蹲在屋簷下
吃著一種叫做月亮的水果
嚼碎的果核吐向空中變成星
冰涼舌尖上
有焚雪的清香
然後踢著石子以三拍子的步度
沿牆垣而南而北而西
而東的一口枯井邊
俯身再也找不到自己的那付臉

(Luo 1975: 137–138)

This is one of the most compelling of the poems because it balances expression with the use of symbol. The image of the mirror appears twice, and it is here that Luo Fu's struggle with the question of identity in alienation is in some ways resolved. The first stanza indicates that the speaker hopes to break the mirror; this represents the possibility of freedom. The second stanza shows him at a "strategic hamlet," basically villages that were turned into prisons to keep the civilian population under control and prevent contact with the Communists. The speaker is surrounded by images of death—the poplar tree is a symbol of death that dates back to antiquity in the Chinese tradition. Midway through the third stanza, we encounter a curious image—the speaker compares his hands to fish, but he cannot say what kind for sure. The answer to the riddle comes in the final stanza when the speaker dances around a well and hopes to see his reflection. This is impossible because the well has dried up, the water-mirror has vanished. He cannot confirm his identity based upon his reflection because the mirror has disappeared.

The mirror having disappeared indicates that any attempt to reflect upon the nature of the self is impossible. In *Death of a Stone Cell*, the identity of the face in the mirror could not be used to confirm the mirror; in the "Saigon Poems," the mirror is lost altogether. This facet of the mirror image in Luo Fu's poetry emerged only after he went to Vietnam. There likely is a strong correlation between his experience of the Vietnam War and the sense of futility or impossibility in establishing the self. Luo Fu encountered war in mainland China and on Quemoy, but the difference in the case of Vietnam is that he was in a foreign country. His exile from China was complete. Conception of the self therefore became impossible outside the context of China.

Chinese culture functioned as the mirror Luo Fu needed to define the sense of self and the Modernist ethos. Without the cultural context, the self could only be defined by its free-floating place in the flux of contingency. And any attempt to recenter the self would only result in further decentering it. Therefore the answer to the riddle of the third stanza is perhaps "a fish out of water." Luo Fu was like a fish out of water. The creative process, the dialectic of self and society, of self and history that gives rise to art, was further disrupted. Luo Fu's Vietnam experience forced him to confront the extreme limits of the Chinese Modernist position. It also forced him to adjust his worldview and poetics, or as Luo Fu said, a change in language is a change in the way we view the world. This readjustment would play out over the coming years.

Magical Songs 魔歌, Luo Fu's fifth collection, followed in 1974—another departure of sorts for Luo Fu. The well-received collection consists of a number of occasional poems and sequences concerned with abstract and metaphysical subjects. He is able to crystallize the abstract in controlled language and rhythm, much like Wallace Stevens, a Luo Fu favorite. He also begins to incorporate elements of classical poetry in his verse and to examine Chinese history, an attempt to reground himself in Chinese culture. Returning home might be impossible, but fashioning a home by situating himself more firmly in the Chinese poetic tradition is not. This shift occurred as the entire island was having doubts about the whole Modernist position, which was being openly attacked by younger poets and critics. His poem "Song of Everlasting Sorrow" 長恨歌, for example, is a modern commentary on Bo Juyi's Tang masterpiece. He also began to write short occasional poems reminiscent of classical models such as "Gold Dragon Temple" 金龍禪寺:

the evening bell	晚鐘
is a small trail travellers take	是遊客下山的小路
down the mountain	羊齒植物
ferns	沿著白色的石階
along steps of white stone	一路嚼了下去
chews its way all the way down	
	如果此處降雪
if this place were covered with snow . . .	
	而只見
but all that's seen is	一隻驚起的灰蟬
a single startled cicada rising	把山中的燈火
to light the lanterns	一盞盞
one by one	點燃
all over the mountain	

(Luo 1975: 165–166)

This poem is reminiscent of the classical theme of visiting a temple such as in Chang Jian's 常建 (fl. 749) "A Buddhist Retreat Behind Broken-Mountain Temple" 破山寺後禪院.

By the time his award-winning *Wound of Time* 時間之傷 appeared in 1981, Luo Fu's life was firmly rooted in Taiwan; there did not seem much chance of ever going home. He had retired from the military and was aging. More grounded in tradition, he sought a balance between the modern and the traditional; excerpts from the title poem cycle illustrate this:

2

A raincoat from before the war
 hangs behind the door
A discharge order in the pocket
The night-blooming cereus on the balcony
Blossoms in vain for one night
The wound of time continues festering
So serious
It cannot be cured even by chanting a
 few lines of the dharani mantra

6

At times I vent my anger before
 the mirror
If only
All lights in the city were extinguished
I'd never find my face there again
I shatter the glass with my fist
Blood oozes out

7

We sang war songs on the
 boulevards that year
Heads high, chins up, we
 proudly entered history
We were stirred to the quick
Like water
Dripping on a red-hot iron
The names on our khaki uniforms
Were louder than a rifle shot
But today, hearing the bugle from
 the barracks nearby
I suddenly rose, straightened
 my clothes
Then sat down again, dejected
Softly keeping time with the beat

2

門後掛著一襲戰前的雨衣
口袋裏裝著一封退伍令
陽台上的曇花
白白地開了一夜
時間之傷在繼續發炎
其嚴重性
絕非念兩句大悲咒所能化解的

6

有時又不免對鏡子發脾氣
只要
全城的燈火一熄
就再也找不到自己的臉
一拳把玻璃擊碎
有血水滲出

7

那年我們在大街上唱著進行曲
昂昂然穿過歷史
我們熱得好快
如水
滴在燒紅的鐵板上
黃卡嘰制服上的名字
比槍聲更響
而今, 聽到隔壁軍營的號聲
我忽地振衣而起
又頹然坐了下去
且輕輕打著拍子

8

想當年
背水一戰
  ○ ○ ○ ○ ○ ○ ○
暮色四起
馬群騰空而去

8
Reminiscing about the old days
When we fought with our backs to the sea
. . . .
Twilight falls
Horses gallop away
An old general's white head
Is seen
Slowly looking up
Out of the dust

隱見一位老將的白頭
從沙塵中
徐徐
仰起

(Luo 1981: 61–66)

From the discharge order mentioned in the second poem, we assume the speaker, like Luo Fu, is a retired soldier. In poems seven and eight, he looks back from the perspective of middle age on his heroic youth and contrasts it with his present dejected condition. However, he also looks toward the future and his inevitable death. In the face of death, he contemplates the evanescence of human existence and the vanities of life. The mirror image, so prevalent in Luo's poetry, appears in poem six. The image boldly rejects the search for the individual, iconoclastic self of the Modernist position. The speaker says he would like to break the mirror, presumably because it can only reflect the ravages of time, the impermanence of the individual self. The speaker's aged reflection epitomizes the transience of life. Although he would in a sense stop the flight of time by destroying the mirror—the marker of time's passage—in the end, the self remains mortal, for blood flows from the shattered mirror. There is no stopping time.

Luo Fu is concerned with the abstract and metaphysical but more so with Chinese literary tradition and history as well as his personal history and how it represents that of China, as the title poem connotes. Poems such as "Sharing a Drink with Li He" 與李賀共飲, quoted in part, exemplify this:

I mull over quatrains, quatrains,
  quatrains as if
I were chewing five-piece beans
In your impassioned eyes
Is a jug of newly brewed Huadiao wine
From the Tang dynasty to the Song to
  the Yuan to the Ming and to the Qing
At last it is poured into this small
  cup of mine
I try to stuff the seven-character
  quatrain that you are most proud of

嚼五香蠶豆似的
嚼著絕句。絕句。絕句。
你激情的眼中
溫有一壺新釀的花雕
自唐而宋而元而明而清
最後注入我這小小的酒杯
我試著把你最得意的一首七絕
塞進一隻酒甕中
搖一搖，便見雲霧騰升
語字醉舞而平仄亂撞
甕破，你的肌膚碎裂成片

Into a wine run
I shake it up, then watch as the
　　mist rises
Language dances drunkenly,
　　rhymes clash chaotically
The urn breaks, your flesh shatters
Screeching ghosts
Are heard on a vast plain
The howls of wolves are carried
　　over thousands of miles

Come, sit down, let's drink together
On this blackest night in history
You and I are obviously not from
　　among the run-of-the-mill
We aren't troubled by not being
　　included in the *Three Hundred
　　Poems of the Tang Dynasty*
Of what use are the nine grades
　　of official rank?
They are not worth bothering about
Weren't you hung over that year?
Vomiting poetry on the jade steps
　　of noble houses
Drink, drink up
The moon probably won't shine tonight
For this once-in-an-eon meeting
I want to take advantage of the
　　darkness to write you a
　　difficult poem
Incomprehensible, then let them
　　not understand
Not understand
Why after reading it we look at
　　each other and burst out laughing

曠野上, 隱聞
鬼哭啾啾
狼嗥千里

來來請坐, 我要與你共飲
這歷史中最黑的一夜
你我顯非等閒人物
豈能因不入唐詩三百首而相對發愁
從九品奉禮郎是個什麼官?
這都不必去管它
當年你還不是在大醉後
把詩句嘔吐在豪門的玉階上
喝酒呀喝酒
今晚的月, 大概不會為我們
這千古一聚而亮了
我要趁黑為你寫一首晦澀的詩
不懂就讓他們去不懂
不懂
為何我們讀後相視大笑

(Luo 1981: 161–164)

Luo Fu is writing as much about himself as he is about the Tang dynasty poet. Both poets are misunderstood, but Luo Fu is not whining; his tone is mocking and he seems fairly certain of his place in modern Chinese letters. He has accepted the fact that he will never be a popular poet.

　　Concomitant with the interest and growing influence of traditional poetry was a thematic turn to root-seeking and nostalgia for his home in China, a major trend among émigré mainland poets in Taiwan. Luo Fu's following collections continued to develop these themes. *Wine-Brewing*

Stone 釀酒的石頭 (1983), for example, contains a forty-two-page elegy to the poet's mother that is in fact a lament for China; *Nirvana of Angels* 天使的涅槃 (1990) features a number of poems written after the poet visited the mainland. His return left him feeling like a stranger. The intervening years had distanced him from his homeland. In 1990, Luo Fu also published the collection *House of Moonlight* 月光房子, which contains a large number of occasional lyrics as well as longer, nostalgic poems such as "Cricket's Song" 蟋蟀之歌 (excerpted):

Someone living abroad once said: "Last night I heard a cricket
chirr and mistook it for the one I heard in the countryside of Sichuan."
. . . .

有人說: "在海外, 夜晚聽到蟋蟀叫, 還以為就是四川鄉下聽到的那一隻."
○ ○ ○ ○

Tonight I'm not in Chengdu	今夜不在成都
My snoring is not a longing for home	鼾聲難成鄉愁
And the chirrup in my ears	而耳邊唧唧不絕
Weaves an unending song	不絕如一首千絲萬縷的歌
I can't recall the year, the month,	記不清那年那月那晚
or the evening	在那個城市, 那個鄉間
In what city or village	那個小站聽過
Or in what small train station	唧唧復唧唧
I heard it	○ ○ ○ ○
Chirrup, chirrup	唧唧
. . . .	究竟是那一隻在叫?
Chirrup, chirrup	廣東的那隻其聲蒼涼
Which cricket is it that really sings?	四川的那隻其聲悲傷
The Cantonese one seems the loneliest	北平的那隻其聲聒噪
The Sichuan one, the saddest	湖南的那隻叫起來帶有一股辣味
The Beijing one, the noisiest	而最後---
The Hunan one, the spiciest	我被吵醒的
But	仍是三張犁巷子裏
When I wake	那聲最輕最親的
It's the cricket in Sanli Lane that	唧唧
Sings the softest and most dearly	
of them all	
Chirrup, chirrup	

(Luo 1990: 53–56)

The poem forms an intertextual allusion to a poem by Su Shi, the Song dynasty poet. Interestingly, Luo Fu's poem was one of three written on the same theme using the same central image, along with Liu Shahe 流沙河 (b. 1931) and Yu Guangzhong 余光中 (b. 1928). It is written from the perspective of a traveller listening to the night-time chirping of a cricket, an exile's longing for home.

Another poem from the same collection that crystallizes the tragedy of modern China and the tragic sense of history, while written on a traditional theme, is "Mailing a Pair of Shoes" 寄鞋, a poem that depicts a gift from one lover to another, separated during the long cold war:

From a thousand miles away	間關千里
I'm mailing you a pair of cotton shoes	寄給你一雙布鞋
A letter	一封
With no words	無字的信
Containing more than forty years	積了四十多年
of things to say	想說無從說
Things only thought but never said	只好一句句
One sentence after another	密密縫在鞋底
Closely stitched into the soles	
	這些話我偷偷藏了很久
What I have to say I've kept hidden	有幾句藏在井邊
for so long	有幾句藏在廚房
Some of it hidden by the well	有幾句藏在枕頭下
Some of it hidden in the kitchen	有幾句藏在午夜明滅不定的燈火裏
Some of it hidden under my pillow	有的風乾了
Some of it hidden in the flickering	有的生霉了
lamp at midnight	有的掉了牙齒
Some of it has been dried by the wind	有的長出了青苔
Some of it has grown moldy	現在一一收集起來
Some of it has lost its teeth	密密縫在鞋底
Some of it has grown moss	
Now I gather it all together	鞋子也許嫌小一些
And stitch it closely into the soles	我是以心裁量, 以童年
	以五更的夢裁量
The shoes may be too small	合不合腳是另一回事
I measured them with my heart,	請千萬別棄之
with our childhood	若敝屣
With dreams from deep in the night	四十多年的思念
Whether they fit or not is another	四十多年的血淚
matter	四十多年的孤寂
Please, never throw them away	全都縫在鞋底
As if they were worn-out shoes	
Forty years of thought	
Forty years of blood and tears	
Forty years of loneliness	
Are all stitched into the soles	

(Luo 1990: 159–160)

Luo Fu's most recent collection titled *Driftwood* 漂木 is actually a 240-page poem. In a sense the poet has come full circle from *Death of a Stone Cell*, the antiepic of his youth, to *Driftwood*, the epic summation of the poet's artistic journey, life experience, and philosophy. On the poem, Luo Fu says, "It sums up my experience of exile, my artistic explorations, and my metaphysics. I consider it a personal epic, the greatest achievement of my old age, and a landmark of my career" (Luo 2001). I had lunch with Luo Fu one day in late spring in Taipei in 1992. He mentioned that he had been contemplating a long poem, an epic about the Chinese people and what they had experienced in the twentieth century. He did not actually sit down and write a long poem until years later after moving to Vancouver. Two interrelated factors seemed to have inspired his decision: he wanted to realize an "aesthetics of distance" (Luo 2002: 284) he had been pondering the last few years and his experience of loneliness during his "second exile" (the first being to Taiwan). In the lonely days after moving abroad, Luo Fu began to take stock of his past. He had lived through a good deal of war and chaos: the war with Japan, the civil war, the bombardment of Quemoy, and the Vietnam War. He began to feel that this life experience for all its tragedy was as transient and fleeting as a dream.

The sense of loneliness and tragedy developed into what Luo Fu terms an aesthetics of distance consisting of two qualities: (1) a tragic consciousness—a combined sense of personal and national tragedy, (2) universalism, transcendent of time and space. Initially, Luo Fu had planned to write about the loneliness and deracination to which many overseas Chinese are subject; however, as he wrote, the focus gradually shifted to a more general exploration of the meaning of life. The theme of the poem capsulates the sense of helplessness and transience of life.

The poem is divided into four parts. The first part, titled "Driftwood," establishes the opening theme. Through the agency of a piece of driftwood, the poet examines and critiques contemporary Chinese culture and society in both Taiwan and mainland China. The second part, titled "The Salmon's Encounter with Death" 鮭, 垂死的逼視, deals with the migratory and unsettled life of the sockeye salmon. The fish comes to represent a drifting, unsettled spirit, symbolic of not only the poet's own rootless existence, but also the larger contemporary milieu. The themes of love, life, and death stand in high relief in this part. The third part, titled "Letters in Bottles" 浮瓶中的書札, is divided into four subsections. The first section "To My Mother" 致母親 deals with a mother's love; in the second section "To the Poets" 致詩人, Luo Fu examines his own views on poetry; and in the third section "To Time" 致時間, he delves into the mystery of time; the fourth and final section "To the Gods" 致諸神 investigates religion. The Fourth and final part of the poem is titled

"Homage to the Ruins" 向廢墟致敬 and probes and criticizes the drifting way of life, the anxiety it produces and how it leads ultimately to a decline and even destruction of culture.

As milestones at opposite ends of Luo Fu's career, *Driftwood* and *Death of a Stone Cell* naturally beg comparison. At one point Luo Fu had considered rewriting his first long poem, but soon dismissed the idea. It was a product of its day. In *Driftwood*, Luo Fu sought to maintain the same linguistic tension and purity as those of the earlier work, but without the overly hermetic results arising from the difficult imagery and private symbols. There remain major differences between the two works. In *Death of a Stone Cell*, Luo Fu expressed his thoughts on life and death using a Surrealist technique; in *Driftwood*, on the other hand, he offers a detached, rational critique of the many aspects of the contemporary Chinese-speaking world.

Luo Fu chose the long poem as a recapitulation for several reasons. Although the separate parts are largely written in different forms and styles, opting for the long poem required him to articulate a comprehensive worldview. He had to proceed in a rational way to develop his themes as well as to create the appropriate forms to best convey the content. He had to stretch his linguistic resources. Taiwan has produced few long poems in the last fifty years and the best ones have largely been historical narratives. Many more have been written in mainland China, but they tend to be narrative poems, of an especially political or historical nature. Luo Fu's ambitious project is therefore largely unprecedented in the annals of contemporary Chinese poetry. I quote from the second part of the poem in order to convey a sense of the work:

The moment an eagle swoops down	當河谷上空一隻鷹鷟
Out of the sky above a river valley and	俯衝而下
Seizes	叼去了
A diaphanous layer of moonlight	河面上一層薄薄的月光
from the water's surface	時間噤聲
Time is silenced	故事正要開始
As our tale unfolds	
Once we swim upstream from the sea	我們一旦游進內陸
The Adam's River becomes eloquently	亞當河變成了滔滔的
mute	兩岸草色淒迷
The grassy banks dreary	霧，比想像中更難掌控
The fog harder to control than ever	早晨很淡
imagined	一到下午臉色多變，口齒不清
So pale the morning	一路也不見激噴湍飛沫
Changing by afternoon, speech slurred	體溫漸失的河水

The turbulent waters are gone
The river gradually grows colder
Leaves fall
Autumn floats and sinks
The water's words
Sputter on dangerous shoals
The fallen leaves are silent as autumn
　　sheds tears
There's absolutely no need for such
　　classical cruelty
The road extends to the horizon
Precipices and plains are all part
　　of the course
In the great wave of Change
There is no need for joy or sorrow
And even less need to stubbornly
　　insist that
I'm just a bubble amid Change
Fear is unnecessary
Anger is unnecessary
Excessive concern is unnecessary
Living for a philosophy or death
Also

Unnecessary
God exists in the breaths we take
And in the
Breathing of a
Blood-gorged louse
Reverence is unnecessary
Excessive faith is like extra flesh
Piety is unnecessary
Before constructing the garden of life
We were choked
With all sorts of poisonous weeds
And God
Was silent
Our only enemy is time
Before the dream is done
The course of life is run
A plume of smoke
Rises into the empty sky
Silently disperses
Vanishing into a greater nirvana
To deny illness　　unnecessary
To prevent fading and ageing unnecessary

漂來幾片落葉
秋, 載浮載沉
水的語言
在危機四伏的淺灘下吞吞吐吐
落葉無言秋墮淚
這種古典式的殘酷完全沒有必要
路, 向天邊延伸
險峻與平坦都只是過程
縱浪大化中
喜和憂沒有必要
硬說大化中那粒泡沫是我
更無必要
膽怯沒有必要
冷眼橫眉沒有必要
極終關懷沒有必要
為某種哲學而活, 或死
也

沒有必要
神在我們呼吸中
也在
一隻吸飽了血的蝨子
的呼吸中
敬畏沒有必要
過量的信仰有如一身贅肉
虔誠沒有必要
在築構生命之前
我們內部
早就撲滿了各類毒草
而神
甚麼話也沒說
我們唯一的敵人是時間
還來不及做完一場夢
生命的週期又到了
一縷輕煙
升起於虛空之中
又無聲無息地
消散於更大的寂滅
否定病　　沒有必要
阻止褪色與老化沒有必要
執著, 據說毒性很大
當然沒有必要
揚棄　沒有必要
被揚棄也沒有必要
豁達　沒有必要
超越　沒有必要

To cling it is said is more toxic yet   魔　黑臉白臉黑臉白臉沒有必要
And, of course, unnecessary   佛　拈花一笑也無必要
To sift   unnecessary   短短一生
To be sifted also unnecessary   消耗在搜尋一把鑰匙上
Open-mindedness   unnecessary   根本就沒有必要
Transcendence   unnecessary   門　就讓它開著
Demons, good and bad, all unnecessary   雲　就讓它飄著
The Buddha plucking a flower and
  smiling unnecessary
A short life
Spent looking for the key
Entirely unnecessary
The door   let it hang open
The clouds   let them float by

(Luo 2002: 83–87)

Luo Fu never ceases to surprise as a poet. A zen-like awareness of the pointlessness of life's struggles emerges in this poem. It is the source of his longevity as a poet and his following in Taiwan and China. Yet throughout the ceaseless changes run several threads: Luo Fu has been unflagging in his search to articulate the self in China through poetry as well as to bring the tragedy of the century into consciousness through art. He has sought to transcend the limitations imposed by history in the search for the freedom to be, to exist beyond the bounds of history, to live in the moment. Luo Fu's is a unique vision.

Chapter Six

Steward of the Ineffable: "Anxiety-Reflex" in/as the Nature Writing of Liu Kexiang (Or: Nature Writing against Academic Colonization)

Nick Kaldis

A stereotyped but unconscious despair is concealed even under what are called the games and amusements of mankind.

(Thoreau 1983: 50)

Taiwan's nature writers know that we can't imitate traditional Chinese intellectuals of earlier times, ensconced as they were in their exclusive social circles, immersed in their own private worlds; there's little common ground between us. We have to make concessions to this narrow little urban island culture, grope about for an appropriate new way of understanding . . . . A new ecophilosophy must meet an urgent need— to be endowed with real-life applicability . . . . When the criteria for observation are so complex, perhaps we must recognize that the so-called "anxiety reflex" exhibited in a nature writer's works is an immanent principle; peaceful quietism is a castle in the air, a disavowal of and escape from reality.

(Liu Kexiang 2002: 4)

Wary of the myopia and stoicism that result when the lens of scientific thinking is focused on nature, Henry David Thoreau wrote: "I fear this particular dry knowledge may affect my imagination and fancy, that it will not be easy to see so much wildness and native vigor there as formerly" (1858: 340). Nearly 150 years later, scholarly studies of nature writing struggle to comprehend, conceptualize, and assimilate the imagination, wildness, and vigor extolled by Thoreau, and to reconcile imaginative and affective nature writing with scholastic "dry knowledge"—the rational, logical thought and prose of academic discourse.

This chapter argues that, while some recourse to received academic paradigms in the study of environmental literature is inevitable, scholars of the nascent field of Chinese nature writing[1]—both poetry and prose—will need to develop new and rigorous forms of interpretation and self-interrogation as we apply our "enterprise"[2] to this still largely unexploited genre, select and create its canon, and formulate the parameters of a discourse that will determine how we understand, study, write about, and teach works of nature writing by Chinese authors (in Taiwan, the PRC, and Hong Kong). By bringing to light a common thread of anxiety running through nature writing and arguing for its indispensability in scholastic interpretations of nature writing, this chapter is both an attempt to think through complex issues of creative writing, language, interpretation, ecology, affect, and subjectivity that are integral to nature writing, and an academic intervention into established paradigms for the reception of new genres into literary studies.[3]

These issues are made manifest, as Thoreau intimated, the moment a naturalist puts pen to paper. For no matter how noble one's intentions, to be an environmentalist and nature writer is to live a deeply personal, anxious, and conflicted relationship to nature and one's experiences with it, especially vis-à-vis one's inscription of nature into poetry or prose. One can, for instance, take a stirring or transformative experience in nature and keep it to oneself, as a solipsistic encounter. But one remains anxiously aware that such experiences are drastically underrepresented in public discourse, devalued in contemporary social life, and that the spaces for such encounters are consequently increasingly threatened, violated, and being extinguished. Nature is disappearing. To maintain a private relationship to nature therefore is to reject a responsibility—the importance of sharing and reviving an appreciation of vulnerable or vanishing spaces in and encounters with the natural world. It is also tantamount to abandoning nature to those who would develop and defile it for economic gain. Indeed, the instrumentalizers of nature are arguably the most important audience one could engage and alert to the symbiotic relationship between pristine natural spaces and the urban, suburban, agricultural, industrial, and commercial spaces that threaten to overwhelm or defile them. As Alfred W. Crosby has argued, "[I]f we must live *here*—and there is, for the very long time being, no likely *there* to go to—then we should take an interest in the nest we are building, strengthening, dismantling, and fouling *here*" (Crosby 1990: 1108).[4]

To restate and elaborate the nature writer's paradox: In an age when opportunities for contact with nature are diminishing, while instances of ecological destruction are myriad, none can deny the importance of written records of our vanishing experiences with what lies outside human-industrial civilization. Such works convey experiences that may inspire readers to care about and cultivate their own encounters with nature. But there is much to complicate this understanding of the correspondence between environmental literature and the environment. Most vexing is the medium through which we document and share our encounters with nature—language.

The moment one sets out to share an encounter with nature one must symbolize it, frame it within discourse, and convert it into language. (At yet another further remove comes the scholarly interpretation of this discursive representation of the original encounter with nature—more on this below). First of all, there is the issue of moving from direct experiences in nature to literary reformulations of those experiences. As one converts an experience of nature into language—poetic, prosaic, imagistic, or otherwise—everything from the original experience that cannot be reduced or translated into language vanishes.[5] Even the most compassionate and ecologically sensitive soul is changing the structure of her/his experience with nature the moment s/he filters the experience through the ordering logic of language and its fealty to the ideological imperatives of given narrative forms. During this process of transcription, the person's original experience of the irreducible and always to some degree impenetrable *otherness* of nature[6] is at risk of being colonized by the writing process that records and preserves the moment in a familiar narrative structure. For the essential otherness of nature can never be fully manifested in written form, and literary attempts to convey that otherness and/or one's immersion in it risk reducing nature to a unified and knowable concept within a rational-discursive linguistic format.[7] Furthermore, this linguistic conceptualization is usually processed through documentation technologies hostile to nature, such as papermaking, printmaking, computers, and the like.

On the other hand, we must acknowledge that, as socialized beings, rational thought and language are, to use a hackneyed phrase, "always already" present in our experiences of nature—at work in our sensory perceptions and unconscious cognitive processes—influencing the form, feeling, and meaning of everything that finds its way into our awareness. This process is compounded when we consciously attempt to represent the original experience of nature to others. Any effort to describe, verbalize, vocalize, represent, and share an experience of the outdoors cannot avoid using the structure and tools for communication with which our minds—and souls perhaps—have been colonized during the inexorable course of our socialization.

Nonetheless, the nature writer's recourse to discourse, to the language of literature, involves not only procrustean but creative and liberating processes as well. Granted, she or he must contort the original experience with nature in order to make it conform to the predetermined rules and ways of knowing the world that rational cognitive processes and language prescribe. At the same time, however, he or she can break language out of its pen and let it *mimete*[8] ways of knowing world and self that only experiences with nature offer. Through recourse to creative linguistic exploration, nature writing has the power to intervene in the sometimes glibly affirmed notion that thought and discourse mediate all experiences.

These are not mere semantic arguments. For it is within the realms of representation that societies formulate their attitudes and actions toward nature. If not for their conceptualization and representation, their inscription—literary and otherwise—into social discourse, most of us would not know or have cause to care about many species that arguably have been saved by collective, *textually enlightened* environmental agitation: the snail darter, the sea otter, the river dolphin, the spotted owl, the black-faced spoonbill 黑面琵鷺, and other such species.[9] Nor would we have learned to value, (and tried to) protect, and preserve places we may never see—places that for most people exist only in the imagination: the ozone, the polar ice cap, the Redwood forests, Yellowstone, Yosemite, the Three Gorges, and other places that often are brought to our individual and collective awareness via the intervention of writers who immerse us in places, relationships, and ways of being that we experience nowhere else but in their writings. In the process of reading such works our relationship to living things and natural spaces is literally incarnated or permanently altered, solely through linguistic mediation.

With other genres of literature (namely fiction), a hermetic textuality frequently *is* the author's self-conscious medium. This can be an acknowledged and welcome necessity, as the inner world of the psyche, the world of emotion and imagination, has no concrete physical, geographical, or social province of its own, outside of the forms through which it is represented. From this perspective, many fictional texts are purely representational, having no reference or representative outside of discourse, even at their most mimetic. Nature writing, conversely, is the *intersection* between the emotional, subjective, imaginative mind we discover and explore through other literary genres such as fiction, *at the moment of its immersion in the natural environment*, the latter being an external, concrete place, a *contextual reality* aside from which the writing at hand would have no motivation or inspiration, no cause to be (or be studied).

Nature writing is thus part of a struggle to preserve affective, imaginative, solitary and social encounters with an external, concrete other, nature—a concrete entity that has no discourse of its own and always stands partly *outside* the realms of language and cultural production.[10] While rendering such encounters into literary forms, nature writing seeks to sustain and restore a connection to the world that is necessary for the sustenance of *all* culture, society, and humanity (see Cronon 1990).

If this language smacks of romanticism and idealism, then it only serves to highlight the difficulty of these aspirations and the need for a new way of discussing them, beyond the scope of reigning intellectual paradigms, and resistant to their cooptation. Modes for the reception and interpretation of Chinese nature writing must be novel in form and grounded in a knowledge that our task as academicians is to "help us locate in a given historical situation the critical linkages between people and the ecosystems they inhabit" (Cronon 1990: 1126).[11] Otherwise, academia, namely the field of (modern) Chinese literary studies, will rapidly appropriate a new genre such as nature writing and incorporate it into its/our established practices.

In this inenviable scenario, discussing nature writing from Taiwan would be an easy enough task, merely a matter of introducing another literary genre to a group of academics. We would start with a survey of names, dates, and exemplary texts and provide a sample cross-section of the variety found therein, eventually divvying it into sub-genres.[12] Then we, or a second generation of nature writing scholars, would begin to produce the requisite applications of currently dominant critical theories to selected texts. Canonization—or colonization—would soon follow. In this enterprise, we would be faithful to Davis's critique of the process: "Most professional students of literature are technicians who, like Thomas Kuhn's 'normal scientists,' prove their membership in the [academic] community by putting reigning paradigms into practice" (Davis 1994: 3).

Taiwan nature writing, I hope, will prove resistant to the application of reigning paradigms in the study of Chinese literature. For it, and nature writing in general, demands a more concrete, vital, and self-referential interpretive methodology. As Liu Kexiang 劉克襄 (b. 1956) has written, Taiwan nature writing has struggled to free itself from, among other Western and Chinese traditions, both abstract idealism and eremitism (Liu 2002: 6). Literary scholars approaching this genre likewise must free themselves from received interpretive conventions and instead seek new, dynamic, open-ended paradigms for analyzing nature writing, paradigms that are developed directly out of the principles they find *within each text*.[13] Otherwise, nature writing will soon be just one more "area of specialization" on the CVs of sinologists.

To reiterate, the scholar's task ought to be, I argue, to strive for forms of interpretation that recognize and valorize the irreducible, unfathomable otherness of the nature writer's subject—nature and man's relationship to the environment—while simultaneously bringing to light what is original and insightful about a literary attempt to breach or approach that lacuna. Analyses of nature as (discursive) referent ought to alter or supplement our understanding of *how* and *why* we refer, denote, symbolize, and interpret.

The greatest difficulty in this enterprise lies, perhaps, in remaining aware of what is lost when academia turns its established paradigms onto the discursive product exclusively, as described in the scenario above. For the academic enterprise can be "professional" in the most pejorative Marxist sense of the word, in that texts and competitive display of our mastery over them is often an end unto itself in literary studies. No matter how humbling, it will remain imperative to police the inception of Chinese nature writing into the academy,[14] censoring from our own analyses anything that smacks of the careerist instrumentalization of texts that is often the ticket to publishing and conference venues.[15] We must instead strive to engage with and take up the spirit of each individual nature writing text, even accept it as a direct challenge to our established habits of interpreting and discoursing on literary works. We must scrutinize how in—or out of—sync our academic appropriations of nature writing are with the author's and the text's relationship to nature. And, we must endeavor to tread full circle, away from our computers and conference venues and back into the source of all this discourse and textualizing—nature. Just as cultural immersion is the gold standard for Chinese language studies, so must *natural* immersion become the green standard and sine qua non for scholars and students of nature writing.

In purely discursive terms, how then might one introduce into the *academic context* writings that are deeply connected to and inspired by nature, writings by people that communicate passion, compassion, and concern for the *environmental context* of which they write?[16] In response to this apparent conundrum, this attempt to synthesize two ostensibly opposed contexts, scholars must strive to sublate the contradiction between the two, without attempting to resolve it. We should attempt to treat nature writing as the kernel or residue of and, in some cases, the sole access to a kind of experience that is not reducible or translatable into other ways of knowing, into other discourses. In translating, interpreting, and disseminating Taiwan nature writing we must strive to acknowledge the unique mode of knowing one's natural environment found therein. Nature writing stands at the forefront of attempts to know what has not yet been formulated about man's precarious yet intimate relationship to the natural world, and we cannot begin to collectively understand this relationship until it has been constituted in a form accessible to conscious understanding, such as literature. As the theorist Walter A. Davis has repeatedly argued,

> Forms of art are original ways of knowing, independent principles of perception and cognition, which give us a unique and primary apprehension of the real . . . providing an immediate access to experience that exceeds the limits of the concept and of socialized, rhetorical determinations of meaning. (2001: 216–217)

> [T]he basic problem is to comprehend the forms of literary creation as original modes of access to experience capable of giving us an understanding of the world which other ways of knowing fail to provide. (1978: 97)

Applying Davis's argument to the genre of Taiwan nature writing, I further argue that, outside of nature writing, we have no access to what, for lack of a less wordy term, I call *the avant-garde of the ecological imagination*. What I mean to describe, in the case of Taiwanese nature writing, is its creative synthesis of the emotional perceptions and associative thought processes that Freud associated with creativity and grouped under the term "primary process thinking," as opposed to objective, rational, scientific knowledge, or "secondary process thinking"[17] (this brings us back to the earlier citations from Thoreau).

One writer frequently associated with the birth and development of the genre of nature writing in Taiwan is Liu Kexiang, arguably the island's preeminent nature writer. Liu's prose essays, prose poems, and lyrical poems constitute an impressive argument for an understanding of the sovereignty of environmental literature as a primary way of understanding our relationship to nature, proof that "[artistic] representation is cognition" (Davis 2001: 152).[18] I must add here that, in the case of Taiwan (and the PRC), where nature is radically embattled and diminished, these are far from being idle theoretical concerns.[19]

In Liu's work, the reader experiences the contradictory and emotionally conflicted, subjective yet thoroughly historical, awareness of the desperate current state of ecological crisis in Taiwan, yoked to images of the unique natural beauty of the island, communicated through a deeply personal, anxious, and imaginative worldview. Such writing deliberately ignores boundaries—generic or other—between, in this first excerpt, daydream, autobiography, and reconstruction of an idealized rustic past when modernization had not disrupted the harmonious coexistence of society and nature in rural Taiwan:

> Current of the ocean, island of the continent.
> . . . Please give me back a small station where but one train stops daily, a lone gravel road where the quail and her chicks softly pass at dawn. My home is by the not-too-distant graveyard, by the temple square where spikes of rice are spread to dry . . . my father the grade-school teacher, holding a fishing pole, forever ambling by. (K. Liu 2004a: 122–123)[20]

This autobiographical prose poem, which begins with the speaker's memories of his ageing, terminally ill father taking a train to visit him (in Taipei), is notable for its prayer-like plea, soliciting ageless land and sea to restore an earlier historical stage in the speaker's life and in Taiwan's modernization. It is one of Liu's less overtly ecological poems, yet it aptly represents the subtlety of his poetic imagination as it condenses numerous elements that are all in some way connected to the loss of a more pristine relationship between man and nature. The speaker longs to arrest and reverse development, for the sake of a multilayered personal memory that is at once bucolic and natural, where the comings and goings of wild creatures and a barely industrialized society take place against the backdrop of agricultural, religious, and mortuary settings, the human cycles of life and death. There is a deep melancholy at the heart of this poem, a sense of loss that indirectly associates the processes of advanced ("21st century") development with the loss of the father, yearning for a time when nature, agricultural village, and family coexisted in health and harmony, even accepting and incorporating an earlier stage of modernization—the lone train—into that happy memory. This last inclusion is key to the piece, for Liu acknowledges but rarely laments or protests against the developmental processes. Here he simply allows readers to overhear his impossible plea to the elements, prompting us to make associations with our own nostalgic desires concerning similar developments in our own lives. In the process, the poem precipitates anxiety over those cherished natural features of our current lives that may soon be lost to further social and industrial encroachment.

The lack of angry outbursts is notable in many of Liu's poems and essays that observe ecological devastation. Rarely taking a self-righteous or castigatory tone, his work consistently embodies an acknowledgment and acceptance of—even reverence for—the natural spaces, plants, and creatures that struggle to survive in symbiotic relationship with the sprawling urban-industrial centers that threaten to overwhelm Taiwan's entire western coast. Owing to this feature, Liu's works continually inspire respect and empathy for nature while painting a bleak picture of its precarious state, keeping readers at a distance long enough not to feel accused of complicity in the situation yet putting us in such intimate and moving contact with nature that we cannot help but be infected with an anxiety over the fate of blameless, beautiful, delicate creatures and places, a fate that is connected to our lifestyle:

Exile of the Mangrove Swamp   紅樹林的流亡

A cluster of finely-woven green sprouts   一枚枚綠色的幼苗
Like the crowding of tiny fishes   如小魚群的簇擁
Searching with difficulty for a spot   艱困地尋找著上溯的位置
  against the current   祖先登陸過的地點
The location where their ancestors disembarked   曾經廣闊如海
Once vast as the sea   它們繼續流亡

They continue in exile   在消波塊和垃圾堆間
Amidst vanishing patches of waves   準備躺成腐敗的姿勢
  and mounds of garbage
Preparing to recline into a posture of decay

                              (K. Liu 2004b: 269)

At other times, this sense of anxiety is conveyed through an entirely different method, in prose that borrows from more familiar discourses such as (in the following excerpt) those of cinema and drama, perceiving the world in narratives that create new and unprecedented awareness of connections between self, society, other, and nature, incarnating heretofore unrepresented emotional knowing:

Dusk, setting sun and sand, add some hovering seagulls, some lingering soldiers and fishermen who can't draw themselves away, circling the black whale, watching it struggle, ceaselessly trying to push the whale out to sea, though it diligently beaches again itself each time, on the verge of death. These five days (from its discovery on the 13th to the 17th) news reports on black whales have followed one upon the other like climax after climax in a movie. The backdrop is a beach, and it's the last climactic scene, the last screening of a tragedy . . .

When I'm standing motionless on Da'an beach, a hundred meters from the waves, using my binoculars to confront this "Black Whale," I think of our common mammalian ancestors, and the several million years since we parted ways—the distance between us now seems like an unbreachable chasm dug by history. But watching the spectacle of this whale in its death throes, even with the intervening several million years of evolution separating us into two creatures inhabiting two vastly different environments, the moment of death finds us back where we started—together. Gazing across the distance like this, it also seems as if the whale is right before my eyes, its fate somehow connected to my own. (Liu 2003: 122–123)

Watching birds and humans gather about a beached whale, to scavenge or save it, the author slips into a dreamlike associative state. Stark documentary reality is condensed with emotive cinematic imagery and, as he peers through binocular lenses, his imagination gives rise to an enigmatic yet deep empathy with the suicidal whale. Here, aesthetic perception makes some unlikely and novel associations that lead to a moving conclusion: modern visual technologies (TV, cinema, binoculars), rather than encouraging specular, voyeuristic distancing, can help breach the historical, evolutionary, and geographical distances between man and other species, creating an uncanny and disturbing proximity, producing dramatic images that call for ethical understanding and behavior.

Our task, once confronted with such images, is to "arrest" them as they "flare up at a moment of crisis and attempt to internalize and articulate their significance before they disappear, perhaps irretrievably, in the predictable rush toward [discursive] ideological reaffirmations" (Davis 2003: 128).

These works by Liu Kexiang demonstrate that, although nature writing is a form of cultural production, an albeit reductive but necessary *discourse* of nature, it has nonetheless become a vital contributing factor in the struggle to preserve and restore natural and wild creatures and spaces, tiny and vast. Such works embody a concern for and connection to something that once existed in an independent, self-sustaining form, wholly *outside* the realm of human-industrial civilization and cultural production. But today the coexistence of nature with developed spaces depends in part on the ability of discourses such as nature writing to represent and uphold nature's precarious sovereignty, even while instantiating the impossibility of its exhaustive distillation into words.

This burden of being both steward of ineffable nature and producer of the public discourse of nature infuses much of Liu Kexiang's nature writing with the "anxiety-reflex" mentioned earlier, clearly evident in the excerpts above. In other pieces, Liu borrows from extant genres to precipitate a kind of regression in the adult reader, conflating (or sublimating) the anxiety from our childhood encounters with imaginative narratives into an adult impetus toward social action on behalf of our shared and inhabited environment:

> Over the past several years most cases involving pollution of our environment seem to have taken the form of a behind-the-scenes fairy tale that never reaches a conclusion. It always goes something like this:
> . . .
> Once upon a time there was a happy place. Then one day an ogre suddenly appeared and began to ceaselessly torment the people who lived in the happy place. The people suffered terribly, and tried every known means to rid themselves of this ogre, but to no avail. Finally they had to ask the local magistrate to intercede on their behalf. Who could have guessed that a magistrate would be terrified of such things, not daring to take any action for fear of provoking the ogre? ! . . .
> An ending without ending. The past is precisely a fairy tale of this kind, leaving so many of these environmental degradation issues hanging, suspended like the toxic emissions from the Sanhuang pesticide factory these dozen odd years. However, this year witnessed a turning point when the "Sanhuang" district residents interceded on their own behalf, and are now trying to rewrite this preposterous fairy tale. Even if their attempts fail, they plan to expose the facts for everyone in the country to see. . . .
> To put it another way, who has the right to subject local residents to such prolonged tribulation? This pesticide factory, this ogre, how does it dare so brazenly flout the law? Where is the institution responsible for banning such flagrant acts of pollution? . . . .
> We don't ever again want to come across another of these tales without endings; we've already had too many of them, far too many.
> (Liu 1992a: 66; 67–68)

This real-life story of grass-roots collective action against a major industrial polluter, whether immediately successful or not, is shown to have achieved an overlooked success: the *intervention in shared, collective social narratives* that we tell about the struggle of individuals and local communities against oppressive industrial monsters of mythical proportions. Even when we fail to concretely reform one cog in the machine of industrial development, we have nonetheless permanently "rewritten" the "preposterous" once-monolithic narrative that seemed to have consigned all such tales to a stock doomed dénouement. We need not capitulate to the perceived inevitability of events, whether allegorically in fairy tales or in public narratives of social justice. Liu imaginatively forges the link between our childhood indoctrination into the foregone narrative conclusions of fairy tales and our adult numbing to equally "preposterous" social injustices, then he shows that an outraged community can stand up to its fears of industrial ogres. This brilliant example of aesthetic perception exemplifies, to paraphrase the well-known psychoanalytic process, "regression in the service of the eco."

To summarize, through the social and cultural act of writing, nature writers increase awareness of the fact that society and discursive cultural production are now irrevocably responsible for the continued existence of that which is always to some degree *other* to human-industrial society, and, paradoxically, other to cultural production. Our experience of nature is acknowledged by Liu Kexiang and many other nature writers as being fraught with irreversible choice, permanent loss, and a knowledge of the burden of being responsible for one's fate, as enacted in one's representations of attitudes and actions toward the environmental other.[21]

This awareness is the origin of an anxiety one finds at the heart of much Taiwan nature writing. Liu Kexiang speaks of this anxiety (焦躁和不安) as an "imminent principle" in a nature writer's work (Liu 2002). It is an anxiety that, directly expressed or left implicit, runs like a shudder just beneath the surface of the words, a fear that *not* to talk about nature's beauty and mystery, *not* to turn it into an object of discourse, *not* to symbolize our connection to its fragility, complexity, and independence from us, *not* to do all this will result in a loss from which no act of recovery, discursive, academic, or otherwise, will be possible. Indeed, anxiety for many nature writers is a primary creative impetus and an *affect* that must be imparted to readers at all costs. It is a state of emotional awareness that cannot be resolved through generic conventions such as closure, parody, irony, catharsis, *Deus ex machina*, or any other literary strategy. Nature writing, at its best, creates and sustains unresolved states of anxiety.

This relationship to nature mirrors the state that existentialism describes as humankind's condition. Briefly summarized, it implies that once we undertake sole responsibility for our decisions, actions, and beliefs, humans are overcome by a permanent sense of anxiety. For those who refuse to flee this state, unwilling to ignore or deny their freedom and their responsibility, anxiety is a constant.[22] The world's current ecological crisis has indeed prompted a renewed existential ethic among many nature writers, but layreaders and scholars are yet to be swayed. These writers' works warn us that the natural world has, through technological developments and overpopulation, been given over to man to either destroy—himself with it—or to preserve against overwhelming odds. "Nature," to paraphrase Sartre's famous formulation, "precedes essence."

By invoking and mimetically representing this anxious condition as our relationship to the natural world, nature writing reminds us that confusion and anxiety over one's choices in the world are necessary conditions of an authentic existence, and we cannot look for guarantees that would relieve us of this knowledge. Nor can we seek solace in representations of nature that praise man as benign steward or glorify nature as protective mother. Nature writing today reveals the bad faith behind any attempts to delude ourselves with the triumphant rhetoric of developmental mastery, utopianism, idealism, romanticism, or eremitic escape. Through artistic knowing, nature writing reestablishes our intimate and inescapable connection to something simultaneously vital to our existence and ineffable—something that remains permanently outside the social, the discursive, the objectifiable, the symbolic.[23] Writer and reader share in an anxious and paradoxical awareness that to not write about our relationship to and experiences with nature is to betray one's certainty of the importance of documenting and sharing such events, while writing about them instantiates a removal from the immediacy of such relationships and experiences, translating them into discursive shadows of the original and confining them to the ideological parameters of narrative formulas.

The best nature writing, incarnated in the works of a writer (naturalist, poet, essayist, activist) such as Liu Kexiang, stands as proof that sustaining anxiety does not mean slipping away from reality into a world of private emotions, but that it can crystallize and deepen our knowledge of what it is *to be*. For anxiety always indicates the presence of an existential issue that is of profound importance to us and demands our attention. Anxiety shatters all psychological reassurances and narrative guarantees, while grounding us in those core issues that are essential to our being. In Taiwan and other nature writing, this being is permanently intertwined with and inseparable from *being in nature*.

Notes

1. I will use this term in a somewhat general way throughout this essay, to encompass nature-centered poetry, prose poetry, and essays. An exclusionary definition serves neither nature nor academic understanding; furthermore, this more expansive definition of nature writing is an apt generic classification for the oeuvre of Liu Kexiang, who himself refers to the works I will discuss as of a kind, pointing to their consistent thematic concerns together with his preferred style of combining subjective/imaginative expressivity with objective/observational description; hence,

the general application of the generic term. The original Chinese term itself is a bit more narrowly defined; it is a relatively new prose and prose poetry genre that appeared in Taiwan circa the early 1980s, now known as 自然寫作 or 自然書寫 "Nature Writing" (familiar with and influenced by, but distinct from the well-established American genre of the same name). It has been defined by Wu Mingyi as a category that "manifests a number of cross-disciplinary qualities ([from] literature, philosophy, history, natural science . . .)" and is deeply intertwined with "the natural environment, the social environment, intellectual movements [in the humanities], even politics and economics" (Wu 2004: 38–62). In addition to Wu's description, we could add that Nature Writing contains various mixtures of: prose and poetry; highly subjective, sometimes creative and imaginative observations and reflections on nature; warnings or protests about development and pollution; documentation of personal encounters with nature and/or wilderness [the latter a disputed term in Taiwanese academic analyses of nature writing]; as well as scientific and statistical facts and analyses.

2. A favorite term of Thoreau's; see the "Economy" chapter of *Walden* for Thoreau's tour-de-force appropriation—indeed, wholesale redefinition— of business and economic terminology. I thank Leonard Neufeldt for teaching me how to read Thoreau.

3. I hesitate to treat Chinese (language) nature writing as a genre so unique as to preclude its inclusion within well-established Western traditions. Yet I also believe that the translation and interpretation of 自然寫作/自然書寫 should from the outset retain and respect the genre's cultural, social, and linguistic integrity. In other words, one goal in this process is to avoid marginalizing 自然寫作/自然書寫 as the "Chinese contribution" to an authoritative discourse emanating from America and Europe. Here it may be helpful to recall that the works of Mencius were historically among the first to directly address the ethical importance of sustainable agricultural practices: *Cugu buru wuchi, yu bie buke shengshi ye. Fu jin yishi ru shanlin, caimu buke shengyong ye* 數罟不入洿池、魚鱉不可勝食也。斧斤以時入山林, 材木不可勝用也 "If close nets are not allowed to enter the pools and ponds, the fishes and turtles will be more than can be consumed. If the axes and bills enter the hills and forests *only* at the proper time, the wood will be more than can be used" (Mencius 1970: 130–131).

4. Davis reveals the *unconscious* processes fueling this fouling: "In dominating nature, subjects attain the illusion of inner dominance; in imposing our will on nature we assure ourselves we have triumphed within. Nature becomes that other we must treat with contempt, especially when she shows herself in power, sheer magnificence, radical independence, unravished splendor. And so we go forth subduing nature in order to extinguish something in ourselves we are intent on denying. We must eradicate the spectre by squeezing every energy out of the ecosystem, leaving as testimony to our will the scorched earth at our backs as we rush to greener fields" (Davis 2001: 90–91).

5. Lacanian treatments of this linguistic issue refer to the "primordial signifier," the "structurally necessary" limit of meaning that both energizes the subject's restless quest for relationship to otherness, and reveals an impossible and dangerous desire for complete understanding of otherness, for modes of signification and representation that would reveal otherness without leaving an unknowable remainder, a residue of inscrutability. From this perspective, the desire to understand our experiences with nature through language involves some unwillingness to accept a nature that will always at some level remain impervious to the meanings that we project into it. When taken to a rational, objective extreme, the disavowal and denial of an impenetrable kernel of nonsense in nature is an epistemological, literary, political, and ecological error (see Eisenstein 2004). While I know of no Taiwan nature writers who are committed Lacanians, many of Liu Kexiang's works demonstrate self-consciousness about the impossibility of any signifying quest—literary or otherwise—to capture the full presence and meaning of nature and our experiences in it. The last section of this essay will discuss the pervasive tone of anxiety underlying these works. We might distinguish such works from others that betray a faith in the fullness of representational presence and mimetic completeness (this is not to categorically dismiss all types of nature writing that fall into the latter group, nor those that demonstrate both tendencies).

6. Joseph Grange combines both spiritual and philosophical influences in his discussion of the otherness of nature, perhaps most provocatively in his discussion of space and the "inscape of natural space": "Space is both the most prominent and the most reserved dimension of nature. Its public quality is shown by the way it appears before our very eyes. Its hidden and private character is revealed by the fact that we cannot touch or feel it" (Grange 1997: 91, and passim).

7. This section implies the rejection of a cherished myth among some nature enthusiasts, academic and otherwise, the myth that the alienation of modern/industrial/global life is tolerable in part because there is still an intact and centered other in nature, preserving the possibility of an unspoiled nonexploitative harmony between self and other (in some versions, a relationship between man and nature that existed in the past [especially with certain races, such as the native Americans] and can be revived). Man, the tale goes, only needs to abandon his wasteful, consuming, urban-industrial lifestyle and return to a more "natural" way of living. Discourses that sustain this fantasy of nature as an unexploited entity at the periphery of society, getting along quite well *elsewhere* (in parks, preserves, mountains, forest, deserts, glaciers, oceans, etc.), awaiting our return to her restorative embrace, turn a blind eye to the fact that global ecological devastation is the hidden condition underlying every standard of living, it is the cost of most—if not all—local societal development. Nature is therefore being defiled and diminished with a degree of complicity shared across all (modern) cultural formations, all social strata and lifestyles. This complicity, I'm arguing, is in part sustained by the fantasy of a lost and

recoverable onenesswith pristine wilderness, harmony with the environment, etc. This fantasy forecloses on the necessity of projecting ourselves
into the struggle to confront, arrest, and reverse the globalizing order with
its rapacious need to develop and consume all otherness, including nature.
We must demystify global subjectivity—whether whole or fractured, mainstream or marginalized—and acknowledge that all social structures neces-
sitate complicity in the abuse of nature, some of which is irreversible. For
a rigorous Marxist elaboration of this dynamic, see Dordoy and Mellor,
who argue: ". . . the ecological limits to growth give the lie to capitalism's
promise of (eventual) universal abundance" (2000: 43). For the only
approach to these issues (that I know of) that combines environmental
ethics, poststructuralist critique, queer theory, philosophizing, and nature
writing, see Oates (2003). Perhaps owing to the small size of the island,
overpopulation, urban sprawl, and high levels of pollution, the works of
Liu Kexiang (and other Taiwan nature writers) have demonstrated little
proclivity for the fantasy of an unspoiled pristine wilderness surviving
along the inland periphery of the east coast urban-industrial corridor.

8. Neologism intended.

9. The fate of the black-faced spoonbill was profoundly affected by Liu
   Kexiang's 1992 essay, *Zuihou de heimian wuzhe* 最後的黑面舞者 (The
   last black-faced dancers), which touched off one of Taiwan's most
   successful grassroots environmental movements to date (K. Liu 1992b).

10. A further note on the psychoanalytical specificities of this argument: Julia
    Kristeva's work contains a substantial repository of original discussions
    and analysis of what is sometimes formulated as "the threshold of the
    unnameable," the distinction between the known and what cannot be
    thought, that which every speaker contains yet will "always remain
    unsaid, unnameable within the gaps of speech" (Kristeva 1980: 272).
    While this kernel of linguistic unintelligibility is always present in our
    relationships to others (see note seven above), it functions outside of
    theoretical discourse in radically different ways. That is to say, how I the-
    orize the unknowable and unnameable aspects of my relationship to my
    familial and social others, no matter how conflicted that relationship, is
    vastly different from how I theorize my understanding of nature and the
    environment. Writing about nature, especially about the limits of human
    understanding and discursive attempts to know nature, takes place within
    a larger social discourse that, I am arguing, may very well contribute to,
    facilitate, retard, or even arrest the destruction of real living entities
    and concrete geographical places. On the other hand, psychoanalytic
    formulations of the gaps in language and knowing that intimate an unin-
    telligible other *within the self* may contribute to an albeit traumatic
    confrontation with one's psyche (via a regression to presymbolic aspects
    of one's inner world), but will not concretely affect the very earth, air,
    water, plants, and creatures upon which all beings rely.

11. Terms such as "ecosystem," "environment," "nature," etc. reflect the
    effort, throughout this essay, to embrace as generous a definition of the

environment as possible, in keeping with Wallace and Armbruster's assertion that "Environment need not only refer to 'natural' or 'wilderness' areas . . . environment also includes cultivated and built landscapes, the natural elements and aspects of those landscapes, and cultural interactions with those natural elements. One way ecocriticism can and should widen its range of topics is to pay more attention to texts that revolve around these less obviously 'natural' landscapes and human attempts to record, order, and ultimately understand their own relationships to those environments" (Wallace and Armbruster 2001: 1–25).

12. (For a concise history, for example, see Wu 2004: 83–150; 196–217; and especially 302–584). Wu's magisterial survey reveals a thinker who is deeply conversant with Western and Taiwanese (and [traditional] Chinese) nature writing, environmentalism, and ecological theory. While this type of book cannot avoid instantiating the academic incorporation of nature writing, Wu's is a highly self-critical, introspective, and principled attempt to preserve the unique ethical, intellectual, and creative contribution of nature writing to established ways of knowing self and world.

13. For this reason, the present essay deliberately avoids discussion of the numerous authors who have contributed to the development of Taiwan nature writing, such as Xu Renxiu 徐仁修, Wang Jiaxiang 王家祥, and Hong Suli 洪素麗, among others. In my translating and interpretation of Liu's nature writing, I have attempted to elucidate the specificities of each piece as well as a collective through-line (embodied, I believe, in the "anxiety reflex" discussed below).

14. Here and elsewhere, when referring to the academy, literary studies, scholarly texts, I deliberately conflate these with Chinese literary studies, the sinological community, and its scholarly texts. How the Western academy determines and imposes interpretive and discursive paradigms for studies of Chinese nature writing is a separate chapter of a larger project of which the present essay is but one installment.

15. Our dominant paradigms are paraded forth at nearly every literature panel, often doing little more than demonstrating our intellectual self-censorship and perpetual willingness to reinscribe the narrow boundaries of the interpretive enterprise, rather than actually engaging the world to which literature and its interpretation ostensibly refer. Note, for instance, the jet and auto fuel/exhaust, the shameful heap of nonorganic, nonrecyclable detritus of plastics and styrofoam, uneaten food, wasted water, gas, electricity, and paper generated by conference venues, a vast unaddressed subtext looming over every panel, poster, roundtable, and paper presented (original version of present essay included), as scholars such as myself passionately hold forth on topics like "nature as sovereign other."

16. For a fascinating argument that incorporates this passion for nature as well as the irreducible otherness of nature as the basis for an environmental ethics, see Mick Smith's inspiring and erudite attempt to "trace a conception of ethics as an *excess* that can resist the rationalization and

the disenchantment of the life-world, a power that can sustain that anarchic love of nature that is a characteristic feature of radical ecology" (Smith 2001: 191).

17. In addition to repetition, contiguity, and metonymy, other modes of primary process thinking (linguistic misprision, unconscious "logic") include: metaphor, tropes, figures of speech such as periphrasis, ellipsis, denial, digression, irony, litotes, etc. These and others are touched upon by Shoshana Felman in her discussion of a (Lacanian) *"rhetoric of the unconscious"* (Felman 1985: 119–25, 180–183). Laplanche and Leclaire list "timelessness, absence of negation and contradiction, condensation, displacement" (Laplanche and Leclaire 1972: 248). See also the work of Charles Rycroft for numerous analyses of primary process thinking (1985; 1992).

18. Elsewhere, Davis elaborates on this argument: "[L]iterature is a special mode of knowing which alone, perhaps, gives us an adequate apprehension of concrete experience. Whereas other ways of thinking inevitably compromise life's complexities, literature preserves 'the whole of things' in a nonreductive and concrete totality . . . . So understood, literature, like philosophy, is a comprehensive and autonomous mode of ontological knowing" (Davis 1978: 35).

19. A note on Taiwan's emergent nature writing canon and an as-of-yet still to emerge canon of nature writing from the PRC (as of 2007). Marxist praxis will be essential in our academic considerations of differences between these two versions of Chinese nature writing, which will surely beg comparison and contrast in the future. The literature from each place instantiates the local writer's attempt to constitute, negotiate, and give meaning to encounters with his distinct natural surroundings vis-à-vis— or perhaps, more appropriately, in opposition to—dominant domestic discourses on nature that are saturated with political ideology. Whether Marxist-Maoist or Capitalist, domestic nature writers in each milieu have to take up a linguistic, imagistic, and affective struggle against Taiwan and PRC public discourses on nature that seek to harmonize and domesticate nature to economic, social, and political goals for national development and modernization. Academic studies of nature writing must remain sensitive to these differing local and domestic contexts. Perhaps both places, having been overrun by urban sprawl, pollution, and overpopulation, will produce works that focus on nature's precarious and limited presence within the urban metropolis. Some of Liu Kexiang's work, for instance, repeatedly addresses this unique (non-American, I would argue) sensitivity to, for want of a better term, "urban wildlife."

20. For a much earlier fictional formulation of a very similar type of complexly condensed nostalgia, see Wang Wenxing's short story "Flaw" (Wang 1995: 235–245).

21. The Camus essay "Absurd Freedom," discusses an analogous paradoxical state, the "appetite for the absolute and for unity and the impossibility of

reducing this world to a rational and reasonable principle" (Camus 1966: 297).

22. Depending on the thinker, anxiety may be likened to or grouped with dread, anguish, or nausea.

23. Some readers may wish to contrast my argument with more optimistic assessments of nature writing's ability to reconnect subject and environment in a holistic manner. See, for example, Kandi Tayebi's compassionate discussion of the ways nature writing draws us into "an intense relationship with the environment that unites the intellectual, physical, and emotional aspects of our being" (Tayebi 2003: 1).

Chapter Seven

Opposition and Adaptation in the Poetry of Zhai Yongming and Xia Yu

Andrea Lingenfelter

Only a year apart in age, Zhai Yongming 翟永明 (b. 1955) and Xia Yu (Hsia Yü) 夏宇 (b. 1956)[1] belong to the first generation of Chinese-language women poets who have given themselves license to write frankly about all aspects of their lives. Although each has at some point resisted being labeled as a "woman writer" or as a representative of women as a group, their work is written from a strongly female point of view. Clearly aware of the constraints imposed by traditional conventions of femininity, Zhai Yongming and Xia Yu assert their right to write about anything they choose, independent of traditional limitations on voice or subject matter. Ironically, their liberation from traditional roles has resulted in writing that is strongly feminine (in the sense of being specifically female). Until recently, much of girls' and women's actual experience was deemed an unsuitable subject for literature or art, and women writers could choose either a traditionally "feminine" persona (as defined by patriarchal society), or a gender-neutral persona.[2] A self-assured and sexually aware female persona was not an available choice, although one could argue that there had been a double standard and that the male counterpart of such a persona was acceptable for men. But historical and social forces in both the People's Republic and Taiwan (pre- and post-1949) have weakened many old prejudices and institutional obstacles to women's autonomy, and with the right to self-determination has come the right to self-expression.

While Zhai Yongming and Xia Yu can be said to have cast off traditional constraints, each has engaged traditional Chinese culture in various ways. This chapter will touch on some of these forms of engagement, including their critiques of the traditional institution of marriage, their expression of previously forbidden emotions or subjects (in particular female anger and sexuality), and the ways in which each employs familiar elements of traditional thought and cosmology and shapes them to her own ends, ultimately creating a world that she can inhabit.

Zhai Yongming was born in Chengdu, Sichuan, in 1955 and began publishing poetry in 1981. She spent time in the countryside as a sentdown youth during the 1970s, a formative experience that is both a powerful presence in her early work as well as a touchstone that, decades later, has lost little of its immediacy for her. Although a contemporary of the Misty Poets 朦胧诗人, who came of age during the Cultural Revolution, she is considered a member the Newborn Generation (*xinsheng dai* 新生代), the Misty Poets' successors. Zhai Yongming has been categorized as a "stream of consciousness" poet[3] (Yeh 1992: 394–395), and, like others in this group, she has drawn inspiration from the American confessional poets, especially Sylvia Plath, whose influence is palpable, particularly in the poem sequence "Woman."[4]

Xia Yu was born in Taiwan in 1956 and began publishing poetry there in the 1970s. Xia Yu's educational background is in drama and film, which may account for some of her eclecticism. In addition to writing poetry, she writes essays, song lyrics, stage scripts, and even radio advertisement copy. Xia Yu puts the number of her prose pieces and plays as rather low and describes the bulk of her writing as being private journals and reading notes, saying that these give her the most pleasure, in large part because they afford her complete freedom (Xia 1991: 121). This desire not to be beholden to her readers characterizes Xia Yu's feelings about her poetry as well. When questioned as to whether it concerns her that other people might not fully comprehend her work, she has replied that as long as she herself is satisfied that a passage or poem is successful, what other people think is unimportant: ". . . I really don't care whether or not other people understand [my work], nor whether their way of understanding [the work] is different [from my own]" (Xia 1991: 108). Like many experimental writers before her, she invites readers to make out of her writing what they can. Although I have written elsewhere on the experimental poems that have come increasingly to define her work, my discussion of Xia Yu here will focus mainly on poems from the early 1980s, a period when her works most clearly reflected a concern with women's experience and articulated an unambiguously female point of view.

Although Xia Yu and Zhai Yongming were raised in societies that were determined to be as different from one another as possible, their early works have some similarities in tone and subject matter, and both have intimately described a woman's life in ways that are unprecedented in their bluntness and honesty. Such pieces account for a greater proportion of Zhai Yongming's oeuvre than Xia Yu's; indeed, the bulk of Zhai's works are rooted in autobiography and personal experience. Although she has made forays into collage and borrowed language (popular songs, overheard conversations, clichés) in her later compositions, she remains largely concerned with self-definition and identity, both of which would be particularly compelling to someone who came of age during the Cultural Revolution. Xia Yu, however, is less worried about originality and authenticity and has become increasingly interested in exploring language per se, to the extent that some of her poems are metapoems that probe the nature of poetry in ways that are both formal and thematic.[5] One has to wonder if this relatively light-hearted attitude to originality is partly a product of growing up in a society where the originality espoused by Modernist poetics was a politically acceptable choice. Xia Yu delights in parody and pastiche, which has led at least one critic to refer to her work as postmodern, although one must do so advisedly. Although Xia Yu has declared herself incapable of writing a "sad" poem and seems irresistibly drawn to satire and lampoon (Xia 1991: 120), as Zhong Ling (Ling Chung) has pointed out, even a poet as dedicated to overthrowing and undermining the lyric tradition as Xia Yu nonetheless creates moments of tenderness and lyricism in her poetry (Zhong 1989b). However, the scope of this chapter does not permit me to examine the full range of Xia Yu's expression, and I will focus instead on her more irreverent or socially transgressive side, in particular her powerful critique of tradition, a project that she and Zhai Yongming both engaged in early in their writing lives.

One aspect of tradition that both Zhai Yongming and Xia Yu take on is marriage, an institution that had historically defined a woman's social status and identity. Zhai's poem "The Black Room" 黑房间 (Zhai 1994: 75–76) is especially caustic. This poem is part of Zhai's 1986 cycle "Living in the World" 人生在世, which is largely an exploration of the poet's social role as a woman. Numerous allusions to fortunetellers and matchmakers reflect the view that women's lives are overdetermined, with marriage a seemingly ineluctable fate:

All crows under Heaven are equally
  black, and this
Fills me with fear, they have so many
Relatives, their numbers are legion,
  they're hard to resist
	天下乌鸦一般黑, 至此
	我感到胆怯, 它们有如此多的
	亲戚, 它们人多势众, 难以抗拒
	
	我们却必不可少, 我们姐妹三人
	婷婷玉立, 来回踱步

But we're indispensable, we
  three sisters
Slim and graceful, we glide
  to and fro
Looking like sure winners
But I mean to make mischief,
  I'm cruel at heart
Keeping up a good daughter's
  sweet-tempered appearance
My footsteps retrace my daily
  defeats

Awaiting proposals in our
  boudoirs, we're fair maids
  of good family
We smile resentfully, racking
  our brains
For ways to augment our
  charms
Youthful, beautiful, like fires
  ablaze
Seared black, these
  single-minded snares
(Which of these good men
  with well-sharpened teeth,
  an unwavering gaze
And steady expression will be
  my brother-in-law?)

I sense
Our chamber is beset on all sides
In the night, both cats and mice
  have awakened
We go to sleep, and search in
  our dreams for unknown
  house-numbers
In the night, we women are
  like ripe melons about to
  fall from the vine
Conjugal bliss, et cetera

We three sisters, different
  with each new day
Marriage, still at the crux
  of finding a mate
Lights in the bedroom fill the
  newlyweds with disappointment

胜券在握的模样
我却有意使坏, 内心刻薄
表面保持当女儿的好脾气
重蹈每天的失败

待字闺中, 我们是名门淑女
悻悻地微笑, 挖空心思
使自己变得多姿多采
年轻, 貌美, 如火如荼
炮制很黑, 很专心的圈套
(哪些牙齿磨利, 目光笔直的好人
毫无起伏的面容是我的姐夫?)

我感到
我们的房间危机四伏
在夜晚, 貓和老鼠都醒着
我们去睡, 在梦中寻找陌生的门牌号码
在夜晚, 我们是瓜熟蒂落的女人
颠鸾倒凤, 如此等等

我们姐妹三人, 我们日新月异
婚姻, 依然是择偶的中心
卧室的光线使新婚夫妇沮丧
孤注一掷, 我对自己说
"家是出发的地方"

Risk it all on one throw, I tell
  myself
"Home is the place we leave"

Marriage here is presented as undesirable yet inescapable, a goal for which women nonetheless scheme like "single-minded snares." Lacking any illusions, the sisters seek to press whatever advantage they have, in order to make the best out of a bad situation. The sisters' efforts to present attractive and feminine exteriors mask their resentment and their fierceness: "But I mean to make mischief, I'm cruel at heart / Keeping up a good daughter's sweet-tempered appearance."

More of their true natures come out in the female realm of night, where they are sexually mature and cast a jaded eye on the platitudes associated with marriage: "In the night, we women are like ripe melons about to fall from the vine / Conjugal bliss, et cetera." The cynicism of the voice and the narrator's distrust of pleasant appearances are indicative of her disillusionment and reminiscent of Plath (in whose work smiles almost always masked ill intentions).

For all of her inner resources, the narrator of this poem is trapped in antiquated traditions. Marriage remains the focal point of choosing a mate, although the reality of marriage will be disheartening. The newlyweds will not like what they see on their wedding night. Fatalistically, the narrator speaks of risking everything on "one throw"—marriage—a gamble whose outcome she cannot hope to control.

Images of matchmakers and marriage recur in other poems in the cycle, including "The Schemes of Summer" 夏天的阴谋 (Zhai 1994: 83–84) where the image of a bridegroom is juxtaposed with images of cold, poison, death, and enemies. In this poem, as in "The Black Room," the previously sacrosanct night has been invaded by cruel cats who prey on terrified mice. Sleep, with its restorative powers, is impossible.

"Here and Now" 此时此刻 (Zhai 1994: 91–92) confronts the prospects awaiting a woman who does not marry:

Living in the world, with no sons or daughters	人生在世, 无儿无女
Day in, day out, more damage done	一天天成为一件害人的事情
Loyal yet loathsome the mirror	镜子忠诚而可恶
Faces me	朝向我
A natural-born widow's moment is here	升起一个天生当寡妇的完美时刻

One penalty for remaining single is to be childless; and in the narrator's cultural milieu, a childless state carries some element of danger, inflicting on her unspecified damages. But time for marriage is running out: the narrator sees herself aging in her mirror, which is loyal in that it is always there but loathsome in that it reveals the harsh truth. The officious matchmaker busies herself, "ever coming and going, with a serious expression on her face." Given the alternatives, the narrator gives into social pressure and surrenders her will to fate:

Here and now, I walk among those people in their proper attire	此时此刻, 我走在穿着得体的人们中间
Hands tucked into my sleeves, I brush past, dressed up like a good citizen	袖手而过, 一副良民打扮
The spitting image of a wary woodpecker tut-tutting officiously	活像警惕的啄木鸟咄咄逼人
Living in this world, mocking myself:	人生在世, 自嘲:
At this over-ripe age, it's best to get married	如此奢侈的年龄, 不如结婚

While Zhai Yongming explores the broader social context and repercussions of marriage, it is the marriage ceremony itself that is played out in Xia Yu's poem, "Ventriloquy" 復語術 (Xia 1991: 9). "Ventriloquy" vividly illustrates the psychic splitting experienced by a bride on her wedding day:

I walked into the wrong room And missed my own wedding.	我走錯房間 錯過了自己的婚禮。
Through the one crack in the wall, I see	在牆壁唯一的隙縫中, 我看見
The perfection of all of the proceedings. He's wearing a white jacket	一切行進之完好。他穿白色的外衣
She's holding flowers in her hands, ceremony,	她捧著花, 儀式,
Vows, kiss	許諾, 親吻
I've turned my back to it: fate, the ventriloquy I've practiced so painstakingly	背著它: 命運, 我苦苦練就的復語術
(that warm aquatic animal, the tongue tamely	(舌頭那匹溫暖的水獸馴養地 在小小的水族箱中 蠕動) 那獸說: 是的, 我願意。

wriggles in a tiny aquarium)
The animal says: Yes, I will.

The wedding is a ritual from which the narrator feels so alienated that she is at two removes from the action. As if by accident, she finds herself in an adjoining room, from which she spies on the proceedings; and what she sees is a bride and groom, bedecked in ritual costumes and carrying ritual props, going through the motions. The bride in the ceremony does not fully participate in the wedding either, for when the moment to take vows arrives, her tongue assumes a life of its own, completing the process of dissociation. The tongue of the bride in the ceremony becomes a metaphor for the bride herself, who, like a captive animal that has had the wildness (and authenticity) tamed out of it, simply performs the tricks she has been taught. The arresting image of the tongue as a sea creature in an aquarium has sexual connotations as well, implying that the institution of marriage is a place where the animal of female sexuality can be confined and controlled.

Although the tongue of the bride in "Ventriloquy" has become docile, Xia Yu's own tongue is quite sharp in poems that treat formerly taboo or unseemly subjects such as female sexuality, infidelity, prostitution, and anger at men. A brief glance backward will reveal that, although before the 1980s there were women poets who touched on the delicate subject of love, it remained just that—a delicate subject. While some expressed in their writing their frustration with men and the limitations of the feminine role assigned them (e.g., Xiong Hong 敻虹 [b. 1940]), frustration soon gave way to internalization, which in turn resulted in either despair or sublimation (through religion or other received modes of transcendence). Conversely, for Xia Yu, frustration turns to anger and indignation, which in turn spurs her to seek and obtain redress, as she does in "Sweet Revenge" 甜蜜的復仇 (Xia 1984: 26):

I'll take your shadow and add a little salt	把你的影子加點鹽
Pickle it	醃起來
Dry it in the wind	風乾
When I'm old	老的時候
I'll wash it down with wine	下酒

Although I endorse the notion that Xia Yu's point of view is distinctly female, I would argue that the voice and the sentiments of this poem are gender neutral. Most readers can identify with the narrator's situation. We infer that the narrator was formerly involved romantically with "you," who left her feeling hurt and taken advantage of, and that now she has thought of a way to get even. The revenge is clearly symbolic, as it is the antagonist's "shadow" 影子, or her memory of him, that the protagonist is planning to torture with salt, vinegar, and desiccation before she finally chews him up and swallows him with a burning mouthful of alcohol. The second stanza also presupposes a comfortable old age for the narrator, at which point she would be fully recovered from her psychic wounds and be able to treat her former lover as a trifle.

Xia Yu appears to have been somewhat surprised by the response to "Sweet Revenge," which struck a powerful chord with her audience; and she was unprepared for and uncomfortable with the commercialism that accompanied the immense popularity of *Memorandum* 備忘錄. She was disconcerted by the crass merchandising of the book's second printing; and she was deeply offended when, in a handicraft shop, she came across a number of gift items emblazoned with the text of "Sweet Revenge."

> I saw "Sweet Revenge" written on pencil holders, magazine racks and chair cushions, all in an ultra artsy font . . . [the poem had been given a] cheap, pretentious whiff of sterile culture, for the purpose of mass marketing . . . they'd utterly destroyed the original line breaks . . . I didn't know whether to laugh or cry, [the whole thing] went entirely against my original intent. (The world is full opportunities for disillusionment, but isn't it usually caused by some jerk who can't help turning something into a seat cushion?) The truth is, I like popular culture, popular songs, and so on, but I never thought I'd see my own poetry turned into seat cushions. That's just a bit too much, isn't it? (Xia 1991: 114)

Although Xia Yu the postmodernist enjoys many forms of non-elite popular culture, she makes a distinction between serious art and kitsch masquerading as art. Furthermore, she prefers to maintain control of her work.[6] The sort of commercialization that is described above also violates Xia Yu's sense of privacy; but from a theoretical standpoint, her response is interesting, given her irreverent attitude as an artist.

Michelle Yeh praises the effectiveness of "the ironic thrust of [the] metaphor" in this poem, pointing out the tension between the nostalgia for lost love and the "cannibalistic act of pickling and eating the man's shadow." She construes the image of the shadow as indicative of a sense of loss, and she reads pickling as remembrance of a great love: "pickling implies preservation (she cannot forget him because of her deep love for him)" (Yeh 1991c: 407). I see pickling more as an act of torture than of remembrance, and the speaker seems to be remembering him less for how much she loved him than for how badly he treated

her. There may be a fine shade of difference between these two interpretations, but the second reading places less emphasis on irony and
inclines to take the sequence of actions at face value and as a direct
expression of the narrator's revenge fantasy. "Sweet Revenge" is
indeed at a polar opposite to the lyricism of the earlier generation of
Chinese women poets, especially poets such as Xiong Hong and
Rongzi 蓉子 (b. 1928). This fantasy is not at all "feminine" in the traditional sense of the word, but its overwhelming (and continuing) popularity with readers attests to its authenticity.

Irony is more clearly on view in "Common Knowledge" 一般見識
(Xia 1984: 78), a 1982 poem that presents a critique of traditional
misogyny:

a woman	一個女人
bleeds once	每個月
a month	流一次血
understands the snake's language	懂得蛇的語言
is good at ambush	適於突擊
is not prone to keep appointments	不宜守約

(Yeh [1992] 1994: 226)

The speaker demonstrates the insidiousness of prejudices by citing an
objective fact that is "common knowledge" and then by following a
chain of associations. People do not generally speak of this "common
knowledge"—after all, the thought of blood is unsettling to many—so
that this assumption becomes a hidden one. The narrator proceeds
from the disturbing image of blood to images of snakes and ambush.
At first, we only read that women bleed, which could be a value-
neutral statement, but with negative images of snakes and ambush
following directly after, the implication is that anyone who bleeds in
this way is not trustworthy. In fact, the poem concludes, women are so
unreliable that they tend not to keep appointments.

One could almost stop here and read this as a sarcastically recited
litany of women's faults, with a somewhat biblical cast (snakes, deceit-
fulness). But the poet has a witty last word, because the concluding
statement is disproved by the opening one: because what is menses, if
not a monthly appointment that women are "prone" to keep? In this
way, the poem further demonstrates that if you let a bigot talk long
enough and make enough sweeping generalizations, he or she will
eventually undermine his or her own arguments.

While Zhai Yongming's approach is less pithy, she does not shy
away from expressing negative emotions. Indeed, undercurrents of
anger and resentment at the world's inequalities run throughout her

early works such as "The Black Room," as well as in her ground-breaking twenty-poem cycle "Woman," which was written in 1984 and published in 1985 in Chinese literary journals. The accompanying preface, "Black Night Consciousness" 黑夜意识, amounted to a poetic and feminist manifesto. As Michael Day maintains (2007c) "prior to [Zhai] no other female poet [in China] had ever seriously attempted to stress the unique nature of female experience and perception. The three female poets that have received the imprimatur of Chinese literary tradition and the current literary establishment as exemplar's [*sic*] of the poetess in China [Li Qingzhao 李清照 (1081–? CE), Xie Bingxin 谢冰心 (1900–1999), and Shu Ting 舒婷 (b. 1952)], to a greater or lesser extent, all accept and conform to the male perception of the role of woman in Chinese society." I quote here from Michael Day's translation of "Black Night Consciousness." (The original was not available to me at the time of this writing.)

> Now is the time I become truly powerful. In other words, now I'm finally aware of the world around me and the implications of my presence in it. The consciousness inherent in each person and the universe—I call this the black night—has determined that I must be a carrier of thoughts, beliefs and emotions of the female sex [*nüxing* 女性]; and, furthermore, injects this burden directly into what I view as the greatest work of consciousness. And this is poetry.
>
> As half of the human race, the female sex is faced at birth with an entirely different world [from that of the male sex]. [A female's] first glimpse of the world is necessarily tinged by her feelings and perception, even by a secret psychology of resistance. Does she spare no effort in throwing herself into life and creating a black night? And, in a crisis, does she transform the world into a giant soul? Actually, each woman faces her own abyss—personal anguish and experience that continually vanishes and is continually confirmed—far from every person is able to defy this proportionate form of hardship up until their destruction. This is the initial black night: laid out in a particular way and at a particular angle, and which is unique to the female sex. This is not the path toward deliverance, but the path toward a full awakening . . . (Day 2007a)

More than anything, what Zhai asserts here is her imperative to write from her own singular and unique point of view. This individuality is grounded in her psychosexual and sociocultural awareness of herself as a woman. Nonetheless, Zhai does not claim to speak for all women, although judging by the impact that "Woman" made on other Chinese women poets, a number of them thought that she did. Zhai Yongming appears to have underestimated the universality (at least among women) of her poetry and her point of view, and she was not comfortable with the overwhelming response to the "Woman" cycle and its preface. As she put it, a "Black Whirlwind" 黑旋風 swept over China during the second half of the 1980s, and she was taken aback by the appearance of a crowd of imitators.[7] In March 1989, Zhai Yongming wrote an article, published in the June issue of *Poetry Monthly* 诗刊, in which she commented on this trend: "As a joke I often say that I should change the first line of 'The Black Room' from 'All crows under Heaven are black' to 'All women under Heaven are black'" (Tang 1994: 10–11; Day 2007c).

Without a doubt, "Woman" broke new ground. Women poets had in the past been forced to choose among three modes of expression (the traditional "feminine," the gender-neutral, and the "overtly masculine," to borrow Tang Xiaodu's tripartite scheme) (See Tang 1994 and 1997), so that a writer who wanted to write *as a woman* would most likely have found herself straight-jacketed by the traditional feminine. The limitations of this mode of expression are legion; but what is pertinent here is that it offers no place for passion, anger, or any strong emotion other than the pain of the injured (i.e., the abandoned woman of *guiyuan* 閨怨 poetry).[8]

Rather than taking her inspiration from Chinese poets, she found a model abroad, in Sylvia Plath. It is ironic that Plath's poetry, as empowering an example as it was for Zhai Yongming (and a generation of American women writers, too, for that matter), was unable to defeat Plath's own self-destructive tendencies. Be that as it may, her work was clearly an inspiration to Zhai Yongming, who was able to internalize the powerful voice of Plath's persona, her sharp, hard-edged, "unfeminine" imagery and attitude and then incorporate these into her own authentic voice.

"Woman" consists of four sections, the first of which, "Premonition" *Yugan* 预感 (Zhai 1994: 5–6), introduces most of the themes and images that form the substance of the group of poems as a whole: women, blackness, and night, and the struggle of these female, *yin* forces with the male, *yang* forces represented by the sky and the sun.

The woman in a black dress
  comes deep in the night
Her secretive glances drain me
I suddenly remember: this is the
  season when all the fish die
And every road passes through
  the trails left by birds in flight
	穿黑裙的女人黛夜而来
	她秘密的一瞥使我精疲力竭
	我突然想起这个季节鱼都会死去
	而每条路正在穿越飞鸟的痕迹
	
	貌似尸体的山峦被黑暗拖曳
	附近灌木的心跳隐约可闻

A mountain range is dragged
  away by the darkness like a
  corpse
Nearby the heartbeat of a shrub
  is just barely audible
Those huge birds look down
  on me from the sky
With human eyes
With an air of private savagery
Winter raises and lowers its
  cruelly masculine consciousness

I've remained unusually calm
  throughout
Like a blind woman, I see
  night's darkness in broad
  daylight
Like a baby lacking guile,
  my fingerprints
Have no more grief to offer
Footsteps! A sound now
  growing old
Dreams seem to possess some
  knowledge, and with my own eyes
I saw an hour that forgot to
  open its blossoms
Bearing down on the dusk

Fresh moss in their mouths, the
  meanings they sought
Folded their smiles back into their
  breasts in tacit understanding
The night seems to shudder,
  like a cough
Caught in the throat, I've already
  quit this dead end hole.

那些巨大的鸟从空中向我俯视
带着人类的眼神
在一种秘而不宣的野蛮空气中
冬天起伏着残酷的雄性意识

我一向有着不同寻常的平静
犹如盲者, 因此我在白天看见黑夜
婴儿般直率, 我的指纹
已没有更多的悲哀可提供
脚步! 正在变老的声音
梦显得若有所如, 从自己的眼睛里
我看到了忘记开花的时辰
給黄昏施加压力

薛苔含在口中, 他们所恳求的意义
把微笑会心地折入怀中
夜晚似有似无地痉挛, 象一声咳嗽
憋在喉咙, 我已离开这个死洞

The narrator displays confidence and self-possession mixed with a sense of wounded enervation. Although physically damaged, she has not yet given up hope. The title of the poem hints at things to come, and, like a premonition, it introduces the rest of the cycle. The first line introduces a female figure, the "woman in a black dress," who comes in the dead of night. Even without the preface, "Black Night Consciousness," this image demonstrates the identification of women with night in Zhai's poetic universe. While women may find their power in the night and be at home there, finding in it a time to commune with one another and trade secrets, that secrecy itself is also draining for the narrator. Attendant to this sense of fatigue is a sense of foreboding and impending death: "I suddenly remember: this is the season when all the fish die." As aquatic creatures, fish live in water, inhabiting, like women, the *yin* part of the world.[9] The natural world is simultaneously rich in signs and unreadable, and thus it colludes in the women's secrecy, with the paths of flying birds constituting a sort of invisible history, like that of women.

In the second stanza, the darkness is powerful enough to consume even the mountains, and, in the darkness, the narrator can hear the faint heartbeat of a plant, a small and vulnerable life. Still, she feels threatened by the human eyes of huge birds that look down from the male realm of the sky, and the struggle continues into the narrator's own *yin* territory of winter, where a "cruel and masculine consciousness" is invading. The "raising and lowering" of that consciousness invites numerous interpretations—from rapaciousness to tentativeness.

By the third stanza, the narrator is challenging the masculine power of daylight, asserting that she can see "dark night in the daylight." Comparing herself to a baby, she calls attention to her own innocence and ability to see the world with fresh eyes. The image of dreams ties in with other images of night, and here as in other poems, dreams are invested with superior powers of truth-telling. The reference to dusk suggests that the narrator may be reaching a turning point of some sort: night is coming, the daylight is about to be supplanted by the women's world of the night. And even if the night gets off to a fitful start ("convulsing," "choked back"), the narrator is already on her way to another state at the end of the poem.

The subsequent poems continue the poet's journey through a symbolic landscape. The third poem, "An Instant" *Shunjian* 瞬间 (Zhai 1994: 9–10), takes the narrator back into the night by way of a dusk that "spits blood," in which she claims for herself a "black-stained" sun. By superimposing black on the sun, she is essentially revising its meaning from a woman's point of view and contesting its supremacy. This night is to be a night of revelations, as "all of the constellations on [her] face are rearranged."

Note that although Zhai Yongming's work marks a dramatic break with tradition in her use of imagery, the experiences she describes, and her attitude to those experiences, much of her imagery is drawn from the traditional repertoire of *yin* 陰 and *yang* 陽 (female and male) symbolism, which she reinterprets and turns to her own purposes. A case in point is the imagery of darkness and night that runs throughout

"Woman." Rather than experiencing night and darkness as oppressive, Zhai Yongming transforms them into sources of strength. At the same time, she creates a mythic world in which her speaker is oppressed by and locked in a struggle with forces or natural objects that are traditionally *yang* (male), including the sky and sun. "The World" *Shijie* 世界 (Zhai 1994: 15–16) exemplifies this conflict:

The sun maintains the sweep of
  its anger with a dictator's gaze,
  seeking out the top of my head
  and the soles of my feet
	太阳用独裁者的目光保持它愤怒的广度
	并寻找我的头顶和脚低

    Zhai intensifies the mythic qualities of this poem by alluding to the Chinese creation myth in which the goddess Nüwa 女娲 is "impregnated by the sky." Despite persecution by the sun, the female narrator remains aware of her own life-giving power. She knows that it is she who gives birth to the same male principle that strives to overpower her (although it deludes itself that it can): ". . . raven-black clouds incubate the setting sun, my eye sockets brim with a vast sea / From the depths of my throat grows white coral" (乌云孵化落日, 我的眼眶盛满一个大海 / 从纵深的喉咙里长出白珊瑚). The sea imagery that pervades this poem is indicative of another female force, that of water, in this case the vast, primordial waters of the sea, from which all life on earth has sprung.

    As the poem continues, the narrator changes from a mother to a newborn baby, who feels a "wild joy" as "the world bursts into my body." Zhai Yongming manages this transformation through the use of imagery. First she is the great maternal ocean, and then it is the waves of that ocean (life) that she feels striking her "like a midwife striking my back." The poet is giving birth to herself, creating herself in her own image, as an independent woman free of social constraints. This poem, with its stress on fertility and the female body, makes clear the distinction between woman defined biologically and materially (as female, or *nüxing*) and woman defined socially (as *funü* 婦女 or "feminine"). By embracing the former as a source of identity and power, Zhai Yongming evades the snares of the latter. She concludes the poem with her avowal that the black night of this poem and others is a balm, a blessing.

    Xia Yu's handling of female sexuality tends to be less symbolic and more graphic than Zhai Yongming's. Zhong Ling regards the former's frank treatment of sexuality as truly groundbreaking, and she describes Xia Yu as a woman-centric poet, a rarity among modern women poets in Taiwan. Chung argues that although she is less preoccupied with the biological facts of women's lives, she nonetheless locates a woman's identity in her physical being. Thus, it is inevitable that Xia Yu will touch on the subject of women's sexuality and desires (Zhong 1989b). She does so in "Jiang Yuan" 姜嫄 (Xia 1984: 107–108), which playfully conflates Chinese mythology with an individual woman's consciousness. Jiang Yuan was the mother of Hou Ji 后稷, the legendary ancestor of the Zhou people, and the epigraph to the poem is taken from Song 245 in the *Book of Songs*.

She who gave birth to the people	厥初生民
Was Jiang Yuan	時維姜嫄
How did she give birth to the people	生民如何
She sacrificed and prayed	克禋克祀
To exorcise selfishness	以弗無子
Book of Songs, "Birth of the People"	詩經生民

Whenever it's a rainy day　　　　　　　每逢下雨天
I get a certain kind of feeling　　　　　我就有一種感覺
I want to copulate　　　propagate　　想要交配　　繁殖
descendants spreading　　　them　　子嗣　　徧佈
over the world each with　　　　their own　　於世上　　各隨各的
dialects　　　　　　　　　　　　　方言
　　clans　　　　　　　　　　　　　宗族
kingdoms　　　　　　　　　　　　立國

like an animal　　　　　　　　　　像一頭獸
in a hidden cave　　　　　　　　　在一個隱密的洞穴
whenever it's a rainy day　　　　　每逢下雨天

like an animal　　　　　　　　　　像一頭獸
doing it like a human　　　　　　　用人的方式

"Jiang Yuan" stands as a celebration of female fertility and sexuality that bears as well some of the mythic quality found in Zhai Yongming's poems alluding to Nüwa. Although Xia Yu and Zhai Yongming both find much to deplore in traditional attitudes toward women, each has also found sources of strength in Chinese culture, deliberately and fundamentally recasting much of that cultural legacy. Whether satirically, like Xia Yu, or earnestly, like Zhai Yongming, each engages traditional culture—revising, subverting, and ultimately appropriating ancient concepts to make them her own.

Notes

1. A book-length translation of Xia's work was published under the Wade-Giles spelling Hsia Yü. See Bradbury 2001.
2. Tang Xiaodu adds a third alternative to this list, that of a "masculine persona," but that would not have been a choice open to women until recently, because of social factors. See Tang 1994.
3. Some other "stream of consciousness" poets are Lu Yimin 陆忆敏 (b. 1962), Zhang Zhen 张真 (b. 1961), Yi Lei 伊蕾 (b. 1951), Tang Yaping 唐亚平 (b. 1962), and Wang Xiaoni 王小妮 (b. 1955), all of whom are women; along with the male poets, Liu Manliu 刘漫流 (b. 1962), Meng Lang 孟浪 (b. 1961), Bei Ling 贝岭 (b. 1959), and Xi Chuan 西川 (b. 1963).
4. Although many of Zhai Yongming's poems exist in multiple versions, those cited here are drawn from her 1994 *Collected Works*.
5. Over the past two decades, Zhai Yongming has engaged in an ongoing project of defining the world and her place in it, along with a constantly revisited and revised exploration of what constitutes "women's writing." For her part, Xia Yu has continued to take her writing in an experimental direction, including, at the time of this writing, experiments with machine retranslation.
6. Xia Yu's dismay at others' appropriation of her work bears comparison with Zhai Yongming's reaction to the intense response to her 1984 poem cycle, "Woman".
7. Tang Yaping, Zhai Yongming's fellow "Stream of Consciousness" poet, is one of the women poets whose work reflects Zhai's powerful influence. Tang's poem sequence, "The Black Desert" *Hei shamo* 黑沙漠, is a good example. See Day 2007b.
8. I have discussed elsewhere the way in which a contemporary poet such as Xiong Hong in Taiwan confronts her own anger, sense of injury, and indignation, only to back down from these intense emotions to take comfort in a deeply religious (Buddhist) but also, not coincidentally, traditionally female form of self-denial and self-abnegation. The reader senses her anger but watches as she sinks into melancholy because of her inability to acknowledge that anger. Instead, she turns it in on herself.
9. This aquatic imagery may also bring to mind Xia Yu's poem, "Ventriloquy."

Part II

Contemporary Poetry of
Mainland China

Chapter Eight

The Ghost Enters the City: Gu Cheng's Metamorphosis in the "New World"

Yibing Huang

"Fairytale Poet" and "Rebirth after Death": Gu Cheng's Position in Contemporary Chinese Poetry

Gu Cheng's 顾城 position in contemporary Chinese poetry remains a mystery despite all the seemingly obvious facts surrounding it. Born in Beijing in 1956, and being the youngest of the "misty" (*menglong*) poets, Gu Cheng actually got an early start as a writer. His earliest poems collected in the posthumously published *Complete Poems of Gu Cheng* (*Gu Cheng shi quanbian*) (Gu 1995) are dated 1964, and his youthful yet stunningly beautiful poem "A Fantasia to Life" (*Shengming huanxiang qu*) was written in 1971, when Gu Cheng was only fourteen years old. On top of that, Gu Cheng had been labeled as a "fairytale poet" (*tonghua shiren*) in the 1980s, which was derived from the eponymous poem that Shu Ting dedicated to him:

You believed in the fairytale
  you wove
So that yourself turned into a
  blue flower in that fairytale

你相信了你编写的童话
自己就成了童话中幽蓝的花

(Shu and Gu 1982: 1)

Tethered by the image of a child-prodigy and the label of a "fairytale poet," ironically, somehow Gu Cheng had never been fully recognized as a mature (or adult) poet during his lifetime. Gu Cheng's violent and tragic demise—he committed suicide after murdering his wife Xie Ye in New Zealand in 1993, at age thirty-seven—has only further damaged his reputation. One of the most common posthumous views of Gu Cheng runs as follows: although always knowing how to sing "songs of innocence," he had never learned how to sing "songs of experience." In this light, the term "fairytale poet" hints a *faux naiveté*, if not an *enfant terrible*, and is ultimately a curse rather than a blessing.

But this perception, although sounding valid, can be simplistic. To say the least, Gu Cheng's early poetry is far from a literal, self-evident "fairytale" of "innocence," and the cultivated image of a "child-poet" may be nothing but an inflected expression of a very Chinese experience at a particular historical juncture.[1] Also, between his early and late poetry there appear significant changes and evolutions in terms of both theme and style. Lastly, and most importantly, moral condemnation or aesthetic derogation aside, do not Gu Cheng's fate and poetry— particularly his late poetry—mirror the common predicament that had confronted his contemporaries too, despite their ostensible personal or aesthetic differences? This last question is particularly pertinent if we move our sights to a larger historical fact. That is, since the late 1980s, and particularly since 1989, many of the "misty" poets, Gu Cheng himself included, had either voluntarily chosen or been impelled to live outside the once familiar "China," an exilic life in an unfamiliar "new world" of the West. This encounter with the "new world" hence played a decisive role in terms of redefining "innocence" and "experience" in a post-1989, and one might even say posthistorical, context.

Yang Lian 杨炼 (b. 1955), for example, a fellow "misty" poet who left China at about the same time as Gu Cheng, later acknowledged the extent of the shock and self-doubt he had experienced upon hearing of Gu Cheng's death:

> If you remember, 1993 was the year that Gu Cheng committed suicide, and not long before that I had just written *Darknesses* (*Heianmen*) in New York. The West was a strange land, offering me no linguistic environment, and how could I really go on? How long would I be able to go on? The future was completely in the dark; it really was like hitting rock bottom. (Yang 2003: 247)

Yet it seems that only by going through such a "death experience" can one start a new life both artistically and personally:

> I am witnessing myself setting out for the open sea, which actually contains all the splits that I have experienced, in reality and in language. These splits in a sense are necessary. If Chinese poets did not experience these kinds of splits, this rebirth after death, we would not have sufficient linguistic energy to express the depth of our existence. (Yang 2003: 248)

In other words, what truly stands as a trial for those "misty" poets in exile is both the utter inexperience in inhabiting a posthistorical brave "new world" and a mounting difficulty to reenact an expiring Chinese experience in this "new world." In order to cope with this very real trial, a transformation, or what I would call a metamorphosis, is inevitable. This transformation or metamorphosis, involving successive self-splits and skin-sheddings, asserting not so much an exilic as a postexilic existence, is precisely what Yang Lian means by "rebirth after death" (*si'er housheng*), which had proven equally applicable to Gu Cheng, the erstwhile "fairytale poet."

Gu Cheng's own metamorphosis in terms of negotiating a postexilic poetry is manifested most noticeably in his last two major poem sequences, entitled *The Ghost Enters the City* (*Gui jincheng*) (1992) and *City* (*Cheng*) (1992–1993). While in his early poetry Gu Cheng longs to be a willful child in nature, in his late poetry he yearns for a return to the city—the poet's native "city." Eventually, this child is anything but innocent and nature is anything but natural; and what is born is neither a poetry of innocence nor of experience, but instead a "ghost" poetry. This metamorphosis from "willful child" to wandering "ghost" and the return from "nature" to the "city" are what I explore in this chapter. I also discuss Gu Cheng's "natural philosophy" (*ziran zhexue*), which serves the dual function of possession and exorcism in relation to the specter of the Cultural Revolution that dwells in his "ghost" poetry. I conclude with a final tribute to Gu Cheng and a contemplation upon his native city of Beijing, regarding their different fates.

From "Child" in "Nature" to "Ghost" in the "City": Gu Cheng's Metamorphosis

Two crucial images have dominated Gu Cheng's early poetry: "child" and "nature." For Gu Cheng, both "child" and "nature" designate a prehistorical and precultural state of freedom and spontaneity, and thus the union of the two becomes the perfect starting point for a poetic pursuit of innocence and beauty: "When I first wrote poetry, it was because I had a consonance with nature, and the sounds of nature became the language in my heart, which was a happy thing" (Gu 1995: 920). Moreover, while Gu Cheng emphasizes that he is a child not of culture or the city, but of nature, quite often such nature is synonymous with wilderness as much as with willfulness: "I'm a child who had been wrested away from tradition, and had grown up on a deserted land, and I cannot give up happiness and willfulness" (Gu 1995: 922). Accordingly, Gu Cheng's poetics from the very beginning is one of metamorphosis, with emphasis on "willfulness," or "*renxing*," by which Gu Cheng literally means following (or indulging) one's own inborn nature. Two of Gu Cheng's representative poems from his early period, "A Fantasia to Life" and "I Am a Willful Child" (*Wo shi yige renxing de haizi*) (1981), are excellent illustrations of this poetics.

Apparently, this vision of a "child" feeling entirely at home in nature is largely anthrocentric and anthropomorphized and is "willfully" Romantic. We can easily find among twentieth-century world poets, particularly among those who once found themselves in the "new world" of displacement and exile, a completely opposite understanding of nature. W.H. Auden, himself a naturalized resident in the "new world" of America, once said that nature in European literature "is humanized, mythologized, usually friendly" whereas in America "nature was virgin, devoid of history, usually hostile" (Auden 1975a: 363). According to Auden, the often romanticized golden image of "child in nature" has instead a much more somber and less nostalgic ring for an American poet such as Robert Frost (Auden 1975b). For the Polish poet Czeslaw Milosz, the "impersonal cruelty" of the universe is what quintessentially defines nature, particularly in the form of wilderness, and there is an inherent enmity and mutual alienation between humans and nature (Milosz 1982: 24). Hence the perfect union as achieved in "child in nature" is deemed nothing but a Romantic illusion, or a deceptive fairytale.

The early Gu Cheng seems much less aware of—or deliberately turning a blind eye to—such anti-Romantic and much darker readings of nature and wilderness. But on the other hand, Gu Cheng's idealization of nature has its own raison d'être and is itself a deliberate act of rebellion against any existing and repressive cultural and social order, a sentiment shared by his fellow "misty" poets in a post–Cultural Revolution context.[2] That is to say, this idealized nature serves an "anticulture" agenda and promises fresh possibilities for language, poetry, and human existence in general:

> Of course, at the germinal stage of language, there is a kind of fresh sensibility, like newly emerging leaves and birdsong, which is still a part of nature, remaining at a dangerous place, providing alternative possibilities and choices for human existence. (Gu 1995: 928)

Gu Cheng's "anticultural" and "willful" nature is not purely Romantic in the Western sense, but imbued as well with influences from classical Chinese traditions such as Daoism.[3] Nevertheless, such a view as nature itself is quintessentially culture-oriented, and an irreconcilable dilemma surfaces. The more Gu Cheng moves his poetic scale toward an "anticultural" nature, the more he actually falls back into the realm of culture. As a poetic ideal and as a physical reality standing in opposition to each other, nature becomes self-alienated, and the sheer "innocent" lyricism of "I Am a Willful Child" withers away.

This transition had already started before Gu Cheng's exile (see Li 1999: 184), but its pace accelerated after Gu Cheng left China and changed his landscape entirely in 1987. Just as Gu Cheng finally regained the lost paradise of "nature" on Waiheke Island in New Zealand, this paradise in the "new world" proved instead too wild and too alien for the "willful child" to endure.

Such a change of perspective in the "new world" is duly registered in Gu Cheng's autobiographical novel *Ying'er* (1993):

> The strangely shaped rock outside the window displays its irregularity, revealing its stubborn and rough edges to the gradually lightening blue sky, and baring its uncompromising nature. All this is evil, utterly and bluntly. It stares straight at the blue sky, taking the blow that was struck by the light of Heaven, acknowledging, damning, and resenting this shape and fate imposed upon him by Heaven.[4]

> It shatters my usual tender understanding and appreciation of love, and all those intoxicating fantasies are softly crushed and mercilessly destroyed by this rock. Nothing is left, the normal and taken-for-granted life is no more, nor does love lead to life. Only now do I realize for the first time the horror of freedom and truth. (Gu 1993: 124)

Both time and space have outgrown the fantasized communion between "child" and "nature." Moreover, the raw and alien reality of the "new world" forces Gu Cheng into an epiphanic awareness of an "evil spirit" (*xieling*) lurking underneath his own skin:

> This island, this forest, lure him to leave behind the distant northern continent, leave behind the city, yet he has never become a real man, he has always been a monstrous and naughty child, who has never grown up. (Gu 1993: 128)

In an interview given in 1992, Gu Cheng goes even further:

> Nature is not really as pretty as what people would claim—that's the "nature" seen through the eyes of vacationers. If you want to live a

self-reliant life, not relying upon society, you will have to be dragged
into the war of nature. In my experience, nature is a bunch of mouths,
either you eat me, or you eat him, and there's almost no other way in
between. (Gu 2005a: 229)

This bleak, almost Darwinian realization of nature in the "new
world" echoes Auden and Milosz quoted earlier. Gu Cheng's poetic
metamorphosis thus takes a surprising turn. The formerly "willful
child" wakes up finding his new incarnation as a "monster" (*mogui*)
or a "ghost" (*gui*)—no longer wandering in the wilderness but trying
to enter the city.

The Ghost Enters the City is a sequence of poems Gu Cheng wrote
during his 1992 sojourn in Berlin. Narrating a ghost's daily adventures
during a week, it consists of eight short poems that follow a short
opening section:

The ghost	0点
At 0 o'clock	的鬼
Walks very carefully	走路非常小心
It's afraid of falling	它害怕摔跟头
And becoming	变成
Human	了人

(Gu 1995: 843)

This introduction of "ghost" and "city" may be Gu Cheng's single most
important attempt—both existential and aesthetic—to simultaneously
deny and (re-)assert his exilic reality and identity in the "new world."[5]

In Suizi Zhang-Kubin's interview with Gu Cheng in 1992, there is a
rather intriguing discussion of the terms "human" and "ghost":

Z: Did you write *The Ghost Enters the City* as a human or as a ghost?
G: A human can write ghost poetry without keeping a distance from the
  ghost. That is to say, to completely enter a ghostly state, to exclude the
  human breath of life, and to write poetry as a ghost. This state of
  poetry writing brings one close to death. A human can also write ghost
  poetry while keeping a distance from the ghost. In other words, it's like
  watching TV, watching a ghost story. If one is writing poetry as a
  human, the human will not be harmed in any way. As a ghost I wrote
  poems like "Houhai" and "Zizhuyuan" [in *City*], while as a human
  I wrote the sequence of *The Ghost Enters the City*. (Gu 1995: 4–5)

Here Gu Cheng might appear splitting too fine a hair, but he has his
point. When Gu Cheng says that he wrote *The Ghost Enters the City*
as a human, he is actually positing the "ghost" as a poetic persona, an

aesthetic device, instead of an existential fact. And I see this as Gu Cheng's strategy of balancing himself between the Western "city"—where he finds himself physically located and yet ultimately muted and excluded—and his native "city," which he had left behind and yet he could still fancy reentering. This also means that he could still maintain a certain artistic leverage and human possibility against the morbid and alienating reality, even if already deprived of the magic power of a "child in nature."

On the other hand, when he says that he wrote *City*—a work executed on a much larger scale than *The Ghost Enters the City*—as a ghost, Gu Cheng seems to indicate that he is by now sinking irreversibly into his lost native "city": the walled city of Beijing and himself. Being a "ghost" and thus possessing a certain psychic mobility and double vision, Gu Cheng is nevertheless much sobered by the fact that this "city," once reentered, is utterly unreal and offers no hope of escape or redemption. Hence the "ghost" is much more vulnerable and desperate, no longer just a persona, disguise, device, or maneuver, but a "naked" incarnation of his true existential self trapped in history. And such a "city" is in fact a liminal space, or, a limbo.

Limbo in a Posthistorical Time: Gu Cheng and the "City"

Indeed, if in *The Ghost Enters the City* the focus is still on the "ghost" as a human persona, then in *City* the attention is definitely transferred to the "city" itself, which, however, appears phantomlike.

The relationship between Gu Cheng and the city demands much in-depth investigation. Among existing studies of Gu Cheng, some already have played with the pun on Gu Cheng's name "Cheng"—which means "city"—attested by such a book title as *Gu Cheng Abandons the City* (*Gu Cheng qicheng*) (Xiao 1994). While also employing this pun, I will, however, make a further twist here and propose a radical reading. That is to say, in comparison with "nature," the "city" is equally, if not more, a crucial complex that entangled Gu Cheng throughout his life and poetry. In fact it may well be the city and not nature that metonymically represents Gu Cheng's original—rather than *alter ego*—"self,"[6] from which he had been trying to escape in his early poetry and toward which he had increasingly yearned to return in some of his last works. As for his final move of "abandoning the city," it signifies a tragic and yet apodictic act of "self-abandonment," and the completion of a process

of what he heralded as "from self to nature" (*cong ziwo dao ziran*)
(Gu 2005a: 99–115).

Gu Cheng's relationship with the city never seemed as easy or
intimate as his relationship with nature. To Gu Cheng, the city had
always appeared somewhat alien and intimidating. This remains true
even for his native city, Beijing:

> I returned to the city when I was seventeen, and I saw a lot of people. I
> was embarrassed, I didn't know how to talk . . . The city was like a
> machine, a clock, and every minute and second you would have to obey
> it. I could not get accustomed to it, so I climbed up to the loft to read
> books. (Gu 1995: 920)

> I'm not accustomed to the city, but I live and write in it. Sometimes, one
> after another, walls would unavoidably squeeze into my poetry, and
> make me feel burdened . . .

> I believe that in my poetry the city will disappear, and what will emerge
> at last will be an open pasture. (Gu 2005a: 182)

This constantly confessed uneasiness with and alienation from the
city has convinced some of his critics to view his poetry as "anticity
poetry" (*fan chengshi de shi*) (Yan 1993: 79–80). Nevertheless, what
may have been overlooked is that it is precisely such confessed uneasiness with the city that proves its prevalence as a fundamental subtext
in Gu Cheng's poetry throughout. Actually, ever since his first return
to Beijing from the countryside at seventeen, the city has made its
presence felt through its seeming absence or suppression. Moreover,
from time to time this subtext or meaningful absence would resurge as
a counter-theme: "return to the city." This counter-theme culminates
and achieves supremacy in *The Ghost Enters the City* and, particularly, *City*, where the "city" itself becomes one of the last imaginative
inner spaces in which he regains—at least to some extent—his free
agency as a compensation for, this time, his loss of "nature."

But this "city" is regained only through the eyes of a ghost.
Furthermore, Gu Cheng regains his "city" through his recognition of
foreign cities, specifically, a city such as Berlin:

> My biggest accomplishment in Berlin was to finish writing the sequence
> *The Ghost Enters the City*. I came to Berlin, and it was snowing. I
> walked in the snow, seeming to leave no traces. This reminded me of a
> ghost's life. When dusk fell, the nights in Berlin became thicker and
> thicker. Then I seemed to see a huge hand softly pressing on all the
> lamplights. Not only Berlin's nights, but also its cold and indifferent
> days, and its constant possibilities of madness, reminded me of Beijing.

The ghost is as quiet as still water, but when it is disturbed, it can also destroy everything. I don't want to say words such as "history" and "culture." But I know that the dead don't just disappear. The ghosts melt into the air, the dusk, the lamplights and the bodies of all the people. Things don't just stop there. I've regained my Beijing in Berlin. (Gu 1995: 6)

In another letter written from Berlin in 1992, Gu Cheng further elaborates:

Coming to Germany felt like traveling to the Beijing of my childhood. It had snow, and bare tree branches swaying in the wind. I felt as if I could return home by walking along the street under my window, and that I could see Xizhimen Gate, with the bleak light of dusk shining on the huge silhouettes of the city walls, and fading away.

In my dreams, I often return to Beijing, but it has nothing to do with the Beijing of today, and is where I was destined to go. Taiping Lake or Zhonghua Gate no longer exist, nor do the bricks in the fine sky, the cinder slopes, or the wild jujube trees, but I'm still walking above them, looking down below, and at the future.

I know about one thing, which people won't mention, but they will still give a hint every once in awhile. This thing is about myself, about that murder and the dead ones. I know it's this thing that has made me unable to find exit anywhere in the city. (Hong and Zhao 1993: 195)[7]

The letter ends on a sorrowful and elegiac note, and Gu Cheng sounds like a drowned person, or, a ghost, desperately trying to reach for home:

It is said in the poem: "Following the water you want to go back/Each ticket costs one dime." I stroke the river water with difficulty, without strength, because I am a dead person, living in a moment that is doomed to die.

As for the sequence of *City*, I have only finished half of it, with many city gates yet to be repaired . . . This perhaps will be a new *Seeking Dreams at West Lake* (*Xihu xunmeng*), I do not know, but I often sing a line from a Vietnamese folk song: "how sorrowful—my homeland." (Hong and Zhao 1993: 196; Gu 1995: 856)

Whereas nostalgia for the poet's native city looms large, such nostalgia is another name for the alienation that the poet experiences in foreign cities. It is in fact a familiar theme that can be immediately recognized by all of his fellow "misty" poet-exiles. It certainly strikes a chord with Yang Lian in his *Notes of a Happy Ghost* (*Xingfu guihun shouji*) as Yang contemplates his own exilic experience: "My prose-essay,

'One Man's City' (*Yige ren de chengshi*) is written about myself wandering like a phantom in the city of Auckland, New Zealand, carrying on a non-stop dialogue with myself. This conversation with myself I found later to be the basis of all ghost-talks (*guihua*)" (Yang 2003: 245). It echoes Bei Dao 北岛 (b. 1949) when he states "I speak Chinese to the mirror" in his poem "A Local Accent" (*Xiangyin*), written in Stockholm (Bei Dao 1991: 51). It further reminds one of Duo Duo 多多 (b. 1951), whose first poems written in exile bear the same ghostly recognition of the native land in a foreign city, as shown in "The Rivers of Amsterdam" (*Amusitedan de heliu*) (1989):

After the passing of the
  autumn rain
That roof crawling with snails
—my motherland
 	
On Amsterdam's rivers,
  slowly sailing by . . .
	秋雨过后
	那爬满蜗牛的屋顶
	—我的祖国
	
	从阿姆斯特丹的河上, 缓缓驶过 。。。

(Duo Duo 2002: 106–107)

This ghostly recognition reflects a poignant double alienation. On Gu Cheng's part, when he says that Berlin reminds him of Beijing, an opposite statement rings equally true, that he can neither inhabit Berlin nor return to Beijing. You cannot inhabit the society or city where you are physically present ("seeming to leave no traces"), while the home city that you have left behind very quickly regresses in your perception into a ghost city because of your absence. The only way that you can return is to revisit it in your mind, in an afterlife, or, as a ghost. Gu Cheng once admitted that "I see my life after I enter the city, which is like a specimen pinned down by a needle, its limbs waving" (Gu 1995: 922). Now returning again, Gu Cheng still finds himself trapped—his native "city" is walled, infernal, not existing in reality or the present, only existing in his own mind, and decaying in a posthistorical time. Earlier, Gu Cheng was a child in nature to which he was exiled; now, he is a ghost in the city that was once his home. Here nostalgia rhymes with claustrophobia, and to exist means no exit.

In the direction of "returning to the city," Gu Cheng's late poetry becomes overtly subjective, fragmented, whimsical, and opaque. Dreams of the future that once appeared in "A Fantasia to Life" and "I Am a Willful Child" are replaced with nightmares and ghost stories from and of the past. As if retreating into a cocoon, Gu Cheng gradually retreats from an open, fluid, and natural imagination into a shrinking, morbid, and claustrophobic inner space. Apparently Gu Cheng is still experimenting with a poetics of spontaneity and free association. However, these free associations, unlike the ones presented in his early poetry, often lack any visible logical links connecting the scattered and disjointed phrases and images, and they appear all too arbitrary and idiosyncratic.

For instance, among the fifty-two poems included in the *City* sequence, most use the names of places in Beijing for titles, but such place names and titles usually bear little or no immediate connection to the actual content of the poems. This tendency can be shown in the following two randomly selected examples:

Baishiqiao (Whitestone Bridge)   白石桥

I thank the courtyard those are flying birds	我感谢院子　　是飞着的鸟
When I came here they slept with me	她们在我来时　和我睡觉

(Gu 1995: 875)

Ping'anli (Peace Neighborhood)   平安里

I always hear the best voice	我总听见最好的声音
The light in the corridor can be switched off	走廊里的灯　　可以关上

(Gu 1995: 878)

Such schizophrenic and sleepwalking murmurs at their best invoke the eerie atmosphere of an old city haunted by its decayed past; at their worst, they are too self-absorbed and become almost inaudible and incomprehensible. In other words, as if its roots had been cut off, the "city" that Gu Cheng had been dutifully rebuilding is a city of phantoms, filled with fragmented and floating signifiers.

However, in spite of (or, perhaps, owing to) its lifelessness and all too obvious deficiencies and flaws, most likely Gu Cheng's Babel-like "city" will find its way to continue to stand in contemporary Chinese poetry. This is so because Gu Cheng had distinguished himself in comparison with his peers, through his fully devoted effort to rebuild his native "city," recognize his own childhood dreams, and deposit historical memories. Via this single-minded, almost innocent obsession with "rebuilding," Gu Cheng did succeed, even if just partially, in transforming and condensing his exilic experience into a haunting postexilic literary testament.[8]

In the ideology and mythology of modernism, closed and claustrophobic spaces, such as towers or prison cells have long been invoked as symbols for the celebration of total individual and artistic freedom and autonomy, such as in W.B. Yeats's *The Tower* or Ezra Pound's *The Pisan Cantos*. We frequently see in the practices of modernist poetry this tendency to contrast a stoic and individualistic gesture against a fluid external reality and history. Gu Cheng's "city" could have similarly served as such a site to restage the willful play of the displaced and deprived poet, in the guise of an ultimately individualistic child-ghost. One might even argue that these enigmatic verses are like riddles or even koans, provoking meaningful yet unexpected answers. For instance, one might see in the title "Peace Neighborhood" an allusion to death, which is directly related to the action of switching off the light, as presented in the second line of the poem. All these ambiguities and obscurities make an uncanny text such as *City* enduring reading.

But instead of resurrecting it from a "pure" aesthetic standpoint, I would view Gu Cheng's "city" as, more importantly, a tribute paid to the twentieth-century history of Beijing and China, no matter how overly private or idiosyncratic such tribute might appear at first. Gu Cheng says that "I don't want to say words such as 'history' and 'culture.' But I know that the dead don't just disappear. The ghosts melt into the air, the dusk, the lamplights and the bodies of all the people." Here the "ghosts" can be, in fact, a muted cry of the repressed history.[9] Perhaps only in this light can the analogy Gu Cheng found between Berlin and Beijing be fully grasped—not just as a mere coincidence, but rather as valid evidence of some hidden historical connections.[10] Gu Cheng's seemingly whimsical and spectral vision may in due course be credited for having preserved a phantom refuge for the ghosts that have been possessed and dispossessed by both modern Chinese history and Chinese modernity.

Possession and Exorcism: Gu Cheng's "Natural Philosophy" and the Specter of the Cultural Revolution

We can come back and further explore the duality of "child" and "ghost" as embodied by Gu Cheng in his metamorphosis. Most studies have very conveniently drawn a comparison between Gu Cheng and the Spanish poet Federico Garcia Lorca, as Gu Cheng himself has many times acknowledged his debt to Lorca.[11] I believe, however, more appropriate is a kindred link to Henri Michaux, the modern French poet who had been profoundly influenced by Eastern (particularly Chinese) traditions of mysticism (Daoism and Zen). In his poetry, Michaux also seeks a liberated inner space by wandering through nonexistent lands of imagination and fantasy. He claims that one of the most important functions of his poetry is "exorcism," which is the only way of reacting against hurts and traumas:

> Exorcism, a reaction in force, with a battering ram, is the true poem of the prisoner.
>
> In the very space of suffering and obsession, you introduce such exaltation, such magnificent violence, welded to the hammering of words, that the evil is progressively dissolved, replaced by an airy demonic sphere—a marvelous state!
>
> Many contemporary poems, poems of deliverance, also have an effect of exorcism, but of exorcism through subterfuge. Through the subterfuge of our subconscious nature that defends itself with an appropriate imaginative elaboration: Dreams. Through planned or exploratory subterfuge, searching for its optimum point of application: waking Dreams. (Michaux 1994: 83)

If we apply Michaux's "exorcism" to Gu Cheng, we discover that in Gu Cheng's late poems the increasingly frequent employment of "ghost" and other images of death and violence is not just narcissistic self-display, but also a desperate attempt to exorcise this "ghost" or demon that has grafted itself onto someone who once was a "fairytale poet." This paradoxical realization can be seen in a confession, in a third-person voice, that appears not in any of Gu Cheng's poems but in his novel *Ying'er*:

> He is a well-disguised maniac. His fantasies and energy for realizing any fantasies have all reached the extent of irreversibility. He wants to exclude all exterior things, all men, all of the male world and society, even reproduction and nature, including himself. He manipulates his disguise of extreme shyness and death to cope with the world, to break all secular order. This combination of understanding and madness makes me fearful. One can understand one's own madness and absurdity, while at the same time all of his rationality serves this madness, and step by step pushes life to its limits. This is no longer just madness. He is a monster! (Gu 1993: 116–117)

From "child" to "maniac" (*fengzi*) and finally to "monster," Gu Cheng presents an extremely complicated and entangled self-portrait. Although when we trace the more immediate genesis of Gu Cheng's poetics of innocence/violence and child/ghost, we will once again witness the haunting specter of the Cultural Revolution.

Gu Cheng devised for himself an earlier poetic persona during his transition from "child" to "ghost." This is "Bulin," the protagonist of *Bulin's File* (*Bulin dang'an*) (1981–1987), and a character who, like the "ghost," in many ways resembles Michaux's famous creation of "Plume" in his *Plume* sequence. Within the space of eighteen poems, Gu Cheng establishes a file for Bulin ranging from his birth to his various adventures, which are at times outrageous and at times humorous. In the postscript entitled "About Bulin" (*Guanyu Bulin*), Gu Cheng explains that "Bulin is a character like the Monkey King and Don Quixote, and had been disturbing my mind from the time I was very young. His inborn eccentricity and love of skipping school fascinate me" (Gu 1995: 757). Gu Cheng further says that the sequence is "reflective and antilyrical" (*fansi, fanshuqing*), and that,

> in terms of form, it is very much like a modern fairytale; in terms of content, it is extremely realistic, but it's not a reality that we have been accustomed to. It is a Latin American style of magical realism. In sum, what it exhibits is the human world, not an ideal heaven floating on hopes. (Gu 1995: 757–758)

This "reflective and antilyrical" style, which "is extremely realistic" and oriented to "the human world," may have directly originated from Gu Cheng's disillusionment in the wake of his early ardent social enthusiasms. And this disillusionment is in turn a reaction to his encounter with recent history, namely the Cultural Revolution:

> I cherished this fervor until the end of 1978, when I saw a large number of Red Guards' graves amid weeds and trees in Sichuan. Then I realized that too many people have already had too many naive impulses in history. That first calling and blood were beautiful, but what finally emerged was the dispassionate vault of Heaven—Heaven has no mercy. (Gu 1990: xiv; slightly modified according to the Chinese original adopted in Gu 1995: 920–921)

By the realization that "Heaven has no mercy," Gu Cheng now makes a decisive leap of faith and turns to Zhuangzi in *All Things Are Equal* (*Qiwulun*), appropriating the idea of "no inhibition" (*wubuwei*) in contrast with "nonaction" (*wuwei*):

> His "all things are equal" was not meant to bring human beings down to the same level as all other natural objects but to enable them to obtain greater freedom in their position between Heaven and Earth, to "roam beyond the four seas driving the clouds and riding the sun and the moon."

> This tradition is called "no inhibition," which means that a person might do nothing and at the same time do anything, alone in coming, alone in going. "Where he took his stand could not be fathomed" (*lihu*

buce). This tradition has influenced the tide of Chinese culture from a high and distant place. The Daoism of the Wei and Jin dynasties and ink-splash paintings and the self-proclaimed "Great Sage, Equal to Heaven"—the Monkey King who wreaked havoc in heaven—all bear the traces of this game. (Gu 1990: xv–xvi; slightly modified according to Gu 1995: 921)

Interestingly, Gu Cheng further includes the Cultural Revolution as the most recent example of this game of "no inhibition":

> Mao Zedong and the Cultural Revolution also reveal this tradition of "no inhibition" as something which suddenly embodied all of society. It appeared not as the relationship between Man and Nature, nor as that between Man and History and Culture, but as the relationship between the absolute individual and the universe. "The perfect man follows no rules"—"lawless and godless." (Gu 1990: xvi; slightly modified)

We can juxtapose the paragraph above with Gu Cheng's own explanation of the genesis of "misty poetry" on a different occasion:

> "Misty poetry" was born of the Cultural Revolution, born out of the void after the catastrophe. It appeared like another explosion of the chaos, experiencing the age of innocence of the human race within the blink of an eye. Almost all of the authors of "misty poetry" once told about such innocent expectations and pains as seen from a child's perspective. (Gu 1995: 925)

Here we find a most telling contradiction. That is, while Gu Cheng emphasizes the "innocent expectations and pains as seen from a child's perspective," he reminds his readers that it is the Cultural Revolution and Mao that embody the attitude of "no inhibition" and thus represent an ideal state of spontaneity and free will. For Gu Cheng, Mao and the Cultural Revolution somehow have come full circle and become the very spiritual source and model of "misty poetry" itself.

In fact, as early as in 1987, right after he left China, Gu Cheng had begun to expound upon this tradition of "no inhibition," which he sees as lying at the very core of the Daoist philosophy, and to attribute the birth of "misty poetry" to the Cultural Revolution (see Hong and Zhao 1993: 167; 168–170). This, in turn, testifies to Gu Cheng's earnest effort to conjoin the Cultural Revolution, "misty poetry," and the "no inhibition" tradition and to articulate a new poetics of his own. On July 10, 1993, about three months before his death, at a conference held at Frankfurt University, Germany, Gu Cheng presented probably the most important manifesto of his poetics, "The 'I' Without Purpose: An Outline of Natural Philosophy" (*Meiyou mudi de "wo": ziran zhexue gangyao*). In it Gu Cheng sums up his brand of "natural philosophy" (*ziran zhexue*) and raises the concept of "the 'I' without purpose":

> The "I" without purpose is free, having an unimaginably distinctive personality, because he has been relieved from the bondage of all purposes and concepts, relieved from the bondage of the concepts of life and death. Neither the principles of human existence nor any corresponding moral consciousness concern him. His spontaneous action puts him forever into creation. He takes not only life but also death as a game. (Hong and Zhao 1993: 214)

Gu Cheng cites Zhuangzi and the Monkey King as two examples embodying this attitude. Regarding the Monkey King, Gu Cheng adds that

> it [the Monkey King] is a breaker of all order, and yet also an embodiment of the will to live. He does evil and also good, and he kills and also saves people, not out of any moral concerns—since he doesn't belong to the human world—but purely in accord with his own liking. The figure of the Monkey King is the embodiment of the consciousness of "no inhibition" in Chinese philosophy. (Hong and Zhao 1993: 215)

The third example that Gu Cheng cites, which no doubt dismays many critics, is again Mao himself, whom Gu Cheng regards as the contemporary embodiment of both Zhuangzi and the Monkey King:

> If the Monkey King is just a spirit, then Mao Zedong could be seen as a human who has been possessed by such a spirit . . . The Cultural Revolution that he made was practically the concrete incarnation of Zhuangzi's anti-cultural consciousness. He destroyed his enemies and his own state machinery, which is the application of "wreaking havoc in heaven" in the human world. What is astounding is not his actions, but his playful attitude. He looks at the revolution that he started with sarcasm, like the Buddha looking at the Monkey King who is turning somersaults in his palm. While he says "carry the revolution to the end," he also says: "we will all be laughable after ten thousand years." (Hong and Zhao 1993: 215)

Gu Cheng's final portrait of "the 'I' without purpose" comes down to:

> One who is in the natural state is free. He does not take "I" as the point of departure, or have any purpose beyond himself, and thus has infinite possibilities in reality. He might have a long and peaceful life, or a

violent sudden death; he might be a wise man, a madman, or a fool; he might be philanthropic, or he might be a beast who concerns himself only with devouring his prey. (Hong and Zhao 1993: 215)

This quasi-Nietzschean "superman" of "nonaction/no inhibition" can be seen almost too bizarrely as a prophetic self-projection of Gu Cheng. It explains some characteristics of Gu Cheng's late poetry, in which he freely mixes good and evil, beauty and violence, life and death, wisdom and madness, spirituality and bestiality, love and *ressentiment*. Gu Cheng is actually promoting an antihumanism and nihilism, which in turn is a natural outgrowth of his "natural philosophy."

One supreme version of this "superman" is, of course, the "ghost," as we see in the last section of *The Ghost Enters the City*:

Ghost			鬼		
No trust no righteousness			无信无义		
No love no hatred			无爱无恨		
Ghost			鬼		
No father	No mother		没爹	没妈	
No son	No grandson		没子	没孙	
Ghost			鬼		
Not dead	not alive	not mad	不死	不活	不疯
	not dumb		不傻		

(Gu 1995: 849)

In these few lines, via disjointed phrases and negative statements, Gu Cheng aims at simulating a state of spontaneity and "no inhibition" on the one hand, and a state of nonattachment and "nonaction" on the other. The utter irony of this simulated portrait is, however, that while the "ghost" may appear as an absolutely free spirit who can roam all over the world, in reality he may have no dwelling place anywhere but be forever tumbling in a claustrophobic limbo. Eventually, "no inhibition" circles back to "nonaction," and transgression degenerates into imprisonment. The metamorphosis from "child" to "ghost" thus demonstrates a fateful disproportion between fantasy and reality.

In the meanwhile, we cannot slight Gu Cheng's "natural philosophy" as a mere eccentric fantasy. Instead, we must bear in mind that the most direct source of this "natural philosophy" is historical rather than natural. And it is here that Gu Cheng shows that he had indeed been possessed by the specter of the Cultural Revolution.[12]

But as shown in Michaux's case, such "possession" can be seen as an attempt at "exorcism," an attempt to expel the specter of Mao and of the Cultural Revolution. Even if "exorcism" had never been explicitly spelled out by Gu Cheng, the dialectic of this "possession/exorcism" nevertheless constitutes the paradoxical core of his poetics and its practice.[13] What one critic says about Michaux's poetics equally holds true for Gu Cheng:

> It is an art of compensation, creating possession where there were lacks, a substitute personality where there was an insecure nonentity, relief where there was tension. It is essentially a non-aesthetic poetry, governed not by artistic but by psychological needs, and improvised with whatever fortuitous fragments come to hand. (Broome 1977: 19)

> It may be an instinctive rebellion against sensed dictatorships within himself; or a shaking-off of potential dictatorships from the outside. Most often it is a violent exorcism, performed *"pour se délivrer d'emprises"* [in order to liberate oneself from the influences]: a laying of ghosts and haunting obsessions. (Broome 1977: 25)

In this light, Gu Cheng's case is a good example of the dual mechanism of "possession/exorcism," or of the "reenchantment/disenchantment" of history in contemporary Chinese poetry.

A Final Tribute: Thirteen Years After

Gu Cheng entered contemporary Chinese poetry as a "child" and exited as a "ghost," but surely this exit has also served as his reentrance. "[T]he dead don't just disappear. The ghosts melt into the air, the dusk, the lamplights and the bodies of all the people. Things don't just stop there." As a "ghost" Gu Cheng will continue to linger in his "city."[14]

Taking a bird's eye view of today's Beijing with its mushrooming high-rises and sprawling highways, thirteen years after Gu Cheng's violent end thousands of miles away on Waiheke Island in the South Pacific, anyone would be taken aback by the thought that Gu Cheng might no longer recognize most of the old sites that he once enumerated and described in *City*. Indeed, as it moves further into the new millennium, Gu Cheng's "city" is almost already too far-gone.

> Le vieux Paris n'est plus (la forme d'une ville
> Change plus vite, hélas! que le coeur d'un mortel);
> (Baudelaire 1993: 174)

> [The old Paris is no more (the shape of a city
> Changes faster, alas, than the heart of a mortal)]

Charles Baudelaire once paid this homage to Victor Hugo, who was then in political exile, and lamented the fate of his native city as the latter was rushing toward a modern future, along its widened boulevards, in the wake of several abortive and bloody revolutions. Yet Baudelaire also persisted in the tenacity of human memories:

Paris change! mais rien dans ma mélancolie
N'a bougé! palais neufs, échafaudages, blocs,
Vieux faubourgs, tout pour moi devient allégorie,
Et mes chers souvenirs sont plus lourds que des rocs.
(Baudelaire 1993: 174)

[Paris changes! But nothing in my melancholy
Has moved! New palaces, scaffoldings, blocks,
Old suburbs, all for me becomes allegory,
And my dearest memories are heavier than rocks.]

Now at the beginning of the twentieth-first century, it is Gu Cheng's own native city that is undergoing a similarly drastic transformation. The city has been busy with simultaneous demolition and reconstruction, expelling all of its residual ghost inhabitants from its old neighborhoods as well as from its own history, ancient and recent, and turning itself into yet another postsocialist and posthistorical "new world." It is here that we may suddenly find that Gu Cheng's last and desperate attempt at "ghost" poetry has foreshadowed certain prospects of Chinese modernity and postmodernity in a cunning way.

This is the subtlety of 这就是生命失败的微妙之处
the failure of life

(Gu 1995: 674)

—Is it a whisper from a "child" enlightened in "nature,"[15] or from a "ghost" lost in the "city"?

Notes

1. The "child-poet" connotation is by no means specific only to Gu Cheng: "[I]t seems clear that Nature's Child is a prevalent persona through which Misty Poets express their most ardent dreams and most profound thoughts" (Yeh 1991c: 407). Also, in this regard, Gu Cheng shared a similar fate with another Chinese poet Haizi 海子 (1964–1989). In fact, both Haizi

and Gu Cheng have been seen by their readers and critics as Rimbaudian child prodigies who perished, however, due to a fateful "innocence."

2. Again, this affinity between "nature" and "child" applies to many other "misty" poets as well. "Nature in Misty Poetry is portrayed in a predominantly positive way and is often contrasted to negative social systems. Nature promises freedom from inhibitions imposed by society . . . To be free of societal inhibitions is to be childlike" (Yeh 1991c: 407). For the role "nature" played in Gu Cheng's early poetry, also see Li Xia 1999: 181–185 and passim and Patton 2001.

3. See Gu Cheng: "The Western 'nature' and the 'nature' as presented in Eastern philosophies are different . . . The so-called 'conquering nature' or 'protecting nature' in the Western sense all take nature as an object, which is the approach of scientific analysis, defining nature as 'realm of nature' (*ziran jie*), but it should not be confused with nature in the Eastern sense" (Gu 2005a: 110–111).

4. The confusion of "it" with "him" in this sentence may not be a random spelling error on Gu Cheng's part, but an intentional effort of anthropomorphizing the rock. It reminds one of the "stone" symbolism in *A Dream of Red Mansions* (*Honglou meng*), where the "stone" is incarnated into the protagonist Baoyu. Perhaps Gu Cheng is making a similar self-reference through the rock.

5. This quoted section also opens *Ying'er* (Gu 1993: 9), showing that this "ghost" will be a guide leading readers into a different "new world" of Gu Cheng's late poetry and fiction.

6. Gu Cheng acknowledges "I often dreamed of returning to Beijing, to the place where I lived as a child . . . I'm recently writing a sequence of poems entitled 'City.' 'City' is my name and also Beijing" (Gu 2005a: 230). Wolfgang Kubin renders the title of this sequence directly as "Beijing.I" and notes, "The title of the cycle 'Cheng' (城), a pun on his first name, bears the subtitle 'Liusi' 六四 (June 4th) . . ." (Li 1999: 23).

7. Later used as the foreword to *City* (Gu 1995: 856), in the latter version the phrase "about that murder and the dead ones" is curiously omitted. While this passage might sound almost proleptic, it also can be read as referring to recent Chinese history. For this interpretation, see Kubin: "The omission of the passage . . . is perhaps open to various interpretations . . . but my marginal note points quite clearly to June 4th . . . Gu Cheng is not only dealing with his own personal trauma, but also that of his fellow countrymen, the majority of whom have succumbed to silence, apathy and forgetting" (Li 1999: 25).

8. Joseph Allen argues "These tensions . . . seem to have produced the best of his poetry, as it struggled to draw his innocence and experience together" (Gu 2005b: xii).

9. *City* is indeed open to readings at multiple levels. See Gu Cheng:
   When I wrote about this [*City*], I felt it was really realistic. I don't think it is a "psychological reality," and perhaps it can be called a spectral reality. For instance, my writing of *City* is closely related to

"□□", it absolutely is, I returned again to that city like a ghost, and met again some other ghosts. I wrote Xinjiekou, Xidan, Zizhuyuan, Houhai . . . all these poems are being together with those dead. This is very realistic, so realistic that I was only recording it down literally, sometimes it was like copying down sentences or sounds in dreams. I don't think this is a political concept, but rather a natural phenomenon in my life. (Gu 2005a: 113)

Here one suspects that the "□□," again an omission at the editor's discretion, may actually stand for "*liusi*," or "June Fourth." Besides Kubin, Allen also adopts this reading (Gu 2005b: xii).

10. Gu Cheng's recognition of Beijing through Berlin is confirmed by Yang Lian's own impression: "Since the first day when I arrived in Berlin, I immediately felt this city wasn't that unfamiliar. Its long, dark and cold winter nights, the dusk which came as early as at four in the afternoon, its snow, and the frozen branches in the snow . . . somehow often reminded me of Beijing. Berlin is a city full of history and yet seemingly without time" (Yang 1998: 214).

11. For example, see Yeh 1991c: 405. For Gu Cheng's own accounts, see Gu 2005a: 101; 179–180; 263; 332–333.

12. This "possession" testifies to Yeh's analysis of the correspondence between the "Cult of Poetry" and the "Cult of Mao" in contemporary Chinese poetry (Yeh 1996).

13. The following explanation by Gu Cheng himself of the genesis of his "fairytale poetry" is perhaps the most nuanced and yet most telling we have seen so far in this regard: "My so-called 'fairytale' wasn't completely born out of a natural state. In fact it originated from the fear that the Cultural Revolution had brought to me. When I said 'Heaven and Earth have no mercy' (*tiandi wuqing*), I didn't just have this feeling when I was walking in the desert fields; I already had it in Beijing." "My self-nature (*zixing*) shrinks owing to fear, and is liberated owing to fairytales, which is why in that fairytale world there are not only fishes and birds, but also so many graves" (Gu 2005a: 310).

14. On another occasion in 1992, Gu Cheng said, "A ghost will not be able to die" (*Gui shi meifa side*) (Gu 2005a: 292).

15. The line quoted from Gu Cheng is the ending line of the poem "Nature" (*Ziran*), which is included in the sequence *Praises to the World* (*Songge shijie*) (1983–1985) (Gu 1995: 654–680).

Chapter Nine

Yan Li in the Global City

Paul Manfredi

Humanity can move itself deeply	人类有打动自己的能力
Humanity can't do any worse than humanity	人类不可能做的比人类更坏
Humanity is nothing but a tool for making science	人類人类是制造可学的工具而已
Humanity can't but make some noise	人类必须发出一些声音地
As it walks on past humanity	从人类的身旁走过去

(Yan Li 严力, 1999: 152)

The present era in scholarship on contemporary Chinese culture is in part one of tracing the textual beginnings of contemporary Chinese cultural transformation. Recent efforts to locate the first Obscure poems,[1] the first attempts to display nontraditional art, or the first copies of *Today* 今天 magazine,[2] have all been fueled by a number of texts of remembrance, most notable for poetry being the 2003 publication by Mang Ke 芒克 (b. 1951) entitled *Gifted Generation* 瞧, 这些人.[3] Yan Li 严力 (b. 1954), a poet and painter whose contributions to these historical origins are undeniably substantial, is both surprisingly time-resistant and oddly out of place. Where powerful, even inescapable politicized points of reference frame the various endeavors of Bei Dao 北岛 (b. 1949), Jiang He 江河 (b. 1949), and others, Yan's work seems to skate both above the fray and below the radar. This is not to say that Yan's intentions are any less political than that of his contemporaries. Indeed, thirty years into his career as an artist and poet, Yan is arguably one of the artists most enduringly frustrated by ongoing difficulties to develop free space for expression in contemporary China. Within this same historical period, though, Yan's style, particularly as a poet, strikes a clear contrast to that of his compatriots. Where the other Obscure poets were ponderous, seemingly cognizant of their pioneering legacy even just as they started their work, Yan's work was markedly lighter, almost playful in what were anything but playful circumstances. This light, buoyant quality has remained consistent through his earliest experiments as a painter and poet in the 1970s, in his move to New York in the mid 1980s, and even in his return to China in 2000. During this time Yan's style has also been largely peripheral to many of the mainstream constructions of this literary and artistic historical record.

I am using the global city as a metaphor for the space that Yan Li has inhabited for the past three decades. My characterization of this space draws heavily on two sources. The first is the "global city" identified by Saskia Sassen. Sassen's analysis, which focuses on Tokyo, New York, and London as three examples of such cities, defines global city as an urban center independent of the nation-state that contains it and even the local communities of which it is comprised. These urban centers are instead channels of the worldwide flow of information, concentrations of producer services systems that themselves require centralized command and control. [4] Thus, despite the ever extending—global—reach of goods and, particularly, services, the sites wherein the terms of this reach are shaped and defined are a precious few. [5] The second is somewhat more literal in nature. It is the notion of "grobalism" developed by George Ritzer in which massive corporate "nothing" is expanded to worldwide reach through a global marketing network that leaves no local stone unturned. [6] Combining these two insight provides a lucid picture of the global situation as an interconnected and increasingly commoditized space for, among other things, artists to produce their work. Yan Li, I argue in this chapter, has turned the changes in largely economic systems to the advantage of his art, producing work that circulates effortlessly in the global systems. He does so, moreover, while staying true to a style he developed as early as the 1970s, a style that turns out to have been, in many respects, ahead of its time.

Placing Yan Li

A clear picture of Yan's work begins in the frame of contemporary Chinese poetry of the mid- to late 1970s. Yan Li came of age at a time when his contemporaries Bei Dao, Shu Ting 舒婷 (b. 1952), and others were setting the stage for a major takeover of the mainstream, official poetry establishment in China. The raw subjectivity of their work, a pained and anything-but-"obscure" lyrical voice, derived from the turmoil of the Cultural Revolution and in retrospect strikes a telling contrast to literary fiction whose largely engineered "wounded" response was always more easily managed. Obscure poetry, as it was derisively named by authorities intent on displacing it, was a clearly explosive phenomenon, and *Today* magazine had widespread circulation and impact.

Of note, however, is not so much the fact of Obscure poetry's success, a function largely of strict controls on literary and artistic expression coming undone after the death of Mao, but the extent to which it has had an impact. The reasons we still refer to Obscure poetry as a defining and even continuing moment in modern Chinese poetics, despite the fact that current work bears little resemblance to Obscure poetry style, are located first and foremost in the process of charting poetic literary history in stark and usually inflated contrast to precedents. Though identifying and denouncing aesthetic antecedents is perhaps the single defining characteristic of twentieth-century Chinese poetry (from Hu Shi to the present day), in the context of a rapidly changing contemporary China on social and economic levels, the "overthrow" of figures of the past is almost absurd when said figures themselves are hardly established writers and artists. If we take the mid-1980s as the high-point of this phenomenon, what followed Obscure poetry is what proclaimed itself to be the "New Generation," or sometimes the "Third Generation." This group of writers is indeed distinguishable in terms of life experience, if not also in terms of style. The Obscure work was the first emergence of a politically unfettered (though, again, politically charged) expression, one that was produced by a generation whose experience and, more importantly, education was determined by the Cultural Revolution and its aftermath. The New Generation continued to create in this relatively open environment, but as the authors are not by and large the "sent down youth" of before, their fields of reference are even more open, creating a kind of generational gap in a very short time. What follows afterward, however, is a dizzying array of New that is much less generational in nature. The Third Generation group, for instance, is soon parsed, in a 1988 anthology, into the "They" poets, "Shanghai" poets, the "Petty" poets, "University Poets," and, as the epitome of the confusing predicament, the "Fei-Fei" or "Not-Not" poets.[7] This grand exercise in one-upmanship has continued to the present day, with each new generation seeming to accelerate the transition from old to new until the task of actually distinguishing becomes impossible.[8]

As one of the founding members of the *Today* group, Yan was well positioned to take an authoritative position in this literary fracas.[9] He opted, instead, to remove himself from the scene altogether by leaving

China in 1985. Yan's departure at the high point of drawing the literary lines of scrimmage meant that he kept his position as one of the founding members of China's contemporary literary scene more intact. As the field of contemporary poetry becomes increasingly fractious, the foundation on which all subsequent variations grew becomes the Obscure poets themselves. Yan Li, in particular, for having missed first-hand experience of the intervening decades in China (1985–2000), becomes a dependable spokesperson for the group, a fact exemplified by Yan's June, 2004, appearance on the Shanghai television show *In People* 风流人物. In the interview, Yan is called upon to give his first-hand account of the activities of Bei Dao, Mang Ke, and other major figures of the Obscure poetry movement, a period that, with the benefit of a quarter century's hindsight, takes on a distinctly romanticized quality. The sense of the program is that though those artists were deprived of basic necessities such as ink and copy machines, their idealistic spirits are enviable from the perspective of an affluent and spiritually bankrupt present.

Also related in the *In People* program is the fact that Yan's poetic work emerged roughly at the same time as his activities as one of the founding members of the Stars Art Group 星星画会.[10] In September 1979, this group held its first public exhibition, hanging their work on an iron fence in a Beijing park across from National Art Gallery. The following year, Yan and others were able to hold another exhibition, this time inside the National Art Gallery itself, an occasion that brought 80,000 visitors to the door and was quickly shut down by authorities (Wu 2000: 12). In the following years, Yan continued, as much as possible, to exhibit his art work, an effort that culminated in a one-man show—the first ever of an avant-garde artist in China—in Shanghai in 1984 (Yan 2004: 65).

Once in New York City, Yan's work in poetry and painting continued apace. His appearances at The Poetry Project (St. Mark's Church), the Nuyorican Poets Cafe (with Allen Ginsberg), and at Columbia University in the mid–late 1980s attested to his successful integration in the local poetry establishment, while his one-man shows at the Feng Gallery (1985), Vassar College (1986), Art Waves (1987) suggest the same for his painting career. At the same time, Yan was developing his own literary magazine, *Yihang* 一行, whereby he was providing a venue for poets otherwise unable to publish in China. As *Yihang* grew into an online journal (2001), it has served, among other things, to cut across many of the boundaries, real and perceived, that separated the various camps of artists and writers in China. Yan's contribution through this journal, which is often remarked upon by writers in

China today, was to provide a venue for writers who would likely have been squeezed out of the tight spaces established by emerging poets. This contribution is emblematic of Yan's work as a whole. Yan, since his participation as a poet in *Today*, and as a painter in Stars, has found himself at a kind of periphery of Chinese cultural production. As a poet who left China, Yan was placed outside of the literary encampments discussed above, and as a poet who paints, he is sometimes left out of poetry circles altogether. Yan's well-organized presence online is itself indicative of his achievements, taking the initiative afforded by technology to occupy a kind of peripheral space that nonetheless intersects in both written text and visual image with numerous centers (Taiwan, China, New York City) at once.

Given the outsider quality, we may observe that the *location* of Yan Li is up for grabs, occupying a positionality in-between states, genres, and eras. If life experience is the operative determinative in establishing affiliations in poetry circles of the past two decades, Yan's numerous places of residence outside of China have placed in him a liminal condition, always at one remove from where he in fact is. This results, particularly with his return to China, in difficult situations in terms of Yan's relationship to other Obscure poetry-era poets as well as to other contemporary artists. Liminality is also manifest stylistically in the underlying complexity of often simple-seeming visual and verbal expressions. We may observe, to begin with, that as a visual artist Yan committed to acrylic material and simple, even cartoonish lines. Yan's visual statements are in a sense superficial (on the surface), quickly apprehended and consumed. His paintings also demonstrate a cerebral bent, images that appear to think out loud. Meanwhile, the sentiments of his poetic lines often whisk by in quips, flashing insight as they go and almost denying emotional force itself.[11] The images and poems are similarly "good to go"—consumable, portable, light, and thus well-suited to new media both as a technological format, and as a mode of consumption. How these aspects of Yan's method and style bear on his standing in global terms will occupy the remainder of this chapter.

Global City on Canvas

Denis Mair observes in his introductory comment to a collection of Yan's painting and poetry that it is Yan's experience living in urban centers over the past twenty years that has generated his preoccupation with looking out of windows of large structures (Yan 2003: 3). If so,

Yan is also toying with the notion of the artificiality of the observer herself, for the vision that travels through the window frames (both leading to interiors and to urban scapes beyond) is ultimately implicated in the built structures themselves. The effect is an interpenetration of formerly disparate elements—the individual and her urban environment collapsing into one. The 2002–2003 series of three paintings entitled "Peaceful Evolution" is a case in point. In the following example, a poignant and typical ambivalence is maintained in the contrast between "peace" and "construction" (actually, "construction industry" in Chinese). The ambivalence is manifest in Yan's delicate balance of warm interiors of lush color that invite the human subject, and the mechanized significance of the bricks that repel it at the same time.

The three images of the "Peaceful Evolution" series manage to reach at once toward the comforts of technology and the perils of its widespread application. Taken in the larger framework of Yan's work, we find a recurrent negotiation of contending systems, human and technological, that gradually, imperceptibly blend into one. The brick balloons are the salient case in terms of Yan Li's painting. In a clever conceit, the balloons buoyancy contradicts their weight in a gesture mutually reinforcing and negating.

In this context, Yan's balloons in the "Longing for Nature" series are of particular interest. As an urban artist, one might expect that Yan's deliberate address (because so titled) to the subject of nature would pose an opportunity for stylistic departure. The images clearly suggest otherwise. In the series, the human subjects are indeed freed from the confines of their urban setting, floating in a fully natural environment. A form of alienation is maintained, however, in Yan's still consistent stylistic treatment of the material subject of his paintings. The woods, for instance, are not unlike the highrise buildings of a multitude of urban images:

The consistency of Yan's visual statements suggest that something else is at work rather than the mere "urban/nature" dichotomy. "Mother and Child," an earlier series, captures a kind of celebration of human-ity on superficial, which is to say structured (brick-like), grounds:

Amidst satisfyingly arranged angles that recede in acute perspective there emerges a mother and her child, whose very bond is as much a feature of the built world as the buildings (and moon) that surround them. In this view, the "Longing" series could well be, as its title suggests, a natural product of the human imagination and poesis, the principal builder.

Yan's urban images are also distinctively unspecific in terms of national space or orientation. One is aware of the human condition in juxtaposition to the fruits of its industry. There is, of course, a discourse relating to environmental degradation specific to Chinese economic expansion, but for an artist such as Yan Li, this is secondary. Degradation is a shared operation, not unlike industry. Yan's work formalizes the ambivalence that stems from being both critic of the processes that corrupt or erode our environment and also fully aware of his own complicity in these processes. Beyond this, though, Yan seems to completely erase the distinction between exhausting our natural resources and exhausting our very selves, positing an oppositional relationship between the human and natural that fundamentally unravels in the contemplation of concepts born in his work. The end result seems a kind of negation; Yan's tendency is to draw pictures in word and image that steal from the world of ideas and run with the money.

The refusal to submit to positionality, to render himself subject to an explicit point of view, is one facet of Yan's location in the global city. His work goes with the flow, almost celebrating environmental degradation in the same breath that laments it. Yan's faceless brick-heads, which to begin with eschew ethnicity of any kind, also resist their own humanity. This maneuver would, in the hands of another artist, perhaps, lead to a critique of an automaton phenomenon. In Yan Li's case, though, something more subtle is at work. We observe instead a genuine mixture of impulses, one that emerges from an appreciation of human nature as system itself, a system that is contiguous with otherwise alienating forces—whether they be political, environmental, or technological. In all of these cases there is a sense of mutual dependency, one that is characteristic of the contemporary global city—be it in terms of commerce, or mutual reliance on natural resource exchange. Awareness of these often dubious partnerships deflate activism at the very moment it might be conceived.

Poetry and Painting: Koans of the City

Yan's connection to a global city is from the above examples partly a content or thematic connection—his images are almost entirely of urban landscapes, or refugees from it. The themes of Yan's poetry indeed include considerable amount of urban reference, many of which I will discuss below. More at issue, however, is Yan's methodology. By the early 1990s, Yan was experimenting with what he often calls his "poetry gum" series, a collection of short poems that, in the principal Chinese edition, is titled "Spinning Polyhedral Mirror" 多面境旋转体.[12] These epigrammatic condensations of contemporary experience are, at first glance, a matter of convenience. One can find, for instance, hundreds of such poems online on a variety of Web sites. One can also discover a continuum in the relationship between the "poetry gum" poems and Yan's longer works, where clearly the poet selects particularly successful lines as candidates for the short-form expression or explores elaboration of some shorter poems in expanded format.[13] Beyond these matters of convenience, however, there are further implications of Yan's "poetry gum" method. As he explains in his preface to the Chinese edition, these poems are meant to be read as "the ever revolving mirrors of a disco ball, reflecting human nature in all its facets" (Yan 1999: 5). Yan further describes the approach as providing direct access to the here and now according to the "advertisement-like increments of time" 广告式的时间划分 (op cit) that comprise life at the end of the last century, and the beginning of a new millennium. A striking testimony to this orientation emerges in a recent manuscript[14] in which we find the following heading to the "poetry gum" section:

Production Location: China.	产地: 中国。
If they're tasty, gnaw on them a bit longer,	有味多嚼一会儿,
And if not, just spit them out	没味就吐掉
Producer: Yan Li	生产者: 严力

The commodity orientation can be discovered in many of the "poetry gum" poems, for instance,

When money raises its	当金钱在生活面前
Wall in the face of life	坚起它的高墙时
You have to pocket a few bricks	人必须贪污其中的
In order to dig through.	几块砖才能钻过去
	(Translation by Denis Mair)

There are also overtones of classical poetry here. What these poems have more in common, however, is the tradition of Japanese Koans. Yan Li's poetic epigrams are almost begrudging philosophical snapshots, insights that, holding to his description of the disco ball, reflect light rather than illuminate. They are epiphanies that nonetheless withdraw insight at the very moment they seem to impart it. We are, for instance, given to wonder what Zen understanding resides in:

Every time I look back	我的每一次回頭都
I hurt my neck	摔傷了我的領子
Because both my home and I	因為我和我的家
Ran away from home	一起離家出走了

Yan's "poetry gum" poems lend themselves very well to a logic of infiltration and dissidence, revealing machinations of a dehumanizing system and raising, in the process, the potential for a voice of protest:

Tomorrow	明天
I'll visit a museum	我要在博物館裏

And fix up a few hours of war for fun	修理幾個小時的戰爭作為消遣
Tomorrow	明天
While smuggling peace to other planets	我向其他星球走私和平時
I'll not be taking U.S. Dollars	不收美金

But as suggested above in the case of his environmentally conscious paintings, Yan does not merely give in to this mode of the dissident, the reformer, the artist/individual versus government oppression, or even environmental degradation. His revelations demonstrate a "subtracted" poetics, one that reduces to the essence, driving at the commonality, indeed, the universal in human experience, but one that is also divested of the kind of interest that would lead to explicit points of view or positionality of almost any kind. The koan analogy allows us to find something that distinguishes Yan's sticks of gum from aphorism or, worse yet, from political or commodity advertisement, namely, the types of communication that Yan's poetics undermines.

If we picture such a figure, as Yan does in his work, we might derive the following image:

Fully ensconced in his environment, irrevocably built into its very material, the lyrical quality of Yan's visual figures, as the subjects of his poems, are almost always at home, despite the forces that would seem otherwise to alienate them. At the same time, reading such an image, as reading many of the "poetry gum" series, brings resolutions that are always somehow unsatisfactory. This is a hopeful gesture, when the act of reading, itself a path to justice, to turning the tide, is recuperative. The poem that opens this essay

Humanity can move itself deeply	人类有打动自己的能力
Humanity can't do any worse	人类不可能做的比人类更坏
than humanity	人類人类是制造可学的工具而已
Humanity is nothing but a tool	人类必须发出一些声音地
for making science	从人类的身旁走过去[15]
Humanity can't but make some noise	
As it walks on past humanity	

is a similar case in point. The exchanges are an inevitable part of the picture, and no rupture is found between the detriments of our technologies, our dependence, and the humanized or natural conditions they defile or pollute. In terms of his paintings, perhaps none is better than another tripartite series entitled "Escaping from the Cities" (2004):

In this sequence, Yan's subjects collapse, Dali-style, within the characteristically (for Yan Li) constructed alternatives to our built environment. Again, the satisfying quality of the lines, in this final case augmented by the distinctly manufactured texture of the natural trunks themselves, allows the painter to almost perfectly contradict the idea of escape suggested in the title. The clouds, the moon, even the signature, all say one thing and do another. In this respect Yan's painting and his "poetry gum" approach are highly consistent. Both provide the viewer with conundrums on which to chew for a while and, perhaps, nothing more.

Regular-Length Poems

With the foregoing discussion in mind, we can turn to Yan's full-length poems. Especially in recent years, Yan's 2002 "Untitled" was conceived in this vein:

Coca Cola and I had our picture taken recently	我与可口可乐合拍了一张影像
But friends don't see much compatibility	但朋友们都说看不出有甚么夫妻相
They say he's old, dark, and crazy materialistically	都说他太老太黑太多物质的狂妄
Though we all know he has sold well for a century	虽然百年来他有全球共识的卖
Friends say that for the sake of heredity	朋友们还说为了我那下一代的质量
I should not rate a spouse economically	绝不能光从经济上考虑配偶的优良
With body and soul I brew up affection repeatedly	于是我一次次地把全身心的情感酝酿
Till I start measuring advantages erratically	直到我在各种条件的衡量中乱了方向
Till my youthful advantage starts deserting me	直到我再也没有青春的优势与他人较量
Till the chill of a lonely world settles inwardly	直到我内心只剩下一片天寒地冻的凄凉
Till my repentant cries echo piercingly	直到我最终把忏悔词喊得山响
Till like an ice-cube, I float in cola bobbingly	直到如冰块沉浮在可乐中的我
Now consuming is all, ideals don't appeal to me	不再谈论除消费之外的任何理

(Translation by Denis Mair. Yan 2004: 139)[16]

The poem, an unbroken but clearly identifiable two-segment sequence, opens with the playfully audacious maneuver of anthropomorphizing the well-known soft drink. As a potential spouse, Coke ranks well in notoriety but raises questions in terms of genetic coding in offspring. The turning point, following his friends' advice, rests on "Thereupon," at which pivot the poem locks into an emphatic list of "until," tightening the space between-iang-ending lines that, with the exception of the penultimate line, anchor the poem's meter. Yan thus ratchets up the intensity wherein the anthropomorphized Coke is drawn ever closer into self-identification, "brewing" and "ageing" until the subject becomes "I" thoroughly cured of any ideal. This arguably horrific baptism by Coke is delivered in unsentimental terms, but also, curiously, without explicit irony. In the global city, the logic of consumption replaces the logic of dissent. It is a logic of exchange, one that cuts through ideals with an unfeeling pragmatism that is lamented and celebrated in equal parts. The preoccupation with the manner and the underlying principal of the "flows" of market forces—or capital, which is so literally a dynamic of a transnational entity such as Coca-Cola through global cities of today—is where Yan's consistency of style is most striking. Returning again to one of Yan's earliest works, for instance, we find "Mushroom" (蘑菇):

Who can	谁能
convince themselves	说服自己
That in the darkest places	在阴暗的处境里
Life disappears	生命不存在了
Even with its back to the light	背着光
Rotten wood is impregnated	朽木怀

(Yan 2004: 5)

Moving across the decades to another 2002 poem, "Patent on Fortune" 幸运的专利:

Humanity is very fortunate!	人类真幸运！
The sun is so perfectly far from the earth	太阳离地球不远不近
Coordinated like land and sky, vagina and penis	像阴道与阳具的天地配合
Humanity can't help but be fortunate	人类不得不幸运
After sucking flat the breast of the earth	在吸扁了地球的乳房后
	如今享受着科技的酥胸
	电子游戏转化了千年的良心事业
	弱肉强食是
	软件内老少咸宣的娱乐

We now savor the nectar
of technology
Video games transform a
thousand years of ethics
In games, the strong prey
upon the weak
to the amusement of young
and old
The news of humanity, how
very fortunate!
Full-page ads covered with
name brand skirts
The pop songs of humanity,
how very fortunate!
From just the few hit tunes
held in your tiny hand
Can ignite an inferno of a
billion in CD sales
And that splendid dust-raising
stock market
The jockeys of humanity, how
very fortunate
Each erection can buy
innumerable climaxes
The evolution of humanity,
how very fortunate!
Cloning changed the
supply-demand system
of sperm and ovaries
Humanity comes and goes
Busy picking up goods from
inside desire
No more storehouses for falsity
of a woman's gaze
The fortune of humanity belongs
to humanity!
Humanity can, after making a
huge mistake
Apply for a patent on fortune

人类的新闻多么幸运！
整版整版的广告围绕在 名牌的群下
人类的流行曲是多么幸运！
仅仅几首握着你小手的专集
就能点燃千百万张碟片的畅销的火
还有那么壮观的尘士飞扬的股票市场
人类的骑手多么幸运
数字的勃起能买来多少高潮
人类的进化是多么幸运！
克隆改变了
精子与卵巢的供求关系
人类进进出出地
忙于从欲望里面直接提货
绝不再设一个仓库来留给虚伪的秋波
人类的幸运属于人类的！
人类能在闯下大祸之后
申请幸运的专利

(Yan 2004: 132)

From such a poem we see the ways in which incorporation starts with a recognition that the human will finds a way of asserting itself, naturally. In Yan's work this assertion occurs even against the odds of rapidly disappearing resources on the natural level and also in defiance of the usually unintended outcomes of humanity's own unwise decisions. We are our own nature and our task is to understand just that. In taking what is biologically essential to the continuation of the species to be simulacra of pop music and stock market exchange, Yan puts humans in their place; that place both shares endangerment with other species and claims the high ground—the last man standing when all else is lost. Thus Yan maneuvers between dire predictions of the previous poem to more celebratory utterances, as in "Sun in the Morning Market" (早市的太阳):

You find yourself at the morning market	看着自己在早市上拎着
carrying a bag of food	一袋食品
	一袋
a bag of	各种个样的叫卖声
a myriad seller's calls,	一袋
a bag of	经过精打细算的脂肪蛋白质以及维生素
fat, protein and vitamins all carefully calculated	一袋
	生活的重量
A bag of	
the weight of life.	很久很久地
	我继续站在路品味自己的生命
For such a long time	
I'm there at the intersection tasting my life.	日常是多么自然
	太阳拎着一袋自己的阳光
How natural, everyday	
The sun carries a bag of its own light	

(Yan 2004: 89)

In the first case, Yan is characteristically connecting oil, which humans blithely draw from the natural environment at their peril, to human sentiment. As with snow and mushrooms, which served as mirrors to reflect upon ourselves more completely, oil is little more than an occasion to observe the kinetic or psychologically motivating potential of pain. In the second case, Yan the poet stands on a street corner, surrounded by urban experience, but breaking down the contents of such experience into financial exchange (bargain price) and biological processes.[17] We can easily imagine a Yan Li painting from this poetic image: bricks in hand, in the face of the sun and, though certainly difficult to render, in the light contained in a bag the sun carries. The bricks are that from which our bodies and economies, cities and solar system are built.

In the context of contemporary Chinese poetry, perhaps the most significant element of Yan's work is that it travels well, as does, for that matter, the poet himself. While many other writers' works are quite deeply bound up with specific histories of the admittedly tumultuous decades of late twentieth-century and early twenty-first century China, Yan's work stands somehow outside this frame of reference. Yan's portability stems at least in part from the commodity-like quality of his work, one that adheres in its method—especially the "poetry gum" series—and content to a widely recognizable world image. Yan's urban scenes, in other words, deny the specific gravity of their geographical and historical location in much the way that a widely recognizable name brands do, for the purpose of immediate and effortless application locally.

This is not to say, of course, that Yan Li's paintings and poems necessarily "sell well," just that in their presentation they borrow mechanisms that relate to economic exchange and that in their content often refer to dynamics of this exchange, even if the agents in the transactions are inanimate or something other than human. Yan Li's focus, thus, is on the systems themselves, and this focus has put him thematically and methodologically current in ways that many of his contemporaries are not. Moreover, his work—visually and poetically— is not so much trying to beat the ever-widening global system, of which he is undoubtedly critical, but to get to the bottom of it. In order to do so he orients himself to an increasingly rapid and efficient global flow, disengaging in numerous possible subject positions to explore others sometimes midstream. Getting to the bottom of it is the ultimate challenge, though, in the global context, as the emptying out of content occurs just at the point of traction, where Yan Li meets his readers or those looking at his paintings. When successful, then, Yan's work is a satisfying return of substance to what seems increasingly interconnected points of nothingness. Yet, even if we as readers are able to find him there, we can bet we would not be staying for very long.

Notes

1. The alternative rendering of "menglong" is "Misty," a term that does not well reflect the controversy that the poetry generated on its appearance, nor, for that matter, the ponderous nature of the style itself. I will henceforth use the term "Obscure" to designate this poetry.
2. *Today* began as a handwritten and crudely mimeographed journal that had widespread impact in the late 1970s and early 1980s in China.
3. Another and more recent example would be the *Crisis and Detour: 25 Years of Today* conference that was held at Notre Dame University in March 2006.

4. Advertising, accounting, finance, insurance, business law are a few examples of such services. Obviously, most of these have a long history. Sassen argues, however, that fundamental changes in these services in recent decades warrant a new understanding of their function globally and locally.

5. This, in Sassen's analysis, is what separates the truly global cities from all the rest. It is not my purpose to argue this point at length here, except perhaps to mention that Yan Li is in fact resident of one of the three.

6. Ritzer places "glocalism" and "something" at the alternate pole of the continuum. The notion of a truly "local" entity, independent from the global system, is, in Ritzer's estimation, increasingly difficult to find.

7. Other publications that bear witness to this phenomenon are the 1993 *Post-Obscure Poetry* 后朦胧诗, and the 2003 *Mid-generation Poetry* 中间代诗. Covering roughly two decades of literary production, these two publications demonstrate the voluminizing tendencies of differential poetics in China.

8. Today's encampments are increasingly conceived in terms of geography, though the "academic" 知识分子 versus "popular" 民间 dichotomy has also served to compartmentalize in recent years.

9. His work figures prominently, for instance, in the 1980 issue (8) of *Today* magazine. In that issue Yan Li's two poems "I Am Snow" (我是雪) and "Mushroom" (蘑菇)—the latter of which is discussed a little later in the chapter—are couched between publications by Shu Ting and Shi Zhi 食指 (b. 1948).

10. By his own account, Yan Li was writing poetry by 1973 and painting by 1979 (Wang 1999: 157).

11. A fact that can be observed in the many versions of Yan's poems. Online, for instance, one finds many of Yan's thirty- and forty-line poems condensed to two- and three-line versions. According to the author, this makes them "easier to remember." Correspondence, January 2005.

12. This text is a compilation of roughly five hundred of these short poems composed between 1990 and 1999. Yan continues to compose in this format, however, and has numerous other manuscripts that include these poems.

13. Personal conversations with the author, August 2005.

14. This particular manuscript brings together Yan's short and long poems, many of his paintings, autobiographical essays, and other materials in Chinese and English translation.

15. This work is also a good example of Yan's tendency to rewrite, which the "poetry gum" method makes particularly convenient. The opening lines of Yan Li's section in a collection of contemporary Chinese poetry edited by Wang Ping has the following: "We have the power to change ourselves. / We can't behave worse than people. / Today we are nothing but tools for science. / To walk past the grave, we must make some noise" (Wang 1999: 159).

16. This translation is by Denis Mair. This and the original poem appear on the *Poetry Sky* 诗天空 Web site.
17. The poem was composed on the occasion of the birth of Yan's first child. His preoccupation with nourishment and life was as a consequence uncommonly acute. Personal conversation with the author, August 2005.

Chapter Ten

Poetic Memory: Recalling the Cultural Revolution in the Poems of Yu Jian and Sun Wenbo

John A. Crespi

Certainly the most controversial period in recent Chinese historical memory has been the Cultural Revolution, and the prevailing artistic modes of remembering those "ten years of turmoil" have been the written and cinematic narrative. From the literature and film of "the wounded" in the late 1970s and early 1980s on through to the "seeking roots" and "avant-garde" writing, the Red Guard memoir, and the 1990s' films of Cultural Revolution childhood, those who came of age during that tumultuous era have used one or another mode of story-telling to comprehend in retrospect the forces that dominated and often traumatized the lives of themselves, their families, and an entire society. In these stories' wake has come an abundance of humanistic studies analyzing this ever-growing corpus of fiction, memoir, and film. The most incisive among these perform the following: identify a hegemonic narrative pattern, then discuss a particular narrative text's complicity with or subversion of the hegemonic status quo. In the case of the more sophisticated narratives, complicity and subversion may, of course, be difficult to separate. As a general rule, however, the approach described is grounded in a postmodern mistrust of grand narratives, among which the most prominent are the cold war narra-tive of freedom versus oppression (Zarrow 1999; Zhong, Wang, and Di 2001), narratives shaped by Western-derived postmodern discourse of "sexuality-as-liberation" (Larson 1999; Larson 2000), the linear modernization narrative of nationalist and official Chinese communist historiography (Braester 2003; Wang 2004; Yang 2002), and, corollary to the modernization narrative, the story of China's rapid transforma-tion under the pressures of globalization (Wang 2004; Liu 2004). Alternatives to such hegemonic formations typically come to light as stories that disrupt, defamiliarize, or simply diverge from existing narrative patterns by invoking historical trauma, everyday resistance, or a metafictional self-awareness.

A less readily observed characteristic shared by these critiques of Cultural Revolution representation—overlooked by its very ubiquity—is that they begin and end in the domain of narrative. Due to the predominance of the narrative mode in such texts, or because of an assumed affinity between history and narration, the search for alternative versions of the Cultural Revolution has presumed narrative as a master genre. Further, it seems the study of narrative has slipped into a dominant pattern of its own, one in which narrative meets counter-narrative, such that the poetics of hegemonic story patterns serving a particular ideology can serve as ground to the figure of alternative narrative forms representing resistance, dissolution, and dislocation. Narrative, in short, stands as both disease and cure for recovering meaningful historical experience; nonnarrative genres, meanwhile, are easily dismissed as irrelevant, or worse, part of the problem.

Undeniably, the study of narrative has yielded tremendous historical and aesthetic insights into representations of the Cultural Revolution period, while also speaking eloquently to narrative's power to structure and disrupt memory, identity, temporality, and social belonging. At the same time, however, one wonders what genres have been excluded or rejected as other means for comprehending such a deeply formative era of China's revolutionary past. In view of such concerns, this study posits that for all its powers of figurative representation, narrative does not tell the whole story. In fact, the weight given to interrogating literary form in the analysis of Cultural Revolution narrative seems logically to demand a look at the nonnarrative genre whose identity as well as meaning-making ability depends by and large upon intensity of figurative language: poetry. The question then arises: how might poetry—and in particular the short poem unbound by conventional narrative expectations for character, plot, chronology—rewrite the Cultural Revolution experience? To venture an answer, I turn to two recent sets of poetic texts that explore the memory of childhood during the 1960s and 1970s. One is "Two or Three Things from the Past" 往事二三, a series of twelve poems by Yu Jian 于坚 (b. 1954), the majority of which are set in Kunming, Yunnan province, the city where Yu grew up and still resides (Yu 2003: 106–120). The other is a series of thirty-six poems by Sun Wenbo 孙文波 (b. 1956), collectively entitled "1960s Bicycle" 六十年代自行车, that recalls the people, things, and events in the New Railway Village 铁路新村 neighborhood in Chengdu, Sichuan province, where Sun's family lived during the 1960s and 1970s (Jiang 2002). Although quite different in style and conception, both sets of texts can be called "poetic memoir": brief, almost entirely autobiographical poems that use the generic resources of poetry to configure personal remembrance of childhood, during the 1960s and 1970s in China.

Yu's and Sun's poems are by no means the first to engage actively the Cultural Revolution period. In the immediate post–Cultural Revolution years a loose confederation of young poets created a literary sensation with work now known collectively as *menglong* 朦胧 or "Obscure" poetry. *Menglong* poems have been described as "poetry of retrospection" deeply influenced by "the poets' memory of a particular historical period" (Li and Hung 1992: 94). More precisely, observes Tao Naikan in the same vein, *menglong* poetry arose from "the poets' personal experience of disillusionment and suppression during the Cultural Revolution" and "was shaped in part as a pragmatic device to voice their personal responses to a dehumanizing history" (Tao 1995/1996: 147). These responses typically—but not exclusively—took the form of poems that departed from the dogmatic collectivist-realist extremes of Mao-era art and literature by employing dense symbolism, an individualized point of view, and intentional ambiguity.

Although memory certainly inspired many *menglong* poems, it is important to note that no small number of them were written during the Cultural Revolution period itself (Van Crevel 1996: 42–59), and thus reflect immediacy more than memory. Also, where memory did come into play, it functioned more as impetus than object; that is, the experience of terror, injustice, and suffering impelled the poets to write and to do so in a manner "unified by its open, though often symbolically expressed rebellion against the Cultural Revolution" (Li and Hung 1992: 94). At some risk of generalization, one can thus describe *menglong* poems as primarily rejecting the past rather than attempting to rework elements of memory.

Given *menglong* poetry's status as the product of a groundbreaking literary movement, its significance cannot be denied. Nonetheless, in terms of time of production and inherent conceptual assumptions, and despite the poets' efforts to transcend the times, *menglong* poems were to a large degree *of* their era, and thus not the place to seek a poetic perspective on memory, much less a perspective informed by a significant historical distance. Such poems, concludes Michelle Yeh, were "transitional" in that they cleared a space for a more independent discourse of poetry but, due to built-in limitations, failed to move fully beyond the literary and political "other" they defined themselves against (Yeh 2003).

Poetic innovation beyond the *menglong* movement began with China's Third Generation 第三代 poets—a term devised to gather under one label a broad array of mostly younger writers who, starting in the mid-1980s, began turning against the style of their Second Generation 第二代—that is, *menglong*—predecessors. The Third Generation took poetry in many directions, but as a general rule rejected the *menglong* poets' historical, political, and aesthetic vision as stylistically artificial and ideologically suspect. Yu Jian and Sun Wenbo, whose early work is often listed under the Third Generation rubric, may be viewed as belonging to a subset of writers within that grouping whose poetry is characterized by an "antilyrical style" (Li and Hung 1992: 97) employing a prosaic, everyday language focused on quotidian life (Yeh 1992; Tao 1995/1996). Within this general typology, however, Yu and Sun's poetic styles differ unmistakably and, as must be kept in mind, continue to evolve. Especially since around 1990, Yu Jian has tended to direct his poetic gaze out and away from the poet's individual subjectivity to capture the transient configuration, tenor, and immediacy of seemingly ordinary objects and situations. A beer-bottle top, oil barrels stacked beside a railway, an animal fleetingly illuminated by headlights on a remote highway, snatches of conversation overheard in a hotel—any element of the local, unique, or transient are raw material for poetry that aims to reenchant the everyday by, as Yu himself asserts, "rooting itself in the soil of contemporary life, not upon the illusions of the past" (2004: 3). After emerging as a poet in the late 1980s, Sun Wenbo, too, has consciously moved beyond the *menglong* style. Sun's is a manner of writing that—as he puts it in a self-reflective poem—has gradually left behind "contrived posing" and "bizarre" phrasing in favor of "learning how / to find the words I need in the things around me" (2001: 65). Viewed more broadly, Sun's poetic output has been characterized by a discursive, often narrativistic voicing that frequently expands into extended line lengths and multiple stanzas (Van Crevel 2005). In these loosely structured, sometimes rather long poems, Sun often uses an inward-looking, confessional tone to develop monologic, ruminative explorations of self through descriptions of quotidian situations.

Although the stylistic differences between Yu and Sun still hold in a comparison of "Two or Three Things from the Past" and "1960s Bicycle," the two poets come together in accomplishing an important task: both use the generic resources of poetry to create configurations of time and memory grounded in first-person experience of the Cultural Revolution. Moreover, these configurations stand apart from the narrated forms of temporality and remembrance constructed by the corresponding, and widely read, subgenre of the Cultural Revolution memoir. Such memoirs are frequently structured in complicity with hegemonic discourses both within and outside China. Especially in the case of the popular Red Guard memoir, they narrate the main character's development along a coming-of-age trajectory that moves chronologically from childhood innocence, to political disillusionment, to a postrevolutionary wisdom of self-realization. For the foreign audience, as Peter Zarrow points out, this narrative structure falls into the cold war pattern pitting "freedom" against "totalitarianism" (1999). Concomitantly, such emplotment parallels and reinforces official and popular narratives that stress a transition from a naive and error-ridden socialist era to the presumably mature, accurate self-knowledge of the post-Mao years. By emphasizing the present at the expense of the past, this brand of narrative imagination pushes the Cultural Revolution period back in time, to a place where it can be regarded from afar as a dark, misguided age succeeded by the bright hope of a more rational and materially abundant present.

The two sets of poems by Yu and Sun offer a poetically constructed alternative to this conventional narrative-driven patterning. In terms of what they avoid, the poems offer no beginning, middle, or end for the Cultural Revolution period, no coming-of-age journey to self-realization for their subjects, and no dramatic escape from political and psychological oppression. While both Yu and Sun's poems at times take anecdotal form, they do not, either singly or in series, construct a continuous teleology of history or personal growth, much less a larger narrative trajectory representing the Cultural Revolution as a span of time willingly left behind upon the emergence of a more hopeful "new era." Instead, in both series of poems the reader encounters carefully configured texts that, when taken individually, offer detached yet closely observant perspectives on Cultural Revolution childhood and, when read as a whole, represent a sustained effort to retrieve, reconstruct and unfold complex, discontinuous moments of memory and self in China's revolutionary past. The Cultural Revolution, both poets implicitly insist, was a deeply formative historical episode that irrevocably occurred, an event forgotten, repressed, and even trivialized during the intervening years, but that has not lost its presence or relevance even decades later at the turn of the twenty-first century.

The key to comprehending how the poems express these ideas lies in attending to certain structural features that help distinguish them generically *as* poems. Understanding how they reconfigure time and memory thus requires close attention to patternment in the poetic texts themselves, and the search for pattern calls for close reading of the sort that not only identifies multiple layers of textual structure, but also discerns how such structure can generate specific visions of historical remembrance.

Below I attempt to disclose significant forms of patternment in and among poems from "Two or Three Things from the Past" and "1960s Bicycle." My approach is informed by the "poetic function," a term briefly defined as the manner in which repetitions among various levels of discourse, from the phonological on through the grammatical and syntactic, "enter into complex organization in symmetries, gradations, antitheses, parallelisms, etc., forming together a veritable spatial structure" (Todorov 1981: 47). Despite its name, the poetic function does not apply exclusively to poetry. Rather, it represents a method for identifying the layers of structure that, in a historically and generically determined manner, differentiate artistic from nonartistic verbal messages. Even so, the poetic function is, as the term's inventor Roman Jakobson maintains, "the indispensable feature in any piece of poetry" (Jakobson 1987: 71) because "on every level of language the essence of poetic artifice consists of recurrent returns" (145). Such artifice may be more apparent in the prosodic conventions of fixed poetic forms but can apply with similar force to free verse—the form of choice for Yu and Sun—where it typically appears as "conspicuous repetition of phrases or syntactical forms" commonly used in conjunction with "mechanically typographical" devices (Fussell 1979: 79, 77).

In examining these works of poetic memoir, I will consider first how Yu Jian's poems configure time and memory through free-verse application of the poetic function and then move on to how Sun Wenbo's poems represent memory through creative violation of this same aesthetic principle. Yu's poems can be read as free-verse texts whose emphasis on internal patternment activates the poetic function's effect of "promoting the palpability of signs" and enhancing "the fundamental dichotomy of signs and objects" (Jakobson 1987: 70). What results is an autobiographical exploration of the Cultural Revolution experience, but one whose significance lies in the ability of poetic patterning to recreate personal historical memory of the period as discrete, autonomous, yet internally complex and undecidable moments. Sun's poems, on the other hand, forego intensity of intratextual patterning—and so, it would seem, the poetic function—in favor of a "real world" reference more typical of realist prose fiction. Sun's seemingly counter-poetic acts of reference, however, construct a patterning of their own that, while running counter to the principles of the poetic function, make for an imagination of memory no less distinct than Yu's.

Yu Jian: Moment against Movement

When considered in contrast to many narrativized versions of the Cultural Revolution experience, the temporal imagination constructed by Yu Jian's "Two or Three Things from the Past" stands out for how it avoids representing the period as a linear movement from "here" to "there." Instead, Yu uses the form of the poem series, as well as the resources of the free-verse poem, to emphasize a "spatial structure" of remembrance for the Cultural Revolution years—not as a movement through history, but as an internally complex moment *of* history. Yu's introductory poem of the series creates a frame for conceiving the Cultural Revolution period overall as an internally dynamic historical moment. Subsequent poems—each presented as a discrete, isolated event in the poet's childhood—develop this frame with smaller, personal, unresolved moments that together form a poetically unified, alternative imagination of the Cultural Revolution experience.

The prefatory poem of Yu's series, "So Hot Then" 那段时间多么炎热, differs significantly from the eleven subsequent poems. Instead of giving poetic structure to a singular event, it describes a general atmosphere of the times. In effect "So Hot Then" offers an interpretive frame for the subsequent texts, a frame whose conceptual weight is realized by activation of the poetic function. Formal elements of note here include typography, parallel syntactic structures, reiterated grammatical forms, and recurring metaphor. Although for purposes of clarity I consider each of these more or less discretely, these several levels of textual elements interrelate. Thus, within the iconic form of a typeset poem, a repeated syntactic structure might contain a particular repeated grammatical form, and a grammatical form might be the vehicle for a specific repeated metaphor. It is the interplay among these elements that creates the spatialized tension animating Yu's constructing of poetic memory.

A commonsense observation, yet one not to be discounted, is the nature of written poetry as "typographically defined" (Finnegan 1992: 25). "So Hot Then" is, of course, typeset as a poem, and its rather standard poetic layout acts as the most visually immediate formal element to impede a feeling of linear sequence:

So hot then	那段时间多么炎热
red trucks loaded with	红色的大卡车满载着
adults' burning tongues	燃烧着舌头的大人们
forward forward again	向前　再向前
disappearing down to the core of resolve	消失在意志的核心

escaped schoolchildren pinching	漏网的小学生 捏着
screaming sparrows rolling toward	尖叫的麻雀 滚向故乡
hometown	啊 时代中的夏天 学校停课
Ah the summer of the era schools	电影院关着门 花园荒芜
closed	篮球场上挂着高音喇叭
theaters closed weeds in parks	革命 用普通话进行
loudspeakers hanging over basketball	只有少年 在古代的河岸上
courts	哑哑地感动 一个个解开裤带
a revolution full blast in Mandarin	握住那 总是会带来好感觉的
only teenagers on the bank of	小玩意 向猿人在钻木取火
an ancient river	直到它 喷出白色的火焰
felt the call they opened their	
pants	
gripped that little thing that	
had always brought them	
pleasure like cavemen drilling	
on a piece of wood	
till it spurts white flame	

(Yu 2004b)   (Yu 2003: 106)

The most salient typographic device, and a fundamentally defining element of modern written poetry, is lineation—the technique of ending a line before it reaches the right margin of the page. "So Hot Then" is, of course, lineated as a free-verse poem. However, Yu supplements the standard poetic practice of truncating lines with the insertion of intralinear gaps. A device found throughout Yu's poetry, and one that he refers to as "long-short phrasing" 长短句 (Van Crevel 2000: 23), these gaps allow Yu to parse his sentences without the clutter of standard punctuation symbols. The spaces, however, do not simply replace commas, semicolons, and periods. Just as often as punctuations, these gaps function more actively by creating line breaks *within* a line. These breaks within breaks make for a doubly enhanced sense of discontinuity; that is, they offset the text's syntagmatically generated forward motion and simultaneously compound the awareness of a montage-like accretion of phrases and images, each potentially linked to others around them. Such multiple elements of typographical mechanics prompt the reader to go on an omnidirectional search for manifold levels of similarity and difference and in so doing sense the repetitions that generate a synchronically realized, spatial structure among the poem's different parts.

Moving from the typographic elements to the poem's verbal content, another level of spatiality becomes apparent. Repetition—here in the form of parallel syntactic structures—defines three separate, simultaneous, and thematically juxtaposed worlds. The poem moves from adult revolutionary participation in lines 2–5, to the play of young children in lines 6–7, and finally to the sexual activity of teenagers in lines 12–15. In lines 2–5 and 6–7, syntactic parallelism implies a mirroring of adults and children: while the former are trucked off toward an ideological oblivion to carry out the deadly serious, sometimes fatal play of political activism, the latter "roll" toward hometown while engaged in sadistic play with a "screaming sparrow." The parallelism of action between these two age groups might suggest the influence of state political discourse on both old and young: directly through political command for the adults, and indirectly through imitation of adults for the children. Keeping strictly to the level of structural effect, however, this instance of parallelism configures a sense of simultaneity, and with it an emphasis on synchronic time whose imagination of temporality begins to define the era as a static, but internally complex, historical moment.

Before looking at the third group—the teenagers—one notes that repetition of grammatical form, now at the level of verb aspect, further enhances the poem's temporal configuration by suggesting an atmosphere of stopped time. In lines 2–7, for instance, depictions of adult and childhood activity are both constructed grammatically through use of the durative aspect marker -*zhe* 着, here affixed to the verbs "load" 满载着, "burn" 燃烧着, and "pinch" 捏着. Because it indicates a condition of continuing, uncompleted action, -*zhe* adds to a sense of temporal suspension by suggesting a state of being rather than a state of progression. The effect is compounded a few lines below, where -*zhe* indexes a sense of stillness by its reappearance in the phrases "theaters closed" 电影院关着门 and "loudspeakers hanging over basketball courts" 篮球场上挂着高音喇叭. Through repetition of grammatical form, then, the poem creates an associative link between humans and everyday space, suggesting the immersion of both in the same regime of immobile time.

The third group of actors in the poem, the teenagers, is clearly aligned as a third semantic category alongside adults and children and as such demands comparison with its counterparts according to the syntactic and grammatical patterning already established. Making such a comparison, however, reveals how the dynamics of parallelism generate a significant variation, one that places adolescents in a separate, in-between space as well as in a distinct temporal regime. Most apparent in this regard are the straightforward subject-verb-object syntactic patterns of lines 12–15. Although retaining the effect of syntagmatic discontinuity effected by intralinear spacing, these concluding lines contrast with the sense of durative, static tableau grammatically created in the earlier portions of the poem. Unlike the adults and children, the teenagers engage in a progressive sequence of linked action: they "felt the call" 哑哑地感动; more literally, "are moved to hoarse cries," "opened their pants" 揭开裤带, and "gripped . . . that little thing" 握住那 . . . 小玩意. In one respect, this sequence explains that teenagers, like those older and younger than they, do indeed respond to the political imperative or "call" of the times coming "full blast" from the loudspeaker. Yet the grammatically marked departure from the established verbal pattern effects a difference as well. For while the oldest and youngest move in politicized parallels driven by the amplified, official voice of revolution; the teenagers, although sensing the political imperative of the era, deform the command of ideology by lying idle, sequestered, and utterly self-directed in a separate temporal regime—one defined not by politically created borderless, empty time, but by an apolitical sense of the timeless carried by images of the "ancient river" and primitive fire-making. It is in this alternative space and time that Yu Jian's autobiographical subject moves; as will be shown later on, it is in this regime that the subsequent poems elaborate their alternative, internally dynamic vision of the era.

Further offsetting any sense of diachronic movement in "So Hot Then," and at the same time enhancing the parallels among the three age-defined spheres of activity, are the images of heat that suffuse the poem. As the poem's title already suggests, an associative sense of heat dominates all parts of the poem as it generates multiple intertwined meanings among them. For instance, "burning tongues" suggests physical thirst as well as the figurative heat of political passion. Likewise, the warm summer season that becalms schools, theaters, and other institutions aligns with the political "heat" of the Cultural Revolution that suspended regular patterns of everyday life in China for so many years. Finally, all these imaginations of heat echo the "white flame" of sexual climax that animates the detached world of adolescence. These metaphorical leaps among multiple domains, each enacting a poetics of variation within repetition, represent another level of spatial structure in the poem. The effect of superimposing heat imagery across the parallel domains of childhood, adolescence, and adulthood defines a figurative unity for the Cultural Revolution's historical "then." The poem's spatial structure, in other words, evokes a singular, temporal moment; at the same time, however, the slippages in meaning introduced by the metaphorical play of the poem suggest a life-world of dynamic and unstable heterogeneity.

To sum up, patterned repetition in "So Hot Then" generates the sense of a complex, synchronic moment that includes familiar events of the Cultural Revolution period—political activism, the suspension of everyday life, the hooliganry of teenagers—but in terms of formal structure runs counter to the diachronic conventions of *Bildung* that figure so centrally in the genre of Cultural Revolution narrative, particularly in the autobiographical narrative. As the first of Yu's series of Cultural Revolution poems, "So Hot Then" introduces a larger ambition for the series of twelve poems: not to narrate a "factual" coming-to-awareness and eventual political liberation of an individual or a society, but to immerse the reader in the climate of an era by recreating its time and space in the verbal environment of a poem. Unlike the popular narrative representations of the Cultural Revolution, "So Hot Then" does not claim to reenact a movement toward resolution through catharsis, crisis, or self-realization. Instead, by inviting the reader to work through carefully configured language, the poem recreates history not as a movement from "past" to "present," but as a self-contained but deeply formative poetic moment.

Where "So Hot Then" describes the Cultural Revolution period as a complexly figured moment writ large, most of the remaining eleven poems in the series narrate discrete events presumably drawn from the personal experience of the poet, who at age twelve in 1966 was entering adolescence himself. These memoiristic poems lend closer specificity to the broad strokes of "So Hot Then." In doing so, however, they do not represent the era as a flow of history structuring the growth of the autobiographical subject, but as a collection of personally experienced, though temporally discontinuous, events. Yet, at the same time and within the poetics of recurrence, the individual texts are linked associatively by the repetition of tropes, in particular turns of phrase that defamiliarize situations otherwise easily recognized as elements of a Cultural Revolution "story." The poems, for example, relate instances of death, insanity, fear, betrayal, home invasion—all standard dramatic fare of Cultural Revolution narrative. Yu, however, often ends the poems with bleakly humorous, sometimes startling imagery that leaves the meaning of these events open and unresolved. Thus, an image of the absurd concludes a poem of eighteen lines in which Yu calmly relates how a cousin, stricken by a persecution complex in the spring of 1967, refuses to follow his work unit's order to enter the insane asylum, until finally,

at the end of their wits	单位上的人没有办法
his coworkers　squatted	只好蹲下　像千斤顶那样
lifted him and the bed　like lifting a car	把他连床一起顶起来
and carried him to the madhouse	抬到疯人院去了
(Yu 2004b)	(Yu 2003: 110)

A note of the surreal provides uneasy completion to a brief ten-line poem describing a Red Guard raid on the child's home:

a little nothing for my mother's	一只香皂盒　我母亲洗脸的小东西
face　a box with soap	被一只解放鞋的后跟踩中
stamped under the heel of a	嘭的一声破裂
Liberation sneaker	绿色的胰子
cracked open	像热带植物的眼球
the green soap	被挤了出来
popped out	
like a plant's eyeball	
(Yu 2004b)	(Yu 2003: 108)

At the close of another short poem, Yu combines bizarre imagery with anticlimax. As the child furtively peers into a crack behind a big-character poster pasted to one of Kunming's ancient pagodas,

someone shouted　What are you	有人喝道　看什么看！
looking at	吓得我立即开裂
I was so startled that winter	一个冬天从背脊上长出来
popped out of my cracked back	那人笑着说　没什么好看的
he laughed　Nothing to see	里面是砖头
only bricks inside	
(Yu 2004b)	(Yu 2003: 116)

Finally, poetic device and sudden revelation cross paths most intensely in "The Beautiful Woman Lived Upstairs" 美丽的女人住在我家楼上 where incantatory repetition of the phrase "the beautiful woman" 美丽的女人 heightens almost to abstraction the remembered desire for an older female piano player. Yu, however, breaks the spell of his words to conclude the poem with a surreal vision that leaves the poem's tenuous story line tragically unresolved:

summer became beautiful　roses	夏天美丽起来　玫瑰花美丽起来
beautiful	我的少年时代美丽起来
my teen years beautiful	美丽的女人美丽地看着蓝天
the beautiful woman looked	美丽的女人美丽地看着少年
at the blue sky beautifully	美丽的女人给我一个水果
the beautiful woman looked	美丽的女人伸出羽毛般的手指
at the boy beautifully	摸了摸我的脸　啊　那个夏天
the beautiful woman gave me an apple	我的生命　从作业本上飞翔起来
the beautiful woman reached out	她是女人　我是男孩
her featherlike finger	我想对她说一句男人的话
to touch my face　ah　that summer	我还不会说　我还在读着小学

my life   flew out of my
  homework
she was a woman   I was a boy
I wanted to say something like a man
didn't know how   I was still in
  grade school
I tried for a whole year   from
  the summer
of 1965   to the summer of 1966
when I was finally ready to say it
her neck hung from the bloody sky
  turned into a frozen scarf
    (Yu 2004b; translation modified)

我想了整整一年   从1965年
的夏天   到1966年的夏天
我终于想好说什么的时候
她的脖子从血红的天空中垂下来
变成了一根冰冻的围巾

(Yu 2003: 115)

Sun Wenbo: Remembrance and the Real

Where Yu Jian's poems configure memory of the Cultural Revolution by constructing a constellation of self-contained, internally complex, and unresolved moments, the poems of memory that comprise Sun Wenbo's series "1960s Bicycle" place less stress on intratextual structure and more on real-world referents. Given the poetic function's emphasis on self-referentiality, such an orientation would seem contradictory to something claiming to be poetry. Sun, however, attempts to transcend this apparent violation of poetic principle by subsuming his poems' extratextual reference within a poetics of memory. What results is a poetry deliberately concretized, vividly enumerated, and constantly in oscillation between past and present. This poeticized reference, patterned by the back-and-forth movement of memory, defines and unifies the poems of "1960s Bicycle."

Like Yu Jian, Sun establishes this vision of memory in the opening poem of his series, "Overture" 序曲. With original footnotes it reads,

Early morning, indoors, naked,
  gauzy coolness
clings lightly to my skin. I light
  a cigarette,
sit, reopen a book left from
  yesterday;
an Irish village, that of Beckett's
  childhood;
1916. His father took him to
  Dublin,
where shocking bonfires of revolt

早晨, 赤裸着呆在屋内, 凉像薄纱
轻贴在皮肤上。点燃一支香烟,
我坐下来, 把昨天没读完的书重新翻开;
爱尔兰小镇上, 贝克特度过他的童年;
一九一六年, 父亲带他到都柏林,
一场起义燃烧的大火让他惊恐,
嵌入他的记忆, 成为一生都困扰他的情景。
我的童年: 文化大革命。同样目睹了
很多混乱的事件: 大街上呼啸的
汽车上挥舞枪的红卫兵, 破四旧
推掉的皇城坝 ①。这些也深深嵌入

fixed disturbing scenes in his
  memory for a lifetime
My childhood: The Cultural
  Revolution. I, too, witnessed
much chaos: screaming
  truckloads
of rifle-waving Red Guards,
  the razing
of the Imperial City. ① These,
  too, are fixed deep
in my memory, too. I recall
  after an armed battle
at Xixiang Middle School②,
  a half *li* or so away,
a Red Guard in spectacles
  raising a rifle to shoot
a clay pot on a telegraph pole,
  shards scattering
    like birds
I recall a junked lorry at the
  roadside,
on it a corpse coated in tar,
  glistening darkly
in the sun; and Mother,
  wanted by a rival faction
as ringleader of the Industrial
  Army③, fleeing town.
Grandma feared for her from
  dawn to dusk; so
many years since Grandma
  died, but still
I see her face the moment she
  knew mother ran.

① A palace-style structure
  built in imitation of Beijing's
Forbidden City, known locally
  as the "Imperial City."
② A middle school a little
  over one *li* from my home in
New Railway Village.[1]
③ A Cultural Revolution
  period mass organization in
Chengdu, labeled the
  "Royalists" by an opposing
faction,

我的记忆。我还记得离家
半里多路的西乡中学 ②, 一场武斗过后,
一个戴眼镜的红卫兵举枪射击
电杆上的瓦瓶, 瓦瓶被击碎像鸟四
处飞散;
也记得路边一辆废弃的卡车上的
被沥青裹住的尸体, 在阳光下
发出黑黝黝的光亮; 以及我的母亲
作为产业军 ③ 的小头目被另一派通缉,
  逃到外地,
外婆从早到晚为她担惊受怕; 如今
外婆已死去多年, 可我仍能
看见她听到母亲逃跑时, 脸上的表情。
① 仿北京紫禁城宫殿式建筑,
成都人俗称皇城坝。
② 距我居住的铁路新村一里多路
的一中学。
③ 文革时成都一群众组织, 因其
观点被反对 派称为 "保皇派", 成
员多国营大工厂人。

comprising mostly workers in
large state-run factories.

(Jiang 2002: 3–4)

From the opening image of the poet seated naked indoors, the entire surface of his skin sensitive and exposed, "Overture" introduces the autobiographical subject as a palpable presence located firmly in the "now." Soon, however, the reading of Samuel Beckett's biography prompts movement elsewhere, to the "then" of a childhood during China's Cultural Revolution. Enumeration—a form of repetition long prevalent in free verse (Fussell 1979: 78–9)—loosely structures the remainder of the poem. One after the other, Sun calls up from memory a series of vivid images that record specific instances of random violence, anonymous death, and domestic terror.

In contrast to Yu Jian's poems, where memory is implied but not examined as such, Sun foregrounds remembrance as a self-conscious act, a highly mediated movement of the mind underscored by recurrence of the words "recall" 记得 and "memory" 记忆. These two words, which function as the hinges of remembrance in the poem, mark a mnemonic oscillation between "now" and "then," a shifting reference to a present and a past that insists on the objective and material reality of both.

Sun highlights the reality of the "now" by describing it as "fixed deep" 深深嵌入 in the poet's memory. This is memory situated within the corporeal reality of the poet's body, naked, sensitive, alive, and firmly located in the space of present-day, ongoing experience. The reality of the "then," meanwhile, assumes empirical weight in two ways. First, it is "witnessed" 目睹, that is, seen with a first-hand immediacy and photographic intensity that insists on a reference to historical fact "out there." Second, and rather more unconventionally, the places and institutions enumerated in the poem—the Imperial City, the Xixiang Middle School, the Industrial Army—are each referred to beyond the poem by means of footnotes. Footnotes by nature literally point the reader elsewhere, doing so in order to validate or elaborate in ways that, according to conventions of writing, do not fit within the body of a text. The footnotes that appear throughout "1960s Bicycle"—a total of eighteen appended to one-third of the poems comprising the series—perform just such a function: they confirm and explain historical realities the poems seem unable to accommodate. They inform the reader, for instance, of the digging of air-raid tunnels in the 1960s, traitor-villain characters in period films, Sichuan's first large-scale battle between Red Guard factions, old city names, a neighborhood restaurant, and the size and location of a plant nursery. All these factual items are explicated in detail "outside" the poetic texts themselves; and all, by directing the reader out of and back into the poem, further enhance a sense of oscillation between "realities" past and present.

Sun's poetic choices, then, seem deliberately to point the reader away from the intratextual, verbal environment of the poem and toward an extratextual, material context presumably "out there," be it in the "external" world of past events or the "internal" world of the poet's present subjectivity. However, even as this aesthetics of reference would seem to leave the poetic function behind, it realizes another aesthetic effect, one that differentiates the poems from the narrative memoir toward which they gesture. For where the Cultural Revolution memoir is structured by a temporally continuous story of individual and social emergence, Sun's poems attempt to leap a temporal gap that narrative seems no longer able to bridge. Through devices that point beyond the poem itself, he creates a poetics of memory that alternates between the material and historical "realities" of present and past, attempting to fix both in place by means of an almost documentary style of reference.

The irony of this oscillatory movement, however, is that the very effort to anchor memory in a lost past and a present self implies an eroding link between lived experience of the past and that of the present. As if to combat such loss, the poems of "1960s Bicycle" invoke intensely specific people, places, and things: each a site of memory in or near Sun's childhood home in New Railway Village, each altered, destroyed, dead, or missing, but all recovered through acts of poetic salvage. One by one they appear as titles to the poems: "Loquat Tree" 枇杷树—the scene years ago of a murder in Sun's courtyard and now a species of tree that raises a lucid vision of both the victim, an elderly bachelor, and the samurai sword used to kill him; "Stone Columns in the Courtyard" 院子中的石柱—a pair of ancient, ornamental carved-stone pillars around which Sun played as a child, later toppled and broken to clear the lot for a drab building; "Nine-Mile Dike Nursery" 九里堤苗圃—a wooded area thick with groves of cassia, loquat, and bamboo, now transformed into a landscape of gas stations, asphalt paving, and caged-in balconies; "Neighbor" 邻居—an older resident of New Railway Village, remembered fondly for his acts of kindness, but now gone forever after succumbing to acute liver disease.

More than acts of poetic testament, these poems to the places, people, and events of the past are also monuments: not the sort erected to permanently enshrine great events or major figures, but minor memorials designed to refer the reader to myriad elements of everyday life, to fix in place those fragments of experience significant not for the parts they play in any continuous narrative, but because their past reality must be brought back in order to wholly constitute an identity in the present. Through poetry, Sun reconstructs those things from which the poet himself is made. The poems are, to cite the title work of the series, Sun's "1960s Bicycle," objects that he fights to retain, evokes in material detail, and uses as vehicles to revisit a past in the process of fading away:

Mom bought a Red Flag bicycle,
and put an end to my envy of
  the bike-owning few.
When her workday was over
  it was my turn to ride,
    circle the courtyard, hit
      the streets.
I loved to make its bell ring
wild. For a time
it was my plaything, and
  I stood tall
seeing people I knew. Once
  at West End Stadium,
rounding the track proud, fast,
  I drew the jealousy
    of some boys,
who cut me off and demanded
  the bike.
I refused, we fought.
Like a tiger defending its cubs,
I would not give it up. And so,
  many years later,
it gleams before me: chrome
  handlebars, coaster
    brake, 28-inch wheels.
I see myself pedaling around
New Railway Village
spinning, turning, all things beside
  me rushing past and away.

妈妈买回一辆红旗牌自行车,
使我结束对别人家有自行车的羡慕。
当她下班, 才轮到我骑上它, 在院子
  里转圈、上街。
我喜欢把他的铃铛摁得乱响。一个时期
它成为我的玩物, 使我见到熟人
腰都比平时挺得直。一次在西郊体育场,
  骑着它我沿着跑道飞驰, 我的得意
    遭到几个小子的嫉妒,
他们把我拦下来, 让我车给他们,
我没有答应, 与他们打起来;
我就像一只老虎保护自己的幼仔,
没有让他们拿走它。所以很多年过去,
它仍在我的眼前闪亮: 镀铬车把、回
  链刹、二八圈。
我看见自己骑着它在铁路新村周围的
  路上
转来转去, 身边的事物纷纷后退。

(Jiang 2002: 35)

The poem is a story, but one whose brevity focuses down on the culminating capture of a memory image: the bicycle whose possession in the 1960s was as rare and valued as the remembrance of it is for the poet more than thirty years later. Indeed, the vision of the bicycle, its components recalled in exact and loving detail long after it is gone, would seem even more present than the one he rode three decades before. As with so many of the poems in the series, such descriptive precision creates for the reader a concrete image whose singularity signals a desire to reach beyond the poetic text and gestures again to the reflection of present remembrance into past reality. To go a step further, because the poem is eponymous with the series as a whole, "1960s Bicycle" asks to be read as representative of Sun's overall poetic construction of memory. Like its many counterparts in the series, this text turns on specific images of the past, all local, all personal, and all as insistently real in the time of writing as the time of first encounter. It is this recreated immediacy of memory that enables the individual works comprising Sun's series to act as vehicles for oscillation between past and present. Such an oscillation, active all through the series, plays out most strongly in the blur of the real and the remembered constructed by the final two lines of the poem "1960s Bicycle." Just as Sun the child defended the bicycle from loss, Sun the adult guards and preserves the image of the bicycle in memory; just as the child once rode the Red Flag bicycle around his now bygone neighborhood, the adult poet guides the recollected image of the bicycle through a landscape of memory materialized in poetic remembrance.

This brief study is, unavoidably, more suggestive than exhaustive. It suggests closer critical attention to poems as an alternative mode of remembering China's revolutionary past. But beyond such a partisan defense of poetry, Yu Jian's and Sun Wenbo's visions of the past do point toward a larger problematic of memory: the question of *how* to remember versus *what* to remember. Such an opposition, writes Richard Terdiman in his study of the "mnemonic disquiet" in memory and modernity, implies a "delicate dialectic" "between reproduction and representation, between fact and interpretation, between recollection and understanding" (1993: 357). Driven to reach beyond the text to recapture the "real" of the past, Sun Wenbo's poems recollect by reproduction and fact. Meanwhile Yu Jian subjects memory to complex intratextual dynamics, inclining him toward the countervailing mnemonic problems of representation, interpretation, and understanding. The differences here are by no means absolute. In fact, by confronting parallel historical experience through contrasting literary aesthetics, both poets gesture beyond poetry to a gradual but important trend: the unobtrusive but persistent and increasingly pluralistic willingness to creatively recover the many meanings of the Cultural

Revolution era, a span of time whose subterranean influence on the present is equaled only by the current regime's resistance to an open reckoning with its past.

Note

1. According to Sun, the footnote contains a typographical error. The middle school was, as given in the poem, a half-*li* or more (approximately ⅙ of a mile) from his New Railway Village (Personal communication, June 17, 2005).

Chapter Eleven

Naming and Antinaming: Poetic Debate in Contemporary China

Dian Li

Time: April 16 to 18, 1999; Place: Pan Feng 盘峰 Hotel in a Beijing suburb. Purpose: A conference on poetry. Among the forty or so participants were well-known poets and critics from all over the country including the cheerleader-in-chief for contemporary Chinese poetry, Professor Xie Mian 谢冕 (b. 1932) from Beijing University. Judging from the name of the conference—"At the Century's End: A Seminar on the State of Contemporary Poetry and the Construction of New Poetics" 世纪之末: 中国诗歌创作态势与理论建设研讨会— the organizers (the Beijing Writer's Society 北京作家协会, the Institute of Literary Studies of the Chinese Academy of Social Sciences 中国社会科学院文学研究所, and the journals *Beijing Literature* 北京文学 and *Poetry Explorations* 诗探索) intended it to be a high-profile forum for the sorting and evaluating of issues and trends in the past so that new poetics could emerge for the times ahead. The conference, however, never went beyond the first part of its mission. After some polite opening remarks by senior critics, a battle line was drawn between two groups of poets—"intellectual" 知识分子and "popular" 民间.[1] The former group represented by Xi Chuan 西川 (b. 1963), Wang Jiaxin 王家新 (b. 1957), Cheng Guangwei 程光炜 (b. 1956), and Zang Di 臧棣 (b. 1964) and the latter group represented by Yu Jian 于坚 (b. 1954), Yi Sha 伊沙 (b. 1966), Yang Ke 扬克 (b. 1957), and Xu Jiang 徐江 (b. 1967) accused each other of writing "bad" poems that have helped breed an atmosphere of indifference and apathy to poetry in contemporary Chinese society. If the issue of poetic judgment was a serious one and the disagreements between the two groups were genuine, the debate was severely undermined by frequent acerbic exchanges of emotional discharges and personal attacks. The fired-up poets and critics did not end their debate at the Pan Feng Hotel; they continued to air their differences and accusations long after the conference had ended. The Chinese media, literary and otherwise, seeing an opportunity not merely in the interest of poetry, offered a helping hand. As a result, the polemics ensued from 1999 to 2002, during which time an ever-expanding list of interested parties spilled an incredible amount of ink on the problem via several dozens of media outlets.[2] In terms of the exclusive positioning and personal intolerance displayed by the participants, this dispute created a colorful literary spectacle in the cultural life of China unprecedented in the last two decades.

Is there any substance to the debate? What stands behind the ugly personal attacks and rhetorical fights? Are the noises created by the participants merely a publicity stunt or an expression of emerging new poetics? In this chapter, I will revisit the major issues of contention between the two schools of thought, examine their artistic positions through a reading of the respective chief spokespersons and finally offer a critique of the debate in terms of the development of contemporary Chinese poetry. First, let us turn to the theoretical construction of "intellectual writing."

According to the poet and critic Xi Chuan, intellectuals are "those of superior intelligence who are rich in the spirit of independence, the spirit of skepticism, and moral fiber, and who, through the means of literature, write about the most important contemporary affairs for educated ordinary readers. Their chief characteristics are to offer a critique of thought" (Shao 1998: 104). In the same vein, Ouyang Jianghe 歐陽江河 (b. 1956) writes: "Intellectual is never an honorary title, for it is always deeply connected with a sort of doubting individualism, whose position is that of a typical liberal" (Wang 1994: 5). Clearly, this view of intellectuals was borrowed heavily from the West as indicated by the critics' choices of words, but the idea is not foreign to the Chinese *shi* (scholar/official) 士 tradition. There is a close correspondence between the Western maxim "the intellectual is the conscience of society" and the Chinese one "the scholar/official concerns the world" 士为天下忧. This description of the intellectual as a skeptical individual also stands against the Maoist discourse of China's immediate past, which not only took away the intellectual's individual rights but also stripped away his dignity as a human being.

If, however, Xi Chuan and others mean to describe the parameters of the intellectual with one eye on the West and another on the Chinese *shi* tradition, they show some creative and original thinking when they begin to theorize about "intellectual writing" based on their ideas of the intellectual. Explicit political interventions and avowed social responsibilities are two key elements that are ostensibly missing in their propositions of intellectual poetry. Here one sees a clear rupture from the spirit of Misty Poetry even though intellectual poets as a whole often demonstrate, more than any other poets, a true deference to Misty Poetry. Although the idea of intellectual writing was present in various poets around the mid-1980s, the founding of the poetry journal *Tendency* 倾向 in 1988 crystallized the concept. The journal held out the banner of intellectual positioning and the spirit of idealism and gathered a large number of poets and critics including Wang Jiaxin, Xi Chuan, Chen Dongdong 陈东东 (b. 1961), and Cheng Guangwei. In 1993, Ouyang Jianghe published an essay entitled "Poetry Writing in China after 1989: Native Temperaments, Characteristics of Middle Age, and Intellectuals' Identifications" to offer a most complete and definitive narrative for intellectual writing. The following words by Ouyang Jianghe are considered by many the manifesto of intellectual writing:

> [Intellectual writing] does not offer either a concrete view of life or an endorsement of values; it is a quality manifested between rhetoric and reality . . . On the one hand, it considers writing as a process that points to the return of particular and relative knowledge from ultimate things and the grand truth. On the other hand, it maintains a warm feeling towards all sorts of truth. In this time of transition, a basic mission for poets of our generation is to end the dual myths of mass writing and political writing, for they are a legacy of our youthful past. In my view, the intellectual poet has two implications: one is that his writing is career-oriented and professional; the second is that he must identify himself with the marginal. (Ouyang 1993: 178)

In terms of its measured engagement with reality and truth, Ouyang Jianghe's view of literature is in lock-step with postmodernism. Yet it radiates an apparent self-recognition of poetry as a clean, elevated, and referential writing of significance and purpose where he manages to evade a mechanical reflection theory of literature and reality and its utopian pursuit of truth. It speaks both of an immediate past, which needs to be rethought, and of a present that is yet to embrace poetry as an acceptable profession. (No doubt Ouyang Jianghe here is looking at the American model of the institutionalization of creative writing, a tell-tale sign of a Chinese critic's negative take on globalization.) Its postmodernist impulse aside, Ouyang Jianghe's proposal does open up new critical possibilities for the operation of intellectual writing, for he locates it in the aesthetic spaces outside the system, the personal, and the marginal—three slippery and yet consensual terms that in fact bridge, rather than enlarge, the gap between intellectual writing and *minjian* writing.

Minjian has long existed as a common linguistic sign and as a literary concept. *Minjian wenxue* has been used in the twentieth century to refer to folklore 风俗, popular legends 传说, songs 歌谣, local drama 地方戏曲, and historical tales 历史故事, and the like. After 1949, its usage is commonly limited to literary writings created by nonprofessional writers, for example, by anybody who does not carry a membership card from the official Chinese Writer's Association. However, a precise definition of *minjian wenxue* is nearly impossible, for it is a question of many conflated issues ranging from genre, authorship, and sentiment, to position, attitude, and subject matter. In this sense, *minjian wenxue* is not unlike many other literary concepts—always elastic but still communicable.

In the 1990s, *minjian* dropped its linguistic companion "wenxue" and became a critical concept unto itself. This "economization" delinked *minjian* from its particular historical context and gave it an expanded range of meanings whose circulations dominated the Chinese critical discourse in the 1990s. The elevation of, or rather, the invention of *minjian* as a current and meaningful critical concept has much to do with the work of Chen Sihe 陈思和 (b. 1954), a professor of modern Chinese literature from Fudan University. His 1987 book *A Macrocosmic View of New Chinese Literature* 中国新文学整体观 gives a sweeping overview of modern Chinese literature based upon the very construction of *minjian* as a new critical instrument, whose "restoration" becomes a focal point for collecting divergent literary phenomena and cultural narratives. In describing *minjian*, Chen differentiates it from the concepts of "civil society" 民间社会 and "public sphere" 公众空间 as commonly understood in the West and gives it a narrower definition: "*Minjian* is a concept in opposition to the central government; *minjian*'s cultural patterns refer to the cultural space existing on the margins beyond the power center of the governmental control mechanism . . . It makes up the third discursive space along with power, and intellectual and elitist consciousness" (Chen 1987: 112). Riding on the strengths of *minjian*'s oppositional thrust and its referential elasticity, Chen manages to present an insightful overview of Chinese literature from the 1930s to the present day, covering from *minjian*'s "suppression" to its "restoration"—a refreshingly different narrative from the familiar and the official version of the history of modern Chinese literature.

However, there are apparent problems with the construction of *minjian* as a critical instrument, chief among them are its ahistorical applications and its signifying instability, of which even Chen himself is acutely aware. He writes,

> "*Minjian*" is not a historical concept, for various subcultures defined by their distances from state power centers exist in any forms of societies governed by any shape of governmental system. At the other end of the power center is *minjian*. If we use a pyramid to describe their relationship, the bottom level is *minjian*; in-between the bottom level and the top there exists a variety of cultural forms. What's more, the bottom level naturally supports the top. Therefore, *minjian* must be containing the ideologies of the state power. This is to say, *minjian* always prides itself for its inclusiveness so as to collect everything from the good, the bad, and the ugly. (Chen 1987: 112)

In this age of uncertainty and excess when critical discourses often valorize extreme positions and unsubstantiated neologism, it is quite remarkable for Chen to be self-conscious of the potentials and the limits of the very concept he has invented. On the one hand, the use of *minjian* to highlight some major trends and issues in the development of modern Chinese literature is productive and meaningful, which becomes an important part of the collective efforts to rewrite modern literary history in the last two decades, and as a result, the establishment of *minjian* as a third discursive space in relation with that of state power and intellectuals has had far-reaching influence among Chinese critics ever since. On the other hand, the imperfection of *minjian* as a critical instrument, particularly its theoretical deficiencies in its entangled relations with state power and intellectuals that it avowedly opposes, becomes a point of endless debate, which many a *minjian* poetry advocate seems to gloss over.

First of all, even though the lapse of time tempts one to establish a link between Chen Sihe's theorizing of *minjian* and *minjian* poets' promotion of the same concept, their connection remains tenuous at best. If the ideas of *minjian* existed in poetry writing and criticism since the aftermath of Misty Poetry, they were expressed in substitutive terms such as "rude man" 莽汉, "they" 他们, and "college students" 大学生, all names of poetry schools that proliferated in the mid-1980s to demonstrate desirable anti–Misty Poetry sentiments. Even well into the 1990s, *minjian* was mainly used as a convenient but undeveloped critical vocabulary to poke fun at "intellectual poetry" so as to highlight the latter's alleged showmanship in language plays and its unwise disconnection from the ordinary life and the reader. Only after the Pan Feng Conference has the construction of *minjian* as a poetic concept become a focused effort, resulting, no doubt, from the necessity of the debate. Numerous poets and critics on both sides of the debate are probably motivated by "a good fight" and write many occasional and spontaneous essays to explicate and decipher the very meaning of *minjian*, virtually making it a household name overnight in this day of media explosion. Curiously, for those people who write about *minjian*, Chen Sihe remains an unacknowledged source, even though traces of Chen's theorization are evident in quite a few writers' employment of *minjian* as poetic concept. For example, Han Dong 韩东 (b. 1961) emphatically pronounces that a chief characteristic of *minjian* is "independent spirit and free creation." And he continues to expound,

> The *minjian* position is to safeguard literature, and to ensure that in an age more materialistic by the day and with the balance of power as its only standard, literature gets a chance to survive and develop, and to protect the free spirit of art and its capacity for creation. (Han 2007: 27)

Xie Youshun 谢有顺 (b. 1972), the most outspoken advocate of *minjian* poetry, expresses a similar idea: "The meaning of *minjian* is an independent quality. The spirit of *minjian* poetry is that it never depends on any colossal monsters; it exists for the purpose of poetry only . . . The *minjian* position is no more than an expression of the unwillingness to be contained by certain systems or certain institutions of knowledge" (Xie 1999: 21). Han's and Xie's formation of *minjian*, clearly written for the sake of argumentation, if in want of Chen Sihe's scholarly objectivity and theoretical sophistication, contains nearly identical understandings of the term as a third space in separation from the realms of the state (system) and the intellectual (institution of knowledge). Interestingly, qualitative vocabularies such as marginalization, independence, nonconformity, and personalization, which Han and Xie frequently invoke to define the *minjian* poet, are the ones that Wang Jiaxin and Ouyang Jianghe often use to describe the intellectual poet. This is not to suggest that the debate is about nothing, but the differences between the *minjian* school and the intellectual school, however, are really the choices of signifiers and not the definition of the signified.

This is not to say that the choice of signifiers does not matter in critical discourses. Chen Sihe's employment of *minjian* as an effective strategy to rewrite modern Chinese literary history, as mentioned in the above, has already proven otherwise. Among the proponents of *minjian* poetry, Yu Jian is perhaps the only one who is able to fully explore the elasticity of *minjian* as a signifier so as to establish a range of its signifieds approximating a new poetics separated from the aesthetical orientations of the "intellectual poetics." Like almost all participants of the debate, Yu Jian is not immune to distasteful sentiments of factionalism and occasional emotional discharges, which harm his case more than they help. But Yu Jian has a great deal of capital to spend: he is one of the most influential post-Misty poets whose diligent cultivation of a distinguishable colloquial and readable poetry has won him much critical acclaim and popular fame. Such credibility plus a productive contribution to the debate has rendered him a consensual leading voice for the school of *minjian* poetry.

It is widely acknowledged that Yu Jian is the one who first brought the word "*minjian*" into the circulation of poetic criticism. That happened in 1998 when he wrote a preface for the controversial anthology *1998 Yearbook of New Chinese Poetry* (Yu 1999: 1–17), which was a show of force for poems that demonstrated *minjian* aesthetics as defined by Yu Jian and the book's editor Yang Ke. Yu Jian's utterances on the topic since then have been numerous, including frequent speeches and newspaper columns, but he reserved his best commentary for after the Pan Feng Conference in an essay entitled "The *Minjian* Tradition in Contemporary Poetry" 当代诗歌的民间传统 (Yu 2004a). The essay represents Yu Jian's summary thoughts on the conception of *minjian* and serves perhaps as a final rejoinder to the shouting match that occurred at and after the conference. In the essay, Yu Jian first attributes the beginning of contemporary Chinese poetry to the underground literature 地下文学 and unofficial publications 民间刊物 of the 1970s. Even though *minjian* as a literary space was most potently described by its distance from official literature and state power in this particular era, *minjian* always served as the only true source for poetry writing whether that distance was real or imagined. That is to say, *minjian* should not be understood as a mere gesture of opposition; rather, it is an attitude and a position from which the best part of the Chinese poetic tradition from antiquity to the present has employed for its own benefit. Thus Yu Jian has no qualms about recruiting *The Books of Songs*, Li Bo, Du Fu, or any other of his favorites into the *minjian* camp. Clearly unaware of the logical problems for supporting his theory of *minjian* as a poetic position, Yu Jian then makes the following generalization:

> *Minjian* is such that it always only pretends to kowtow to any mainstream cultures. Outside the leftist faction and the rightist faction of the ruling ideology, *minjian* insists upon common sense 常识 and

experience 经验, things that are fundamental and permanent. Ideologies always use and distort common sense, but after all the dust settles down, what emerges from the waters is still the face of *minjian*, ordinary but forthcoming. *Minjian* does not want to change the world; it is only a foundation. *Minjian* believes in the world's constancy but not its changes. Which is precisely the foundation of all literatures. Literature of true value must be of *minjian*. Or at least it is created against the background of *minjian*. What Kafka's lifelong writing activities demonstrate is a *minjian* position because his so-called avant-garde quality exposes precisely "the fundamental absurdity" of the world, but not "the absurdity of a certain era." (Yu 2004a: 553)

The keywords in Yu Jian's argument are obviously "common sense" and "experience." Their precise meanings are undefined—perhaps Yu Jian does not feel the need for it because they are so familiar and conventional. Nevertheless, they are cornerstones of his overarching *minjian* poetics, for they work as self-containing aesthetical categories in separation from ruling ideologies and systems of knowledge. We seem to be hearing an echo of Chen Sihe in Yu Jian's separation of *minjian* as a third aesthetic space. Unlike Chen Sihe, however, Yu Jian empties *minjian* of its political and ideological contents, making it "fundamental and permanent" in the process of literary creation, which points to a vision of universal humanity beyond time and particular historicity within the Chinese context.

"Opposition" 相对 is a distasteful word for Yu Jian. While the intellectual poet is always self-conscious of his oppositional status, the *minjian* poet in Yu Jian's version wants to preclude any traces of opposition from his poetry. "*Minjian* does not oppose anything," Yu Jian says (Yu 2004a: 552), in his characteristically authoritative tone. Yet for *minjian* to be a credible and executable alternative critical position, it has to be differentiated from existing ones such as official literature and intellectual poetry. Yu Jian's way of arguing for this differentiation is to "separate"; to separate but not to oppose, that is, to separate not to challenge or subvert, but to conserve and to restore. The object for this conservation and restoration finally emerges as the attractive but nebulous signifier: Chinese tradition, which returns Yu Jian to the center of the familiar and time-honored debate about Chinese tradition, Western values, and modernization. "*Minjian* society always keeps company with conservative and traditional thoughts," Yu Jian writes. "In this time of radicalism, *minjian* means a conservative position. It is *minjian* but not the state nor the mainstream culture that has protected the foundation of traditional China" (Yu 2004a: 552). It is here that we see a pronounced difference between Chen Sihe and Yu Jian in their identical public pleas for the restoration of *minjian* in contemporary Chinese literature. For the former, the restoration is a way of examining historical truth and a strategy for recovering meaning from neglected texts. For the latter, the restoration is a return to lost values, a promotion of indigenous aesthetics, and a protest against the forces of globalization, all of which fit perfectly in the rising tide of nationalism in contemporary China's cultural discourse.

The attempts to describe their differences at the macrocosmic level by the intellectual school and the *minjian* school are only the beginning of this influential debate. To an objective observer, however, their contending conceptions of poetry share more similarities than both sides care to acknowledge. This is not say that they have nothing to argue about but that they share the same concerns of upholding poetry as a serious and meaningful art form in an era of uncertainty and excess and of locating its cultural functions vis-à-vis other social and political forces. Because of this and also probably due to a general dissatisfaction with some publicity-hungry debate participants with entrenched and extreme positions, many cool-minded Chinese critics and those on the sidelines in particular have pointed out a signifying commonality between intellectual and *minjian* poets, such as the following perceptive remarks made by Zhang Qinghua 张清华 (b. 1963): "In today's linguistic context, intellectuals and *minjian* are supplementary but not oppositional to each other, particularly in the sense that they both exist outside the system. From the perspective of writing, one emphasizes vitality, the other depth; one orients towards deconstruction, the other construction. Each complements the other in its own strengths and weaknesses" (Zhang 1999: 26).

Zhang's remarks, which bear the marks of disinterested professionalism and scholarly objectivity, are interesting in two ways. On the one hand, he seizes upon the intellectual and the *minjian* poets' shared marginal status and highlights their supplementarity while downplaying their differences to allow room for inclusiveness and tolerance. On the other hand, he offers a list of distinguishable characteristics of the two schools that validates their claims to different poetics. Zhang qualifies this list with the phrase "from the perspective of writing," by which he probably means artistic tendency and aesthetic value as embedded in the act of poetic creation. This is an interesting but also a popular way for a Chinese scholar to talk about poetics at the basic operational level regarding a poet's prewriting choices and a critic's after-writing judgment. If we call the previously mentioned debate about the poet's self-positioning vis-à-vis the state power and mainstream cultures a sort of "theoretical poetics," we may call this different perspective on writing a kind of "practical poetics," which is mainly concerned with concrete and practicable value orientations in the writing process, and it is here that one sees a concentrated display of differences between the intellectual poet and the *minjian* poet. Chief among these differences is the problem of poetic language, which stands at the center of this debate and, judging by the attention it has received, has overshadowed any other single issue of interest.

Following the tradition of isolating poetic language as a primal aesthetic issue by Misty poetry, both the intellectual poet and the *minjian* poet have expressed a sustained and focused interest toward creating a new and satisfactory poetic language. Both Yu Jian and Han Dong have repeatedly stated their adherence to this well-known maxim: poetry starts with language and ends with language. Wang Jiaxin's desire to poetically reach the inner power of language is legendary. This is how he poetically describes his unusual relationship with words: "They are something from the purgatory / sharp, bright, unsurpassable / until the knife edge shifts / we suddenly tremble / for we have finally been touched" ("Words"). Similar interests, however, do not mean similar opinions. In fact, the intellectual poet and the *minjian* poet have gone their separate ways on the road of poetic language ever since after Misty poetry, and the debate becomes a perfect staging ground for their divergent opinions. That the problem of poetic language occupied a central place is evidenced by the frequent occurrence of the phrase "yuyan ziyuan" 语言资源 during the debate. Yuyan ziyuan, or resources for language, pertains to both the question of language and the question of language-in-use, approximating the Saussurean divisions of langue and parole. During the debate, the question gradually evolves into two subissues: where does poetic language come from and how should language be used in a poem. Answers to these two questions show the sharpest differences between the intellectual poet and the *minjian* poet.

Resources for language is foremost a question of writing strategy. Guided by his fixation on the *minjian* position, the *minjian* poet advocates a "looking-back" attitude and tries to find inspirations in cultural resources that stand for the East, the primitive, the indigenous, and the traditional, which not only are configured to contest the state and the mainstream culture but also are employed to contrast with the orthodox, and the modern, and the West. Thus poetry writing for him has acquired the meaning of cultural renaissance, for it is given the grand mission of restoring the dignity of the Chinese language. To be true to this mission, poetry must locate itself on the coordinates of the traditional (read: an essential Chineseness emptied of its modern corruptions) and the native (read: a separated Chinese identity freed from Western influences) and must find writing material in common sense, experience, and daily living, which, more than anything else, constitute the real foundation of literature. In this connection, it is quite easy to understand that the word "life" 生活 has become a banner word for the *minjian* poet. Slogans such as "to be close to life" 逼近生活 and "restore the essence of life" 还原生活本质 point to an experience-centric and naturalistic poetics that advocates a sort of photorealistic representation of the quotidian and the mundane and rejects any reference to the transcendental, the metaphysical, and the sublime.

The *minjian* poet's valorization of life, which calls for a "looking-at-the-present" attitude, is paradoxically integrated into his desire for the traditional, which requires the attitude of "looking back." On the one hand, he takes life as a happening of the present with its specific time and place references; on the other hand, life is an ahistorical and universal concept that unifies and validates a long-standing but somewhat hidden Chinese tradition. In other words, if life is a cultural construct, its very culturality must be deemphasized for the *minjian* poet to function. The advocacy of colloquial style 口语 represents a conscientious exploitation of this paradox by the *minjian* poet, which has become an easily identifiable artistic yardstick against which the intellectual poet's perceived valorization of the written word 书面语 is measured. Ideas about "colloquial writing" 口语写作, which are often more impressionistic than theoretical, diverge among many *minjian* poets such as Han Dong, Xu Jiang, and Yi Sha. Yu Jian stands out as the only one to demonstrate a persistent pursuit of the topic. Even before the Pan Feng Conference, he published a series of essays offering something approaching a theorization of colloquial writing, chief among which was "The Hard and the Soft Tongues of Poetry: On Two Different Directions in the Languages of Contemporary Poetry." With his characteristic interest in binary oppositions, Yu Jian constructs the contrasting pair of the "hard tongue" and "soft tongue" of poetry's language-in-use, with the former equating to modern Mandarin (Putonghua) and the latter to regional languages 方言. The reason that Putonghua is a "hard tongue" is because "it is an official language far removed from lived experience and it makes the poet's tongue stiff [hard] in his subconsciousness" (Yu 1999: 462). Regional languages, on the other hand, are a soft tongue in the sense that they are the goldmine of life and therefore they help to preserve life's true, uncorrupted original state. Yu Jian's use of regional language is actually singular—the examples are all from the Yunnan regional language with which he is most familiar, but this does not prevent him from lauding a region-based colloquial writing in general:

> Colloquial writing is in fact to restore a worldly tendency that links tradition with the Putonghua-centric contemporary Chinese language. It softens the language which, because of its past focus on ideological struggles, has become stiffened and belligerent and therefore unfit to express the experiences of spontaneity, temperament, mediocrity, softness, concreteness, quotidian in mundane living; it means to restore the language's relations with things and ordinary senses. Colloquial writing enriches the Chinese language's textures, giving it back the qualities of humor, gentleness, this-worldliness, and transitivity. It rediscovers the connection with a corporeal language excelling at describing eat drink man woman in life's routines that were common in Song poetry and the fiction of the Ming and Qing dynasties. (Yu 1999: 463)

Yu Jian's passion and eloquence are evident in this remarkable passage. One can hardly fault him for unabashedly advocating colloquial writing, for it has been the path of development for modern Chinese literature. The remaining question is about language resources for colloquial writing. The May Fourth generation of writers invented a new literature that used the vernacular and rejected classical Chinese, and now Yu Jian wants to rediscover the vernacular in regional languages. There is no doubt that Putonghua is deeply embedded with all sorts of traces that could be deemed "official" and "foreign"—if Maoist discourse is only temporary and has since dwindled into a faint echo, the Europeanization of the modern Chinese language was a formative force at the very beginning and has all the signs of becoming even greater today. Indeed the very existence of Putonghua gives life to dialects. In addition, they do form a binary pair that validates Yu Jian's *minjian* poetics: in relation to Putonghua's unshakable centralized position—which, as Yu Jian rightly points out, has profound implications for the Chinese mind about culture, ideology, and geopolitics—regional languages survive on the margins, representing a pristine aesthetic space that the *minjian* poet is seeking. However, if Putonghua opposes dialects, does that automatically make it oppose the vernacular and the colloquial? Are both the spoken word and the written word not part of Putonghua? For that matter, is it not true that any major living language, official or otherwise, always contains elements commonly considered colloquial and written? The real valid question is what constitutes the colloquial and the written within one language, a question in which Yu Jian shows hardly any interest. Instead, he relies on the substitution of the colloquial with dialects to communicate his worthy pursuit of colloquial writing, a substitution that not only is contrary to the creative practices of the *minjian* poets including his own[3] but also serves to reduce a very significant poetic question into an inoperably simple formula.

The charge that the intellectual poet values the written word is true to some extent, but he does not exclude the spoken word in the same way that Yu Jian tries to expel the written word from poetry. There are many intellectual poets who also passionately talk about the desired goal of colloquial writing. Chen Dongdong believes that "colloquial language is the real reason for the vivacity and energy of the modern Chinese language" (Chen 2000: 115). Zhang Shuguang 张曙光 (b. 1956) thinks that the tonality and rhythm of colloquialisms are indispensable in poetic language, because "this so-called 'colloquial rhythm' 口语节奏 greatly enables me to encompass experiences of the present and to dissolve readers' feelings of distance due to the high-brow status of poetry" (Zhang 1999: 246). Still other intellectual poets accept the inclusion of colloquial language into poetry in a qual-ified manner, among whom Xi Chuan's view is representative. "Today as in the past I have always believed that colloquial language is the only language for writing," he avers.

> It is almost impossible now to use traditional language to create brand new poems. However, here we must first define colloquial language. There are two kinds, one being a language on the street, which is close to regional language and gangster society slang, and the other being written language, which has something to do with civilization and the universality of things. My choice is the latter. (Xi 1997: 24)

Xi Chuan's subsuming written language under colloquial speech is surprising, but his purposeful confusion of familiar concepts reflects a common position held by most intellectual poets: colloquial speech must first be processed before it can become poetic speech. This process, as Xi Du 西渡 (b. 1967) puts it, is "extraction" 提炼, whose end product is a purified and rectified colloquial language. Xi Du further admonishes, "It is quite suspicious to indiscriminately use colloquial language [in poetry], for doing so is in fact to surrender a poet's responsibility towards language. The result would be a reduc-tion of poetry to language, but not an elevation of language to poetry" (Xi 2000: 29).

The difference between the *minjian* poet and the intellectual poet regarding language resources, however, goes far beyond what constitutes colloquial language. It is the latter's Western-looking posture—from open acknowledgment of foreign poets and frequent allusions to non-Chinese cultural sources to borrowed complex writing techniques and Europeanized syntax—that has raised the ire of the former. As Yu Jian puts it, life is always elsewhere for the intellectual poet (Yu 2004a: 553). Another *minjian* poet is even more blunt:

> Intellectual writing is a backward movement among the camp of pure poetry. It not only has lost the spirit of Misty Poetry but also falls into the old traps of language elitism and word play. In the present paucity of spiritual and language resources, it worships Western poetry and creates unaccountable poetic texts that pay tribute to Western masters. (Xie 2004: 454)

Most intellectual poets acknowledge that Western poetry serves as an important inspirational source for their work, but few would agree that they write merely to "pay tribute to Western masters." They describe whatever Western traces that occur in their writing as evidence of complex intertextuality, a concept to which Wang Jiaxin gives full explanation in its Chinese context:

> It is worth pointing out that an acknowledgement of intertextuality in contemporary writing is not tantamount to the poets' abandoning of "Chinese identity" or "Chineseness." From a careful look at the development of poetry in the 1990s, one would find that poetry has undergone a transformation vis-à-vis the West, i.e., "influence and being influenced" has changed into a relationship of dialogue and intertext. In other words, poets have stopped receiving influences passively and have begun to self-consciously, effectively, and creatively construct an intertextual relation with the West. This intertextual relation creates both a link and a distance between the poet and the Western text at the same time. (Wang 2002: 120)

That the theory of intertextuality is itself a Western invention is worth noting, and Wang's application of it in a cross-cultural context is certainly not without problems. Nevertheless, the realization that "Chinese identity," "Chineseness," and the West are not exclusionary terms contends directly with the *minjian* poet's stale and unsubstantiated nativism. In this sense, intertextuality as a self-willed act rather than as a forced act has the potential theoretical energy with which new writing space can be greatly expanded for the Chinese poet, for, unlike the *minjian* poet who is infatuated with regional languages and ill-defined colloquial language, the intellectual poet locates his language resources in all possible existing human utterances from speech to text and intertext, with intertextuality as his thread and as his guiding aesthetic principle.

The renowned Chinese poet Wang Xiaoni 王小妮 (b. 1955) says that if naming is a way to monopolize truth, then poetry is always antinaming. Indeed, contemporary Chinese poetry beginning with Misty Poetry has been a battleground for naming and antinaming. While Misty Poetry focused its fight on external political forces and earned its name along the way, Chinese poetry since then has engaged in a battle of its own making—the battle of how to name itself in the changing cultural and social landscape of China. "Pass Bei Dao!" 超越北岛 or 超过北岛 was the first shot by a younger generation of poets who were determined to be rebels more than the rebel Bei Dao had been. If this was an expression of the anxiety of influences, it relished rupture and rejected the immediate past for the sake of maintaining a continuous fighting spirit. I think it was this fighting spirit that stood behind the proliferation of poetic schools in the mid-1980s. The over one hundred named poetry groups displayed on the *Shenzhen Youth Daily* offered an unforgettable literary spectacle, but few of them contributed distinctive and meaningful theories about poetry and therefore had hardly any lasting impact. Still, a culture of factionalism and infighting among Chinese poets has survived.

The 1990s saw poetry undergoing major adjustments—some would argue that it experienced a decline or even a crisis, judging by its dwindling readership and social influence. Many established poets went abroad for reasons of exile or temporary residence, and young poets had not yet earned their place. Curiously, the lack of major poetic works in the fashion of Misty poetry in the earlier decade was compensated by an industrious production of writings about poetry. Most of these writings had become explicitly polemical, and neologism was frequently invented to describe one kind of poetry to the exclusion of others. Poetic debates broke out one after another among poets and critics over aesthetic positions and writing strategies such as narrativity 叙事性, lyricism 抒情性, middle-age writing 中年写作, personalization 个人化, nativism 本土化, woman's poetry 女性诗歌, and other such categories. It is in this context that the debate between the intellectual poet and the *minjian* poet happened to dominate the poetic scene at the turn of the century. Doubtless, this was a continuation of the now familiar culture of debate and was also a realignment of Chinese poets' desire for naming and association. Even though many of the views voiced during the debate are not really new, either to critical theory or in the context of modern Chinese poetry, they are being kept current by reenergized signifiers and recalibrated aesthetic positions. Misunderstanding and misreading of each other's positions are an integral part of any debate, and this debate is no exception. Once the personal animosity cooled down, the debate clarified many vexing issues and identified a few intractable problems facing Chinese poetry today. This was, after all, a valiant collective effort by Chinese poets and critics to reconfigure the meaning of poetry in China's cultural discourse on tradition and modernity in the age of commercialism and globalization.

Notes

1. The translation of "zhishi fenzi" to "intellectual" is a precise equivalent, but the translation of "minjian" to "popular" is problematic. There are several options available, such as "folkic," "people's," "mass," and "public," but none of them could neatly cover the complex meanings of "minjian" as its advocates have described. Maghiel van Crevel wrestled with this intriguing translation problem (2007) and chose "popular," but I cannot accept the suggestion of "popularity" that this word evokes. Absent an equivalent English term, I will simply use "*minjian*" throughout this chapter. This translation problem itself reveals two contrasting value-orientations, one of accessible universality and the other of intractable nativism.

2. Maghiel van Crevel (2007) offers an exhaustive description of the polemic in which he details almost every participant's—major or minor—stated position. His research is tremendously helpful to the writing of this chapter. I should point out, however, that although the polemics ended in 2002, judging by the "cease-fire" declared by several original Pan Feng conference participants, critics and scholars are writing about this debate in academic journals to this day.

3. For example, the critic Cao Wenxuan has observed Yu Jian's not realizing his own theories in his poetic work (Cao Wenxuan 2002: 287). Without suggesting that Yu Jian must be consistent in his double roles of poet and critic, I am interested in this "inconsistency" only insofar as one reads it as an indication of, perhaps, the impossibilities of his theory of colloquial writing.

Chapter Twelve

Online Avant-Garde Poetry in China Today

Michael Day

Net Servers	网侍
On a silver screen	银光屏
A crowd of young men and women	一群少男少女
In confusion	一群混杂之人
Here	在这里
Play and frolic	游玩, 嬉戏
Here	在这里
Practice evil and randomly do over others	恶搞, 乱整
Here	在这里
Run mad, go wild, stir up emotion	发疯, 撒野, 激情
The silver screen	银光屏
Modern technology	现代科技
A crystallization of human wisdom	人类智慧的结晶
Crystallizes in man, the soul of all things	结晶于万事万物之灵的人
Here	在这里
There's darkness and enlightenment	既有黑暗, 也有光明
worship of the lofty and the low	既有崇高, 也有崇低
embellishment and anti-embellishment	既有妆饰, 也有反饰
bright things and trash	既有亮物, 也有垃圾
Poetry	诗
This long-forgotten thing	这个早就被人们忘却了的东西
Finally finds	终于
Here a field for her to be	在这里找到了她生存的园地

(Artisan of Flowery Rocks 花岩匠人 2006)

According to a recent estimate by the poetry critic Chen Zhongyi 陈仲义 (Chen 2006), there are approximately two million new poems produced annually on Web sites in China today. My own research (Day 2006) lends credence to Chen's rather conservative claims that there are at least three hundred poetry Web sites operating online in

China and to his estimate, based on conversations with Web site operators, that on average twenty new poems appear daily on such sites. Chen's numbers refer to all poetry activity on the Internet in China, the great bulk of which is in "new poetry" forms. Poetry lovers and scholars seeking to "discover" poetry that meets their tastes or interests are bound to be initially nonplussed by such profusion and at a loss as to how to approach what at first glance can be described only as an anarchic state of poetry.

A large portion of the poetry Chen addresses in his article, and that which the poem above refers to is what I term "avant-garde". My preliminary research indicates there are over one hundred poetry Web sites that may be so termed, and several times that number of blogs by poets who contribute to these Web sites. Preliminary research into this area has been begun by Michel Hockx under the self-explanatory title "Virtual Chinese Literature: A Comparative Case Study of Online Poetry Communities" (Hockx 2005) in which the layout and procedures of one mainland Chinese poetry Web site are compared to current Western (U.S.) practice. Since 2002, my interests have led to a focus on avant-garde poetry activity on the Internet in China. What follows is a brief overview, ultimately focusing on recent events that hopefully will help readers make some sense of the seeming confusion.

The Internet as a space for poetry production became an integral part of the avant-garde poetry scene in China during 2000. It was at this time that *Poem Life* 诗生活 and other influential poetry Web sites were established and began to attract the participation of recognized avant-garde poets, previously interested only in paper publication, official or unofficial (in self-published journals with limited circulation), as well as newly emergent poets aspiring to "recognition" and avant-garde status. Earlier, access to such forums had been largely restricted to technology-savvy, "amateur" poetry enthusiasts and university students.

Chinese language poetry Web sites began to appear in North America (*The Olive Tree* 橄榄树 is a comprehensive literature site with poetry as a major component), Taiwan, and Hongkong in 1995, 1997, and 1998 respectively (Sang 2001). In China, this activity was retarded by the later development of Internet infrastructure and because individual access to computers was largely limited to places of work and study. This situation began to change in the late 1990s as a result of growth in personal disposable income among city dwellers and a state-led emphasis on the development of high technology in general and the Internet in particular.

Before 1999, the Internet in China had no dedicated poetry Web sites. However, from the mid-1990s, simple discussion forums that specialized in literature in general or poetry in particular existed as part of Web sites attached to commercial entities and universities. Among the most influential was Qinghua University's *Water and Wood Qinghua* 水木清华; forums on commercial sites such as *Sina* 新浪, *Netease* 网易, and *Under the Banyan Tree* 榕树下 (for an examination of this site and a comparison with pre-1949 literary practices see Hockx 2004) also proved popular and influential.

Before a dedicated poetry Web site would appear, there was a first poetry webzine, *Limits* 界限, edited by the Chongqing poet Li Yuansheng 李元生, the first edition of which was published online in March 1999 as an adjunct to the *Chongqing Literature* 重庆文学 Web site (Li Yuansheng 2002). The *Limits* Web site was opened in November 1999, and its influence spread nationwide as a result of this and the publication of a reformulated third edition of the webzine, no longer primarily devoted to the work of Chongqing poets. The site also contains a section in which a selection of outstanding poetry of the 1990s is stored, effectively constituting an anthology, and a section containing scanned covers and introductions to various unofficially published poetry journals. *Limits* later opened a number of poetry forums, and the Web site and webzine were the first to carry a forum and a section for translations of foreign poetry. This much imitated innovation is carried over from an increasingly common practice among unofficial poetry journals since the mid-1980s, a tradition to which *Limits* clearly links itself.

A key figure in the development of avant-garde poetry on the Internet in China is the Heilongjiang poet Sang Ke 桑克. Having begun to use the Internet at his job in 1997, in October 1999, with the help of net-friends, Sang became one of the first poets to have his own "column" 专栏 for poetry and essays hosted within a large commercial site (no longer extant, see Sang 2001). Not long thereafter, a visitor to Sang's site introduced him to a poetry forum where he met several Internet poets, such as Lai Er 莱耳. Ultimately this resulted in the establishment in February 2000 of the *Poem Life* Web site with Sang as content manager, Lai Er as administrative manager, and White Jade Bitter Melon 白玉苦瓜 as the chief forum moderator. Until 2005, a webzine was published on the fifth of each month—the first true webzine, in that it was *not* also published in a paper format—and both this and the design of the Web site have since been much imitated by new Web sites and webzines. The Web site also opened dozens of columns for poets and critics and was the first to offer a poetry news service, carrying up-to-date information on publications, activities, and prizes, both domestic and international.

Most Web sites and poetry forums tend to be formed by groups of like-minded poets with a shared *illusio*, the very establishment of which amounts to a position-taking activity in the avant-garde subfield of poetry as defined by the French sociologist of culture, Pierre Bourdieu (Bourdieu 1993 and 1996). On the Internet in China, this tendency is confirmed by the names of some sites (such as *Object-ism* 物主义 and *Vulgar World Being Here-ism* 俗世此在主义) but is more likely to be found in explicit statements of poetical tendencies located on the forum or in the site's webzines (such as Moved Writing 感动写作, Lower Body 下半身, Trash 垃圾, and the so-called Low Poetry 低诗歌 movement in general).

However, unlike the "sub-field of high literature" dealt with by Bourdieu, the subfield I refer to as the "Second World of Poetry" (Day 2005) possesses only an avant-garde and lacks any form of stable "establishment." This Second World is largely unseen by the public inside China and was inaugurated and inspired by the founding of the unofficially published (or "underground") Beijing-based literature journal *Today* 今天 in 1978. When young, experimental (or avant-garde) poets found their avenues to official publication blocked by editorial fiat during the early-1980s, many turned to similar self-publication activities as individuals or as groups, and this phenomenon has continued and grown since that time. In this unique situation, the only valid legitimizing agents are the participating poets and their unofficial publications—poets may attain greater prestige and thus greater cultural authority than others due to longer histories of publication or longer histories and greater accumulated prestige within the Second World. In this sense, the Misty poets of the 1970s and early 1980s (the most influential of whom were contributors to *Today*) can be seen as taking on the role of an "established (or 'consecrated') avant-garde," as they are to some degree legitimized as a target for attack by newcomers to the subfield on account of their earlier and more frequent official publication, and due to subsequent recognition by literary critics and sinologists. Since 2000, the Internet has created a situation in which both avant-garde poetry webzines and Web sites function as "unofficial publications" and as part of the Second World.

Thus, paradoxically, the appearance of acceptance and occasional publication of the Second World poets in the CCP-dominated First World of "official" media in the PRC has a potentially delegitimizing effect, especially in the eyes of ambitious newcomers to the Second World. This is, in fact, the political element touched on only briefly in the Western-oriented model constructed by Bourdieu. To an extent, this situation mirrors the Western avant-garde's reaction against the accumulation of popularity and economic capital through art, which in post-Mao China is often overshadowed by the accumulation of the sociopolitical capital necessary before anything else. As in the West, there is little money to be made in being an avant-garde poet in China today.

Given the inherent instability of the unofficial Second World that arises from the pressurized, borderline illegality and the economic uncertainty of these poets' publication activities, as well as fragile interpersonal relations, internal legitimizing agents and a resultant "establishment" cannot enjoy more than a fleeting existence. What cultural legitimacy can be attained is therefore tenuous and frequently reliant on external sources, such as, during the 1980s in particular, translated foreign poetry and critiques that may be soon destabilized by translations of newer, antagonistic poetical tendencies and critiques as thrown up through the mechanisms of the Western avant-garde, as described by Bourdieu. A further paradox results from the universal desire for recognition that leads avant-garde poets in the PRC to seek or accept publication in official media, which thereby potentially undermines their own moral authority and position-takings against the CCP-dominated literary establishment. (In recent years, numerous print anthologies of poetry specifically culled from Internet sites have been published in China, and official poetry journals have taken to online solicitation of the work of Internet poets for publication.) Furthermore, the more ambitious the grouping, the more liable it is to internal divisions and, in the case of the Internet, the establishment of offshoot Web sites.

The Internet gives newcomers unprecedented, direct access to publication and avant-garde status. Poets can publicly challenge established positions and liaise more easily with like-minded poets than was the case heretofore in the Second World in China. An example of this is the "Low Poetry Movement" 低诗歌运动, which involves several poetry forums and associated poets and paper journals. The "movement" is not only an attack on establishment poetry and the recognized avant-garde, but also on the emergent Internet avant-garde, such as the *Poem Life* Web site, which is considered to be weighted toward "intellectual" poetry or poetry in the received "Western" metaphysical tradition (Zhang 2004).

The original *Low Poetry* forum was the no longer extant *Low Poetry Movement Forum* 低诗歌运动论坛, opened on March 29, 2004, by the poets Long Jun 龙俊, Zhang Jiayan 张嘉彦, and Hua Qiang 花枪. The *Low Poetry Network* 低诗歌网 was opened in November 2005 and is a clearinghouse for the forums and Web sites linked to the movement. Among these thirty-plus poetry sites and forums are the *Trash Movement Forum* 垃圾运动论坛, the *Poetry Vagabonds Forum* 诗江湖论坛, and the *Them Literature Net* 他们文学, all of which preceded the establishment of the *Low Poetry Forum* (2003, 2001, and 2002, respectively).

The majority of the poets involved in this "movement" belong to the self-styled generations of poets born during the 1970s (70后) and 1980s (80后) and identify closely with the "popular" or "among-the-people" 民间 poetry writing tendency that emerged very publicly during the 1998–1999 polemic between adherents of this tendency and those of the "intellectual" 知识分子 poetry tendency (Van Crevel 2007).

Yet, in a recent essay, Zhang Jiayan addresses all these issues and acknowledges the limitations, if not the death, of Low poetry as a "movement" (Zhang 2005). The genesis of the movement is linked to the appearance in 2001 of the Web site *Poetry Vagabonds*, its webzines and unofficial paper journals, and the "Lower Body" style of poetry championed by its poets (such as Shen Haobo 沈浩波, Yin Lichuan 尹丽川, and Wu Ang 巫昂). Zhang sees this as a successful smashing of the taboo on the writing of sex and sexual activity. Two years later, the Trash Movement appeared, also with webzines and paper journals, but now the focus was on smashing the taboos on writing about the basest bodily functions. As with Lower Body poetry, there was an aspect of reaction against the lofty, obscure subject matter of the "intellectual" poets who are seen as importing Western standards of metaphysical poetry alien to modern Chinese culture and language. In this sense, the Low Poetry Movement is seen as an effort to purify Chinese poetical language, bringing it closer to the lives and language of the people of China. Moreover, in his essay, Zhang championed the smashing of a final taboo, politics—thus seeking the depoliticization of language—and established a forum dedicated to this purpose (*China Low Poetry Tide* 中国低诗潮 2005). Zhang acknowledges that no "movement" similar to that which accompanied Lower Body or Trash poetry is possible at this time and places the burden of responsibility on the "Individual Avant-Garde" 个体先锋. This translates into poetry that smashes through political taboos being posted by individual poets on poetry forums, the managers of which are willing

to run the risk of posting it, or in personal blogs or Web sites. For
example,

Notes on June 4, 1989	**1989年6月4日记事**
1	
The 4th of June 1989	1989年6月4日
What all I did	我都干了些什么
I'm not entirely sure now	现在有些记不清楚了
It seems I was on a train	我好象是在一列火车上
A train	那一列火车
Travelling from Shenzhen to Nanchang	是由深圳开往南昌的
I remember in the sleeper car	我记得卧铺车厢里
There were mostly middle-aged and older people	中老年乘客居多
Everybody a stranger to the other	大家彼此陌生
But I had two companions	而我有两个同伴
One my 18-year old girlfriend	一个是我18岁的女友
The other a	另一个是一名
Cadre in the organization department of a provincial Communist Youth League	共青团 X 省组织部的干部
For some reason	由于某种原因
We'd broken off our business in Shenzhen	我们中断了在深圳的公干
Were hurriedly backtracking	匆匆返程
. . .	。。。
5	
The setting sun kissed the roof of the carriage goodbye	落日吻别了车顶
The night grew deeper	夜色开始由浅变深
At Zhuzhou station	株州火车站内
As many as 10,000 passengers were gathered	已云集了上万名乘客
We sat on the tracks	或坐于铁轨上
Or wandered about not far from the car	或游走在车厢不远处
Some asked in the station when the train would go	有人向车站询问列车何时开走
The answer was a shock:	答复令人诧异:
Either return to Shenzhen	要么开回深圳
Or just wait for orders from Beijing!	要么只有等来北京的指令!
The night grew grimmer	夜色更加深重
The hour hand moved toward zero hour	时针刺向午夜零点
I returned to the carriage	我回到了车厢里
Hugging my sleeping girlfriend	搂着入睡了的女友
	冥冥之中
	我感到了火车向右拐的律动
	并飘浮于
	夜色的更深处

In the dim light
I felt the rhythm of the train turn
  to the right
And float into
A deeper spot in the darkness

(Person of Inferior Health 亚健康者)

The penname effectively hides the name of the author and there is a gradual, indirect approach to the subject—still a necessity in the current political environment. The massacres on June 3 and 4, 1989, in Beijing and Chengdu remain the most sensitive subject matter for poetry in China, while the Cultural Revolution, Mao Zedong, and Marx, for example, are increasingly popular subjects.

Another aspect of this "Low" style of poetry is increasingly topical approaches to politics, as demonstrated by the following:

Chairman Hu's Speech Stirs Hearts　　胡主席的讲话激动人心

When the curtain of night descends
And birds are sweetly falling asleep,
In my home, I watch television,
And together with me,
Is my friend.
At seven o'clock, the news starts,
And we're still talking

. . . .

I like Chairman Hu's words
The speech of politicians is
  unusually staunch,
Rich in benevolent thought,
Displaying the talents of wise
  rulers.
He speaks of the importance of
  culture, of people having greater
  need of spirit,
Of the relationship between the
  spirit and harmony.
He speaks of the work of the
  Chinese Writers Association,
The mission of the Writers
  Association.
I see a multitude of cultural
  workers
A multitude of Party leaders,

当夜幕低垂下来，
众鸟儿要甜甜睡觉，
在我的家里，我看电视节目，
和我在一起的，
是我的朋友。
七点钟的时候，新闻开始了，
我们还在说话。

。。。。

我喜欢胡主席的话，
政治家的言论，却非常坚定，
富有仁爱的思想，
显示英明君主的才能。
他说文化的重要，世人更需要精神，
精神和和谐的关系。
他说中国作协的工作，
作协的使命。
我看见众文化工作者，
看见众位中央领导人，
看见他们严肃的神态，
我感到新生的希望了，
我心中的欢乐在沸腾着。
我想说：多年等待的愿望，
今天终于实现了，
我们是可怜的诗人，
以前不被人注意，
今天才感到了关怀。

Their serious posture,	胡主席, 我们的许多中央领导人,
I feel the hope of a new life,	你们关怀我们,
The joy in my heart is welling up.	我们多么激动。
I want to say: A long-awaited desire	。。。
Has finally been realized today.	
We are wretched poets,	
Nobody paid us heed before,	
But today we feel the love.	
Chairman Hu, our many Party leaders,	
You're concerned over us,	
And we're so excited.	
. . .	

(Little Moon 小月亮 November 11, 2006)

Here, the poet (a woman) immediately responds to the television broadcast of a speech given by CCP chairman Hu Jintao. This rather long poem is heavily ironic, listing many events that have occurred on the avant-garde poetry scene in recent years—events of which Chairman Hu would not be aware and for which, if he were, he would be unlikely to have benevolent thoughts. The surname Hu is replaced by an asterisk in the title of the original forum posting in an apparent effort by the poet or the managers of the forum to avoid attention from the authorities (his name appears in the poem itself). In other poems, there are incidences of hyphens or dashes being inserted between the characters of names, leading to Marx being rendered as 马-克-思 or Prime Minister Wen Jiabao as 温/家/宝, for example—apparently to decrease Internet searchability.

Another style championed by the Low Poetry Movement is the poetry of menial workers. The experiences and emotions of workers—a low, unpoetic form of life by consecrated poetical standards—are desirable given the relationship such poetry has with universal, China-specific experience and colloquial language. One of the more prominent of the Web sites related to such poetry is *Menial Worker Poets* 打工诗人.

I Write in the Dark of Night   **我在黑夜里写下**

我在黑夜里写下路灯, 街道和一个四处奔波的外乡人
我在黑夜里写下制衣厂的女工和她们命运中的咳嗽
我在黑夜里写下五金厂的炉火以及一截让机器吞掉的手指
我写到路灯, 它孤独, 是啊, 它多象一个乡愁病患者
我写到街道, 它宽广, 灯火辉煌, 但是哪里又有我站立的地方
我写到五金厂的炉火, 它暗淡的光啊, 照亮我苍白的青春
我写到爱情, 它甜蜜的味儿, 它不知明天会怎样的辛酸
我写到黄麻岭, 这个收藏我三年青春的沿海村庄

啊，我最后将写到自己，一个四处奔波的四川女孩
啊，这打工生活——我将要忍受怎样的孤独与命运

(郑小琼)

In the dark of night I write down streetlights, streets and a stranger rushing about
In the dark of night I write down women workers at a clothes plant and the
  coughs of their destiny
In the dark of night I write down the furnace fires of ironmongery and a finger
  swallowed by a machine
I write a streetlight, it's solitary, yes, it's so like a homesick person
I write a street, it's broad, lights burning bright, but where's a place for me to
  stand
I write a furnace at an ironmonger's, it's dim light illuminates my pallid youth
I write of love, its sweet taste, it doesn't know how bitter tomorrow will be
I write of Jute Ridge, this costal village that's taken in three years of my youth
Ahh, finally, I'll write of myself, a girl from Sichuan rushing about
Ahh, this menial-worker life—what sort of loneliness and fate must I endure

(Zheng Xiaoqiong)

The woman poet Zheng Xiaoqiong is one of the most successful and best-known practitioners of poetry in this vein. She also has written topical poetry on the death of coal miners, for example.

Another aspect of avant-garde Internet poetry is a tendency among some poets to refashion "found" texts, which may consist of placing nonpoetic texts within the text of a poem or artfully editing nonpoetic texts into poetry.

How the Steel was Tempered	钢铁是这样炼成的
Goat City Evening News reporter Zhao Shilong	羊城晚报记者赵世龙 湖南日报记者徐亚平
Hunan Daily News reporter Xu Yaping	中国妇女报记者邓小波
China Women's Press reporter Deng Xiaobo	网易部落
Tribes on the Netease site	联合报道
In a joint report	
Hunan Province Yueyang City Huarong County	湖南省岳阳市华容县 年仅12岁的女童 段英
After Duan Ying	被人拐卖到
A girl only twelve-years old	岳阳市区廖家坡后
Was sold	
Into Liaojiapo in Yueyang	在3个月内 共有700余名嫖客
Inside three months	强暴过
A total of over 700 whoremasters	她
Brutalized	
Her	而150多名老板

And	
Over 150 bosses	从中作了
Made their introductions	介绍
Little	小
Duan Ying	段英
Secretly made notes on this all	偷偷地把这一切作了记录
What's shocking is that	令人吃惊的是
Over a period of more than three months	总共850多名作恶者
	竟在长达
Out of over 850 reprobates	3个多月里一人未抓
Not one has been caught	全部
All	逍遥法外
Remain at large	

(Blue Butterfly Purple Lilac 蓝蝴蝶紫丁香)

Blue Butterfly Purple Lilac is a male poet who writes and publishes exclusively on the Internet, and the foregoing poem is an example of tendencies toward spontaneous topicality, colloquial language, and social responsibility advocated by Low poetry. The title of the poem is taken from the 1934 novel by the Soviet writer Nikolai Ostrovsky, later made into a popular film in 1956 and produced as a TV series in China in 2000—to which this poem seems to be an ironical response.

Poem Written on June 4th	**写在6月4日的诗歌**
1	
Today	今天
Is	是
The 4th of June	6月4日
Today	今天
Is	是
The 4th of June 2005	2005年的6月4日
Today	今天
Is not	不是
The 4th of June 1989	1989的6月4日
2	
Today	今天
Is	是
The 4th of June	6月4日
Today	今天
Is	是
The 4th of June 2005	2005年的6月4日

Today	今天
I don't remember a thing	什么都不记得了
Today	今天
I remember	就记得
Pissing the day away on the Internet	在网上泡了一整天
3	
Today	今天
Is	是
The 4th of June	6月4日
Today	今天
Is	是
The 4th of June 2005	2005年的6月4日
Today	今天
I pissed the day away on the Internet	在网上泡了一整天
But not	不是在
In a chatroom	论坛
Chatrooms	论坛
Are like spittoons	就像一个痰盂
Spit out	吐
A mouthful of phlegm	一口痰
Then leave	就可以走人
4	
Today	今天
Is	是
The 4th of June	6月4日
Today	今天
Is	是
The 4th of June 2005	2005年的6月4日
Today	今天
Is not	不是
The 4th of June 1989	1989年的6月4日
Today	今天
Was entirely spent	一直都在
Playing games	玩游戏

(Blue Butterfly Purple Lilac)

This handling of the June 4 topic is notable for linguistic reasons. Aware of the taboo on the mere mention of this date on the Internet, much less in polite conversation, the poet's repetition of it becomes something of a mantra that effectively reduces the date to a seemingly harmless game. Yet, in the context of the discourse field of CCP-dominated China and its Internet, this can be regarded as both subversive and liberating, and as an attempt to "normalize" the "saying" of the date as a possible first step toward writing about it in a more meaningful manner. Blue Butterfly is also noted for creating poems out of numeric codes and for the introduction of Chinese Internet terms into his poetry, such as "ou" 偶 instead of "I," or "wo" 我.

Amateur–avant-garde interaction is among the factors that have led to the development of Internet writing styles. This trend is evident in the work of those who have learned to write poetry or primarily publish in Internet forums such as Blue Butterfly. Writing about computers and the Internet, featuring terminology that is commonly used there, is an inevitable result:

Program of Life	**生命的程序**
Plug in the universal port	接上统一的插座
Connect to the machine's power source	连通机器的电源
Open the device of life	打开生命的机子
Enter the username on the ID card	输入身份证的用户名
And the self-centered code we've cooked up	与我们编造的自私密码
Bring up the desktop of lies	刷新谎言桌面
Arrange the icons of authority	排列权力图标
Cooling sperm and eggs	冷却的精卵
Stiffening hands and feet	僵化的手脚
Create a new file	新建成一个文件夹
Copied greetings	复制的问候
Pasted happy faces	粘贴的笑脸
Sent to the body's other	发送到身体的另一个
Stored on hard drive	硬盘保存
The soul of error code	错码的心灵
Place in an attachment and zip	打包压缩
Delete at a set time	定期删除
Dump it in the recycle bin and	放入回收站等候清空
wait for it to clear	思想经常被
Thought is often	新的国家指令
Fully formatted	全盘格式化
By new state directives	精神的病毒
Viruses of the spirit	通过盗版软盘
Invade the operating system of the brain	侵入大脑的驱动程序
Through pirated software	侵入大脑的驱动程序
The system is infected	世界黑屏
The world is a black screen	然后强行关机
Turn off the machine by force	人生资料因此
And all data of life	全部丢失
Are lost as a result	

(Little Prince 小王子)

Women poets have taken advantage of the Internet to reach a larger readership in establishing forums devoted exclusively to women's poetry. For example, *Wings* 翼 forum and *Women's Poetry Paper* 女子诗报 are both unofficially published poetry journals that use their forums to attract new poets and poetry.

Women poets are also very active in the developing move into poetry blogging. Wu Ang, Yin Lichuan, Chunshu 春树, Mo Xiaoxie 莫小邪, and An Qi 安琪 are among the more prominent of those who began blogging in 2005. In fact, the most notable event on the avant-garde poetry scene in China during 2005 was the great increase in the use of Internet blogs by poets. While Internet forums are still heavily used and increasing in number, a growing proportion of avant-garde poets are turning to blogs to initially publish poetry and engage in relatively private conversation with readers, as opposed to the ready partisan support easily received on the forums with which they may be associated.

This phenomenon may also be recognition on the part of some poets that Internet forums—in particular those of the avant-garde— can be intimidating places for "readers." In this sense, this development can be seen as positive and part of a "natural" maturation process for Internet poets and poetry as they learn and adapt to their Internet *habitus*. That said, the plethora of blogs in fact increases the importance of a continued presence on forums, as poets post poems with blog addresses in apparent attempts to attract readers to their blogs. The more successful bloggers in this respect tend to be woman poets, such as Wu Ang, Yin Lichuan, and Mo Xiaoxie, who post personal essays and photography, allowing readers to get closer to the poets and their poetry. The "stickiness" of their sites has apparently reduced the need for them to appear on poetry forums. Male poets, such as Sang Ke and Shen Haobo, tend to be less personal and include critical essays along with poetry in their blogs. Correspondingly, they tend to be far more active on avant-garde poetry forums than their female colleagues.

Critics have spoken out against the seeming anarchy of poetry on the Internet, among other things citing "nonpoetic" topics such as sex, drug-use, and unseemly bodily functions. Coarse language and earthy humor are also frequently present and criticized as unpoetic, as is poetry on topical issues. In fact, similar criticisms were leveled against elements of the avant-garde during the 1980s, but then the targets were groups and individuals such as Sichuan's Macho Man 莽汉 and Not-Not 非非, Zhou Lunyou 周伦佑 and Liao Yiwu 廖亦武, and Tianjin's Yi Lei 伊蕾. Other aspects are unique to or exacerbated by the

Internet and computers, such as cataloguing and the "postmodernist" technique of inserting nonpoetic texts into poems.

The "consecrated" avant-garde and other self-appointed guardians of highly selective aspects of poetic traditions (either Western or Chinese) are, as always, trying to halt or slow change, and thereby protect their positions on the poetry scene, while newcomers and experimenters continue, as always, to push the limits, seeking support through appeals to the "people" and common experience and language.

In the West, computers and the Internet have led to what is generally called "medium-specific" experimentation with poetry that synthesizes pictures and film, music and sound, with or without written characters, through use of FLASH technology. In China, the lack of finances and technical abilities is the biggest impediment to this. The poet-philosopher Illiterate 文盲 was one of the first avant-garde poets to develop his own Web site with graphics and sound. Recently, poets have begun to take advantage of Web sites that will allow them to podcast and make use of streaming technology. One of the first avant-garde poets to utilize this technology is Yi Hushui 伊湖水, who has placed online a recitation of his latest work—"The Merits and Faults of Marx"—together with atmospheric music and accompanying graphics. To date, little has been done in the area of e-poetry or cyber poetry, as it is called in the West. Moreover, whether e-poetry "happenings" can still be considered poetry and not a new art form birthed by and for computers is still subject to debate, and an issue that is beyond the scope of this chapter.

The Internet in China has opened up a vast new subfield within the larger field of poetry. Pressures of submitting poetry texts to far-off, anonymous editorial committees at official and even unofficial publications are being circumvented by the immediacy of the publication of poetry on internet forums and blogs. The fact that there are now published books of Internet poetry indicates that even Internet poets like to see their names in print and that some factions of Internet poets are seeking somehow to solidify their highly liquid Internet reputations via traditional methods. Moreover, some webzines are also still printed in unofficially published paper editions, and many official and unofficial journals and periodicals now operate or visit poetry forums to collect material for publication.

If anything, all around the world the Internet is leading to more poetry being written and published, in whatever form, than ever before. New poets and new poetry are emerging everyday and are waiting to be found by those who have the time and interest to seek them out. In this regard, critics and sinologists no longer need rely on the recommendations of the widely read few, who have access to otherwise unseen paper publications, to find the gems they seek. Conversely, it is perhaps also for this reason that paper publication is of continuing value, functioning as it does as a snapshot of brief moments in time and space in an ever onward-rushing tide of poetry, more visible now than ever before in the history of humankind.

The appearance of emergent poets jockeying for positions in the fluid subfield of avant-garde poetry continues apace, as illustrated by the following poem posted on the *Poetry Vagabond* forum on November 29, 2006:

Manifesto of Post-1990s Poetry

I'm the last soul born into the post-1980s
I'm the first post-1990s person to become
  a dragon of the times
In this time of a wild poetry scene
The post-1990s   Young hearts
Will take up historical responsibilities
We are not blind
We want to guide China's poetry
  toward regularity
Looking back on the confusion of
  the post-1920s and -1930s
Laughingly viewing the hopes of
  the post-1940s and -1950s
We want to open the closed door of
  the post-1960s and -1970s
And see through their profound
  expressions
The innocence of the post-1980s
Innocently taking on the responsibility
  of innovation
And us a new generation
Young hearts
Wanting to see the current state of
  China's poetry
Our hearts fuse all epics
And raise a torch
Illuminating all roads opened by
  our predecessors' hardship
And by this fire
Gain a road on which to advance and
  pass our lives

90后诗歌宣言

我是出生在80后的最后一个灵魂
我是90后第一个时世成龙的人
在这个诗风狂乱的年代里
90后   年轻的心
要担起历史的责任
我们不做盲目的人
我们要引导中国诗风走向正规
追忆20、30后的迷茫
笑看40、50后的希望
我要打开60、70后封闭的门
透视他们深邃的眼神
80后的纯真
纯真地担负了创新的责任
而我们 新的一代人
年轻的心
要看到中国诗歌的现状
心融起所有史诗
擎一把火
照亮所有前人艰辛开拓的路
并借此火
得度我们一生前进的路
来   来   来
快   快   快
90后   90后
新的一代人
年轻的心
联合起来
担负起历史的责任
引导中国诗歌走上正规
走上正规

Come   Come   Come
Quick   Quick   Quick
Post-1990s   post-1990s
A new generation
Young hearts
Come together
Take up this historical responsibility
Guide China's poetry towards regularity
Into regularity

(Dragon of Cold Times 寒时世龙)

Serious or not, a challenge from newly emergent poets is bound to come, and a quest for "regularity" or "proper standards" 正规—a rejection of seeming Internet anarchy—would appear to be an easy position to take for a start. Under current conditions in China, lacking a generally acknowledged domestic institution of consecration, the avant-garde poets themselves act as the shop stewards of poetical standards and traditions. All position-takings are valid and potentially effective (and affective) in such a situation.

So, ambitious young hearts and minds—welcome to the free-for-all.

Bibliography

An, Qi 安琪 et al., eds. 2003. *Zhongjiandai Shi* 中间代诗 (Mid-generation poetry). Fuzhou: Haixia wenyi chubanshe.

Artisan of Flowery Rocks 花岩匠人. "Net Servers." In *Low Poetry Tide* <http://my.ziqu.com/bbs/666023/>. Accessed November 11, 2006.

Auden, W. H. 1975a. "American Poetry." In *The Dyer's Hand and Other Essays*, 354–368. London: Faber and Faber.

———. 1975b. "Robert Frost." In *The Dyer's Hand and Other Essays*, 337–353. London: Faber and Faber.

Ballard, J. G. 1970. *The Atrocity Exhibition*. London: Granda Books.

Barlow, Tani E., ed. 1993. *Gender Politics in Modern China: Writing and Feminism*. Durham: Duke University Press.

———. 1994. "Politics and Protocols of *Funü*: (Un)Making National Woman." In Gilmartin 1994: 339–359.

Barmé, Geremie, and John Minford, eds. 1986. *Seeds of Fire: Chinese Voices of Conscience*. Hong Kong: Far Eastern Economic Review.

Baudelaire, Charles. 1993. "Le Cygne" (The Swan). In James McGowan, tr., *The Flowers of Evil*. Oxford: Oxford University Press, 172–177.

Bei, Dao 北島. 1991. *Old Snow*. Bonnie S. McDougall and Chen Maiping, trs. New York: New Directions.

Benjamin, Walter. 1979. *One-Way Street and Other Writings*. London: New Left Books.

Bing, Xin 冰心 (Xie Wanying 謝婉瑩). 1923. *Fanxing* 繁星 (Myriad stars). Shanghai: Commercial Press.

———. 1931. *Chunshui* 春水 (Spring waters), reprint. Shanghai: Beixin shuju.

———. 1949. *Bing Xin shiji* 冰心詩集 (Collected works of Bing Xin). Reprint, Shanghai: Kaiming shudian.

Booth, Allyson. 1996. *Postcards from the Trenches: Negotiating the Space between Modernism and the First World War*. New York and Oxford: Oxford University Press.

Borges, Jorge Luis. 1999. "The Argentine Writer and Tradition." In Eliot Weinberger, ed., *Selected Non-Fictions*, 420–427. New York: Viking Press.

Bottomore, Tom, ed. 1983. *A Dictionary of Marxist Thought*. London: Basil Blackwell.

Bourdieu, Pierre. 1993. *The Field of Cultural Production: Essays on Art and Literature*. Cambridge: Polity.

———. 1996. *The Rules of Art: Genesis and Structure of the Literary Field*. Cambridge: Polity.

Braester, Yomi. 2003. *Witness Against History: Literature, Film, and Public Discourse in Twentieth-Century China*. Stanford: Stanford University Press.

Broome, Peter. 1977. *Henri Michaux*. London: The Athlone Press.

Camus, Albert. 1966. "Absurd Freedom." In William V. Spanos, *A Casebook on Existentialism*, 297–307. New York: Thomas Y. Crowell.

Cao, Wenxuan 曹文轩. 2002. *Ershi shiji Zhongguo wenxue xianxiang yanjiu* 二十世末中国文学象研究 (A study of Chinese literary phenomena at the end of the twentieth century). Beijing: Beijing daxue chubanshe.

Chambers, Ross. 1991. *Room for Maneuver*. Chicago and London: University of Chicago Press.

Chase, Cynthia. 1985. "'Viewless Wings': Intertextual Interpretation of Keat's 'Ode to a Nightingale.'" In Hosek and Parker 1985, 208–225.

Chen, Dongdong 陈东东. 2000. "Huigu xiandai Hanyu" 回顾现代汉语 (Looking back at modern Chinese). In Wang Jiaxin 王家新 and Sun Wenbo 孙文波, eds., *Zhongguo shige: jiushi niandai beiwanglu* 中国诗歌: 九十年代备忘录 (Chinese poetry: Memorandum of the 1990s). Beijing: Renmin wenxue chubanshe.

Chen, Li 陳黎. 2003. *Daoyu bianyuan* 島嶼邊緣 (On the edge of the island). Taibei: Jiuge chubanshe.

Chen, Sihe 陈思和. 1987. *Zhongguo xinwenxue zhengtiguan* 中国新文学整体观 (A macrocosmic view of new Chinese literature). Shanghai: Shanghai wenyi chubanshe.

Chen, Yizhi 陳義芝, ed. 1999. *Taiwan wenxue jingdian yantaohui taolun ji* 台灣文學經典研討會討論集 (Collected proceedings from the conference on Taiwan literary classics). Taibei: Lianjing.

Chen, Zhongyi 陈仲义. 2006. "Xinshiji wunian wangluo shixiang guancha" 新世纪5年网络诗象观察 (Observations on Internet poetry phenomena during the five years of the new century). <http://www.yanruyu.com/jhy/author/69892.shtml>. Online posting accessed December 3, 2006.

Cheung, Dominic, ed. and tr. 1986. *The Isle Full of Noises*. New York: Columbia University Press.

Chiu, Julie. 2005. "Free-verse Poems in Fixed Forms: Tracing the 'Silhouette' of Zheng Chouyu's Early Poems." *Texas Studies in Literature and Language* 47.2 (Summer): 188–218.

Chow, Rey. 2002. *The Protestant Ethnic and the Spirit of Capitalism*. New York: Columbia University Press.

Cronon, William. 1990. "Modes of Prophecy and Production: Placing Nature in History." *The Journal of American History* (March) 76.4: 1122–1131.

Crosby, Alfred W. 1990. "An Enthusiastic Second." *The Journal of American History* (March) 76.4: 1107–1110.

Culler, Jonathan. 1985. "Changes in the Study of the Lyric." In Hosek and Parker 1985, 38–54.

Dagong shiren 打工诗人 (Menial worker poets). <http://sh.netsh.com/bbs/8832/>. Accessed December 3, 2006.

Dai, Wangshu 戴望舒. 1989. "Wo sixiang" 我思想 (I think). *Collected Works of Dai Wangshu* 戴望舒全编. Liang Ren 梁仁, ed., Hangzhou: Zhejiang wenyi chubanshe.

Davis, Walter A. 1978. *The Act of Interpretation: A Critique of Literary Reason.* Chicago: University of Chicago Press.

———. 1994. *Get the Guests: Psychoanalysis, Modern American Drama, and the Audience.* Madison: University of Wisconsin Press.

———. 2001. *Deracination: Historicity, Hiroshima, and the Tragic Imperative.* Albany: State University of New York Press.

———. 2003. "Death's Dream Kingdom: The American Psyche After 9/11." *Journal for the Psychoanalysis of Culture and Society* (Spring) 8.1: 127–132.

Day, Michael. 2005. *China's Second World of Poetry: The Sichuan Avant-Garde, 1982–1992.* <http://leiden.dachs-archive.org/poetry/md.html> (e-book version of doctoral thesis, University of Leiden). Accessed December 3, 2006.

———. 2006. "China's Second World of Poetry: Web Site List." <http://leiden.dachs-archive.org/poetry/list.html>. Accessed December 3, 2006.

———. 2007a. <http://leiden.dachs-archive.org/poetry/translations.html>. Accessed January 15, 2007.

———. 2007b. "The Poetry of Tang Yaping 唐亚平." <http://leiden.dachs-archive.org/poetry/MD/Tang_Yaping_trans.pdf>. Accessed January 15, 2007.

———. 2007c. "Zhai Yong-ming: China's First Poet of the Female Sex." <http://leiden.dachs-archive.org/poetry/MD/Zhai_Yongming_trans.pdf>. Accessed January 15, 2007.

Dishige luntan 低诗歌论坛 (Low poetry forum). <http://my.clubhi.com/bbs/661612/>. Accessed December 3, 2006.

Dishige wang 低诗歌网 (Low poetry network). <http://www.dpoem.com>. Accessed November 15, 2006.

Dordoy, Alan, and Mary Mellor. 2000. "Ecosocialism and Feminism: Deep Materialism and the Contradictions of Capitalism." *Capitalism Nature Socialism 43* (September) 11.3: 41–61.

Duo, Duo 多多. 2002. *The Boy Who Catches Wasps.* Gregory B. Lee, tr. Brookline, MA: Zephyr Press.

Eisenstein, Paul. 2004. "Visions and Revision: Aronofsky's π and the Primordial Signifier." In Todd McGowan and Sheila Kunkle, eds., *Lacan and Contemporary Film.* New York: Other Press: 1–28.

Felman, Shoshana. 1985. *Writing and Madness Literature/Philosophy/Psychoanalysis.* Martha Noel Evans, Shoshona Felman, and Brian Massumi, trs. Ithaca: Cornell University Press.

Felman, Shoshana, and Dori Laub, eds. 1992. *Testimony: Crises of Witnessing in Literature, Psychoanalysis, and History.* New York: Routledge.

Finnegan, Ruth. (1972) 1992. *Oral Poetry: Its Nature, Significance and Social Context.* 1st Midland Book edition. Bloomington and Indianapolis: Indiana University Press. Original edition, Cambridge University Press.

Fussell, Paul. 1979. *Poetic Meter and Poetic Form.* Revised edition. New York: Random House.

Ganlan shu 橄榄树 (The olive tree). <http:www.wenxue.com>. Accessed December 3, 2006.

Gilmartin, Christina K. et al., eds. 1994. *Engendering China: Women, Culture, and the State*. Cambridge: Harvard University Press.

Grange, Joseph. 1997. *Nature: An Environmental Cosmology*. Albany: State University of New York Press.

Gu, Cheng 顾城. 1990. *Selected Poems*. Sean Golden and Chu Chiyu, eds. Hong Kong: Renditions.

———. 1993. *Ying'er* 英儿 (Ying'er). Beijing: Zuojia chubanshe.

———. 1995. *Gu Cheng shi quanbian* 顾城诗全编 (Complete poems of Gu Cheng). Gu Gong 顾工, ed. Shanghai: Shanghai sanlian shudian.

———. 2005a. *Gu Cheng wenxuan* vol. 1 顾城文选 (卷一) (Selected works of Gu Cheng). Harbin: Beifang wenyi chubanshe.

———. 2005b. *Sea of Dreams: The Selected Writings of Gu Cheng*. Joseph R. Allen, tr. New York: New Directions.

Haft, Lloyd, ed. 1989. *A Selective Guide to Chinese Literature 1900–1949, Volume III: The Poem*. Leiden: E. J. Brill.

Han, Dong 韩东. 2007. "Lun minjian" 论民间 (On the popular). Quoted and tr. in Van Crevel 2007.

He, Jipeng 何寄澎. 1981. "Zheng Chouyu zuopin shangxi" 鄭愁予作品賞析 (An appreciation and analysis of Zheng Chouyu's works). In Lin Mingde 林明德 et al., eds. *Zhongguo xinshi shangxi* 中國新詩賞析 (An analysis and appreciation of modern Chinese poetry), 241–278. Taibei: Chang'an.

Heidegger, Martin. 1962. *Being and Time*. John Macquarrie and Edward Robinson, trs. New York: Harper & Row.

Hockx, Michel. 2004. "Links with the Past: Mainland China's Online Literary Communities and Their Antecedents." *Journal of Contemporary China* 38 (February): 105–127.

———. 2005. "Virtual Chinese Literature: A Comparative Case Study of Online Poetry Communities." *The China Quarterly* 183 (September): 670–691.

Hong, Ying 虹影, and Zhao Yiheng 赵毅衡, eds. 1993. *Muchuang: Gu Cheng Xie Ye haiwai daibiao zuoping ji* 墓床: 顾城谢烨海外代表作品集 (Grave bed: Representative overseas works of Gu Cheng and Xie Ye). Beijing: Zuojia chubanshe.

Hosek, Chaviva, and Patricia Parker, eds. 1985. *Lyric Poetry: Beyond New Criticism*. Ithaca and London: Cornell University Press.

Hsu, Kai-yu, ed. and tr. 1973. *Twentieth-Century Chinese Poetry: An Anthology*. Ithaca, New York: Cornell University Press.

Jakobson, Roman. 1987. *Language in Literature*. Krystyna Pomorska and Stephen Rudy, eds. Cambridge, MA: Belknap Press.

Jameson, Fredric. 1985. "Baudelaire as Modernist and Postmodernist: The Dissolution of the Referent and the Artificial 'Sublime'." In Hosek and Parker 1985, 247–263.

Jiang, Hao 蒋浩, ed. 2002. *Xinshi: Sun Wenbo zhuanji* 新诗: 孙文波专集, "六十年代自行车" (New poem: Sun Wenbo special edition, "1960s bicycle"). Beijing: Self-Published.

Jiao, Tong 焦桐. 1999. "Jiangou shanshui de yixiangren: lun Zheng Chouyu Zheng Chouyu shiji" 建構山水的異鄉人: 論鄭愁予《鄭愁予詩集》(The alien creator of landscape: On Zheng Chouyu's *Collected Poems of Zheng Chouyu*). In Chen Yizhi 1999, 286–295.

Jiexian 界限. "Limits." <http://www.limitpoem.com>. Accessed December 3, 2006.

Johnson, Barbara. 1985. "*Les Fleurs du mal armé*: Some Reflections on Intertexuality." In Hosek and Parker 1985, 264–280.

Knapp, Bettina. 1991. "The New Era for Women Writers in China." *World Literature Today* (Summer): 433–439.

Kristeva, Julia. 1977. *About Chinese Women*. Anita Barrows, tr. London: Marion Boyars.

———. 1980. *Desire in Language*. Leon S. Roudiez, ed.; Thomas Gora, Alice Jardine, and Leon S. Roudiez, trs. New York: Columbia University Press.

Laji yundong luntan 垃圾运动论坛 (Garbage movement forum). <http://my.ziqu.com/bbs/665500/>. Accessed December 3, 2006.

Laplanche, Jean. 1999. *The Unconscious and the Id: A Volume of Laplanche's Problématiques*. Luke Thurston and Lindsay Watson, trs. London: Rebus Press.

Laplanche, Jean, and Serge Leclaire. 1972. "The Unconscious: A Psychoanalytic Study." In Laplanche 1999: 224–272.

Larrain, Jorge. 1995. "Identity, the Other, and Postmodernism." *Transformation: Marxist Boundary Work in Theory, Economics, Politics and Culture* 1 (Spring): 271–289.

Larsen, Neil. 1995. *Reading North by South*. Minneapolis: University of Minnesota Press.

Larson, Wendy. 1999. "Never this Wild: Sexing the Cultural Revolution." *Modern China* 25.4: 423–450.

———. 2000. "Women and the Discourse of Desire in Postrevolutionary China: The Awkward Postmodernism of Chen Ran." In Arif Dirlik and Xudong Zhang, eds., *Postmodernism & China*, 337–357. Durham & London: Duke University Press.

Leung, Laifong, ed. 1994. *Morning Sun: Interviews with Chinese Writers of the Lost Generation*. Armonk: M. E. Sharpe.

Li, Fukang, and Eva Hung, trs. 1992. "Post-Misty Poetry." *Renditions* (Spring): 93–149.

Li, Rui 李鋭. 2000. "Forget Joyce, What about Lu Xun?" *China Daily*, July 24.

Li, Xia, ed. 1999. *Essays, Interviews, Recollections and Unpublished Material of Gu Cheng, 20th Century Chinese Poet: The Poetics of Death*. Lewiston, NY: The Edwin Mellen Press.

Li, Yuansheng 李元生. 2002. "Jiexian de muhou gushi" 界限的幕后故事 (The behind the scenes story at *limits*). Accessed December 3, 2006 <http://limitpoem.online.cq.cn/shalong/show.asp?id=96>.

Li, Ziyun. 1994. "Women's Writing and Women's Consciousness." Zhu Hong, tr. In Gilmartin 1994, 299–317.

Lin, Huiyin (Lin Whei-yin) 林徽因. 1990. *Lin Huiyin* 林徽因. Chen Zhongying 陳鍾英 and Chen Yu 陳宇, eds. and comps. Hong Kong: Joint Publishing.

Lin, Julia. 1985a. *Essays on Contemporary Chinese Poetry*. Athens (Ohio) and London: Ohio University Press.

———. 1985b. "Cheng Ch'ouyü [Zheng Chouyu]: The Keeper of the Old." In Julia Lin 1985a, 1–11.

Lindley, David. 1985. *Lyric*. London and New York: Metheun.

Link, Perry, Richard Madsen, and Paul Pickowicz, eds. 1989. *Unofficial China*. Boulder: Westview Press.

Liu, Kexiang 劉克襄. 1992a. "Guaishou tonghua" 怪獸童話 (Monster stories). In *Xiaoshizhong de yaredai* 消失中的亞熱帶 (Vanishing subtropics), 66–68. Taibei: Chenxing.

———. 1992b. "Zuihou de heimian wuzhe" 最後的黑面舞者 (The last black-faced dancers). In *Ziran lüqing—jingyu, mihou, yu niaolei de guancha jishi* 自然旅情—鯨魚, 獼猴, 與鳥類的觀察記事 (Emotive natural excursions—observational notes on whales, macaques, and birds). Taibei: Chenxing.

———. 2002. "Yige ziran xiezuozhe zai Taiwan" 一個自然寫作者在臺灣 (A nature writer in Taiwan). Paper presented in March at the annual meeting of the Association for Asian Studies, Washington, DC.

———. 2003. "Heijing zhi si" 黑鯨之死 (Death of the black whale). In *Liu Kexiang jingxuanji* 劉克襄精選集 (Selected essays of Liu Kexiang), 122–123. Taibei: Jiuge chubanshe.

———. 2004a. "Haiyang zhi heliu" 海洋之河流 (The ocean's flow). In *Xiao wushu de kanfa* 小鼯鼠的看法 (Little flying squirrel's opinions), 122–123. Taibei: Chenxing.

———. 2004b. "Hongshulin de liuwang" 紅樹林的流亡 (Exile of the mangroves). Nick Kaldis, tr. *ISLE: Interdisciplinary Studies in Literature and Environment* 11.2 (Summer): 269.

Liu, Xinmin. 2004. "Play and Being Playful: The Quotidian in Cinematic Remembrance of the Mao Era." *Asian Cinema* 15.1: 73–89.

Luo, Fu 洛夫. 1957. *Ling he* 靈河 (River of the soul). Taibei: Chuangshiji shishe.

———. 1965. *Shishi zhi siwang* 石室之死亡 (Death of a stone cell). Taibei: Chuangshiji shishe.

———. 1967. *Waiwaiji* 外外集 (Poems from beyond). Taibei: Chuangshiji shishe.

———. 1974. *Moge xu* 魔歌序 (Preface to magical songs). Taibei: Zhongwai wenxue yuekanshe.

———. 1975. *Luo Fu zixuanji* 洛夫自選集 (A personal anthology). Taibei: Liming wenhua shiye youxian gongsi.

———. 1981. *Shijian zhi shang* 時間之傷 (Wound of time). Taibei: Shibao chuban gongsi.

———. 1990. *Yueguang fangzi* 月光房子 (House of moonlight). Taibei: Jiuge chubanshe.

———. 2001. Personal communication with John Balcom. March 15, 2001.

———. 2002. *Piaomu* 漂木 (Driftwood). Taibei: Lianhe wenxue.

Mang, Ke 芒克. 2003. *Qiao, zheixie ren* 瞧, 这些人 (Gifted generation). Changchun: Shidai wenyi chubanshe.

Marney, John. 1991. "PRC Politics and Literature in the Nineties." *World Literature Today* (Summer): 383–387.

McDougall, Bonnie S. 1994. "Preview: Modern Chinese Poetry (1900–1937)." *Modern Chinese Literature* 8: 127–170.

Mencius. 1970. *The Works of Mencius*. James Legge, tr. New York: Dover.

Michaux, Henri. 1994. "Preface to *Ordeals, Exorcisms*." In David Ball, tr., *Darkness Moves: An Henri Michaux Anthology, 1927–1984*, 83–84. Berkeley: University of California Press.

Milosz, Czeslaw. 1982. Richard Lourie, tr. *Visions from San Francisco Bay*. New York: Farrar Straus Giroux.

Morin, Edward, ed. 1990. *The Red Azalea: Chinese Poetry since the Cultural Revolution*. Honolulu: University of Hawaii Press.

Nüzi shibao 女子诗报 (The women's poetry paper). <http://www.sunpoem.com/nzsb/>. Accessed December 3, 2006.

Oates, David. 2003. *Paradise Wild: Reimagining American Nature*. Corvallis: Oregon State University Press.

Ou, Wai'ou 鷗外鷗. 1998. "The Second Obituary for the World." In Zheng Shusen 鄭樹森, Huang Jichi 黃繼持, and Lu Weiruan 盧瑋鑾, eds., *Zaoqi Xianggang xinwenxue zuopin xuan* (1927–1941) 早期香港新文學作品選 (1927–1941) (Anthology of early modern literature of Hong Kong [1927–1941]), 57–61. Hong Kong: Tiandi tushu.

Ouyang, Jianghe 歐陽江河. 1993. "Bajiu hou guonei shige xiezuo: bentu qizhi, zhongnian tezheng yu zhishifenzi shenfen" 89後國內詩歌寫作: 本土氣質, 中年特徵與知識分子身份 (Poetry writing in China after 1989: Native temperaments, characteristics of middle age, and intellectuals' identity). *Jintian* 今天 (Today) 22: 176–185.

Palandri, Angela C. Y. Jung, ed. 1972. *Modern Verse from Taiwan*. Berkeley, LA, and London: University of California Press.

Patton, Simon. 2001. "The Forces of Production: Symmetry and the Imagination in the Early Poetry of Gu Cheng." *Modern Chinese Literature and Culture* 13.2: 134–171.

Plath, Sylvia. 1998. *Ariel*. Reprint, New York: Harper Perennial.

Prose, Francine. 1998. "Scent of a Woman's Ink: Are Women Writers Really Inferior?" *Harper's Magazine* 296 (June): 61–70.

Ritzer, George. 2004. *The Globalization of Nothing*. Thousand Oaks: Pine Forge Press.

Rycroft, Charles. 1985. *Psychoanalysis and Beyond*. Peter Fuller, ed. London: Chatto and Windus.

———. 1992. *Rycroft on Analysis and Creativity*. Washington Square: New York University Press.

Sang, Ke 桑克. 2001. "Hulianwang shidai de Zhongwen shige" 互联网时代的中文诗歌 (Chinese language poetry in the Internet age). *Shi Tansuo* 诗探索 (Poetry explorations), 1–2. <http://www.cnrr.cn/cnrrwx/shownews.asp?newsid=1059&name=%E8%AF%97%E8%B7%AF%E8%8A%B1%E9%9B%A8>. Online version accessed December 3, 2006.

Sartre, Jean-Paul. 1968. Hazel E. Barnes, tr., *Search for a Method*. New York: Vintage Books.

Sassen, Saskia. 1991. *The Global City: New York, London, Tokyo*. Princeton: Princeton University Press.

Shao, Jian 邵健. 1998. "Zhishifenzi 'ziwo pipan' de yiyi" 知识分子 "自我批判" 的意义 (The meanings of intellectuals' "self-criticism"). *Zuojia* 作家 350: 98–105.

Shen, Qi 沈奇. 1995. "Meili de cuowei: Zheng Chouyu lun" 美麗的錯位: 鄭愁予論 (A beautiful dislocation: On Zheng Chouyu). In Shen. *Taiwan shiren sanlun* 臺灣詩人散論 (Scattered essays on Taiwan poets). Taibei: Erya.

Shi jianghu luntan 诗江湖论坛 (Poetry vagabonds forum). <http://my.clubhi.com/bbs/661502>. Accessed December 3, 2006.

Shi shenghuo 诗生活 (Poem life). <http://www.poemlife.com>. Accessed December 3, 2006.

Shu, Ting 舒婷. 1994. *Selected Poems*. Eva Hung, ed and tr. Hong Kong: Renditions Paperbacks.

Shu, Ting, and Gu Cheng 顾城. 1982. *Shu Ting, Gu Cheng shuqing shixuan: 1971–1981* 舒婷、顾城抒情诗选: 1971–1981 (Selected lyric poems of Shu Ting and Gu Cheng: 1971–1981). Fuzhou: Fujian renmin chubanshe.

Smith, Mick. 2001. *An Ethics of Place: Radical Ecology, Postmodernity, and Social Theory*. Albany: State University of New York Press.

Sun, Wenbo 孙文波. 2001. *Sun Wenbo de shi* 孙文波的诗 (The poetry of Sun Wenbo). Beijing: Renmin wenxue chubanshe.

Tamen wenxue wang 他们文学网 (Them literature net). <http://www.tamen.net/>. Accessed December 3, 2006.

Tan, Wuchang 谭五昌 et al., eds. 2004. *Zhongguo xinshi baipishu 1999–2002* 中国新诗白皮书 1999–2002 (A white paper on new Chinese poetry 1999–2002). Beijing: Kunlun chubanshe.

Tang, Qi 唐祈 et al., eds. 1984. *Zhongguo dangdai nüshiren shixuan* 中国当代女诗人诗选 (Selected poems by contemporary Chinese women poets). Guiyang: Guizhou renmin chubanshe.

———, ed. 1990. *Zhongguo xinshi mingpian jianshang cidian* 中国新诗名篇鉴赏辞典 (A guide to the appreciation of famous works of the new Chinese poetry). Chengdu: Sichuan cishi chubanshe.

Tang, Xiaodu 唐晓渡. 1994. "Nüxing shige: cong heiye dao baizhou—du Zhai Yongming de zushi 'Nüren'" 女性诗歌: 从黑夜到白昼—读翟永明的组诗"女人" (Women's poetry: From the black night to daylight—reading Zhai Yongming's poem sequence "woman"). In Zhai 1994: 233–238.

———. 1997. "Shei shi Zhai Yongming?" 谁是翟永明? (Who is Zhai Yongming?). *Jintian* 37: 49–64.

Tao, Naikan. 1995/1996. "Going Beyond: Post-Menglong Poets." *The Journal of the Oriental Society of Australia* 27/28: 146–153.

Tayebi, Kandi. 2003. "Editorial." *Academic Exchange Quarterly* (Winter) 7.4: 1.

Terdiman, Richard. 1993. *Present Past: Modernity and the Memory Crisis.* Ithaca and London: Cornell University Press.

Thoreau, Henry David. 1983. *Walden and Civil Disobedience.* Middlesex: Penguin Books.

————. January 1, 1858. Journal Entry. <http://www.library.ucsb. edu/thoreau/writings_journals_pdfs/J13f1.pdf> Manuscript Vol. 25: November 25, 1857–June 4, 1858): 33. Accessed March 18, 2007.

Todorov, Tzvetan. 1981. R. Howard, tr. *Introduction to Poetics.* Minneapolis: University of Minneapolis Press.

Van Crevel, Maghiel. 1996. *Language Shattered: Contemporary Chinese Poetry and Duoduo.* Leiden: Research School CNWS.

————. 2000. "Fringe Poetry, But Not Prose: Works by Xi Chuan and Yu Jian." *Journal of Modern Literature in Chinese* 3.2: 7–42.

————. 2005. "Rhythm, Sound, and Sense: Narrativity in Sun Wenbo." *Journal of Modern Literature in Chinese* 6.1: 119–151.

————. 2007. "The Intellectual vs. the Popular—a Polemic in Chinese Poetry." In Raoul Findeisen, Bernhard Führer, and Maghiel van Crevel, eds., *Chinese Texts, People and Procedures*, 59–113. Wiesbaden: Harrassowitz.

Vendler, Helen. 1995. *The Given and the Made: Recent American Poets.* London and Boston: Faber and Faber.

Wallace, Kathleen R., and Karla Armbruster. 2001. "Introduction: Why Go Beyond Nature Writing, and Where To?" In Kathleen R. Wallace and Karla Armbruster, eds., *Beyond Nature Writing: Expanding the Boundaries of Ecocriticism*, 1–25. Charlottesville: University of Virginia Press.

Wan, Xia, 万夏 et al., ed. 1993. *Hou menglong shi* 后朦胧诗 (Post-obscure poetry). Chengdu: Sichuan jiaoyu chubanshe.

Wang, Ban. 2004. *Illuminations from the Past: Trauma, Memory, and History in Modern China.* Stanford: Stanford University Press.

Wang, Duqing 王獨清. 1974. "Wo cong *Café* zhong chulai" 我從Café 中出來 (I came out of the café). In Zhang Manyi 張曼儀 et al., eds. *Xiandai Zhongguo shixuan 1917–1949* 現代中國詩選 一九一七~一九四九 (Modern Chinese poetry: an anthology 1917–1949), 2 vols. Hong Kong: Hong Kong University Press, Vol. 1: 281–282.

Wang, Jiaxin 王家新. 2002. *Meiyou yingxiong de shi* 没有英雄的诗 (Poetry without heroes). Beijing: Zhongguo shehui kexue chubanshe.

Wang, Jiaxin, and Sun Wenbo, eds. 2000. 中国诗歌：九十年代备忘录 (Chinese poetry: memorandum of the 90s). Beijing: Renmin wenxue chubanshe.

Wang, Ping, ed. 1999. *New Generation: Poems from China Today.* New York: Hanging Loose Press.

Wang, Wenxing 王文興. 1995. "Flaw." Chen Zhuyun, tr. In Joseph S. M. Lau and Howard Goldblatt, eds., *The Columbia Anthology of Modern Chinese Literature.* New York: Columbia University Press, 235–245.

Wenmang 文盲 (Illiterate). *Wenmang lingdu kongjian* 文盲零度空间 (Zero-degree space of the illiterate). <http://www.wenmang.com/>. Accessed December 3, 2006.

Williams, Raymond. 1976. *Keywords: A Vocabulary of Culture and Society.* New York: Oxford University Press.

Winckler, Edward. 1994. "Cultural Policy in Postwar Taiwan." In Stevan Harrell and Huang Chün-chieh, eds., *Cultural Change in Postwar Taiwan,* 22–46. Boulder: Westview.

Wong, Wai-leung. 1979. "'The River at Dusk is Saddening Me': Cheng Chou Yü [Zheng Chouyu] and *Tz'u* [ci] Poetry." *Renditions* 11 and 12 (Spring/ Autumn): 265–279.

Wu, Hung. 2000. *Exhibiting Experimental Art in China.* The David and Alfred Smart Museum of Art. Chicago: University of Chicago Press.

Wu, Mingyi 吳明益. 2004. "Ganxing de ziran dizhi: wenxuexing ziranshuxie de tezhi" 感性的自然地誌: 文學性自然書寫的特質 (Emotive natural history: The elements of literary nature writing). In *Yi shuxie jiefang ziran: Taiwan xiandai ziranshuxie de tansuo* 以書寫解放自然: 臺灣現代自然書寫的探索, 1980–2002. (Liberate nature by writing: Exploration in modern nature writing of Taiwan, 1980–2002), 38–62. Taibei: Da'an Press.

Xi, Chuan 西川. 1997. *Rang mengmianren shuohua* 让蒙面人说话 (Let the masked man speak). Beijing: Dongfang chuban zhongxin.

Xi, Du 西渡. 2000. "Xiezuo de quanli" 写作的权利 (The right to write). In Wang Jiaxin and Sun Wenbo, eds., 2000.

Xi, Mi 奚密 (Michelle Yeh). (1996) 1998a. "Bianyuan, qianwei, chaoxianshi zhuyi: dui Taiwan wuliushi niandai xiandaizhuyi de fansi" 邊緣, 前衛, 超現實: 對台灣五、六十年代現代主義的反思 (Marginality, avant-garde, surrealism: Reflections on modernism in Taiwan in the 1950s and 1960s) *Jintian* 3: 34–52. Reprint. In *Xiandangdai shiwen lu* 現當代詩文錄 (Essays on modern Chinese poetry), 155–179. Taibei: Lianhe wenxue.

———. 1998b. "Taiwan xiandaishi lunzhan: zailun 'yichang weiwancheng de geming'" 台灣現代詩論戰: 再論〈一場未完成的革命〉 (The modern poetry debate: Reflections on "an incomplete revolution"). *Guowen tiandi* 國文天地 13.10 (March): 72–81.

Xia, Yu (Hsia Yü) 夏宇. 1984. *Beiwanglu* 備忘錄 (Memorandum). Taibei: Self-Published.

———. 1991. *Fuyushu* 腹語術 (Ventriloquy). Taibei: Xiandaishi jikanshe.

———. 1995. *Moca.wuyi mingzhuang* 摩擦. 無以名狀 (Rub. ineffable). Taibei: Xiandaishi jikanshe.

———. 2001. Steve Bradbury, tr., *Fusion Kitsch*. Brookline, MA: Zephyr Press.

Xiao, Xialin 萧夏林, ed. 1994. *Gu Cheng qicheng* 顾城弃城 (Gu Cheng abandons the city). Beijing: Tuanjie chubanshe.

Xie, Youshun 谢有顺. 1999. "Neizai de shige zhenxiang" 内在的诗歌真相 (The inner truth of poetry). *Nanfang zhoumo* 南方周末: April 1.

———. 2004. "Shei zai shanghai zheng de shige?" 谁在伤害真正的诗歌 (Who is hurting true poetry?). In Tan Wuchang et al. 2004. 450–456.

Xin, Di 辛笛 et al. 1981. *Jiuye ji* 九叶集 (Nine leaves). Nanjing: Jiangsu renmin chubanshe.

———. 1984. *Baye ji* 八葉集 (Eight leaves). Hong Kong: Joint Publishing.

Xiong, Hong. 敻虹 (Hu Meizi 胡梅子). 1968. *Jin yong* 金蛹 (The golden pupa). Taibei: Lanxing shishe.

———. 1976. *Xiong Hong shiji* 敻虹詩集 (Collected poems of Xiong Hong). Taibei: Xinlixiang chubanshe.

———. 1983. *Hong shanhu* 紅珊瑚 (Red coral). Taibei: Dadi chubanshe.

Ya, Xian 瘂弦. 1981a. "Xiandaishi de Xingsi" 現代詩省思 (Reflections on modern poetry). In Ya Xian 1981c, 3–43.

———. 1981b. *Ya Xian shiji* 瘂弦詩集 (The collected poetry of Ya Xian). Taibei: Hongfan.

———. 1981c. *Zhongguo xinshi yanjiu* 中國新詩研究 (Studies in modern Chinese poetry). Taibei: Hongfan.

———. 2002. Interview with Steven L. Riep, Davis, CA, May 29, 2002.

Yan, Chunde 阎纯德 et al., eds. 1983. *Tamen de shuqing shi* 她们的抒情诗 (Lyric poetry by women). Fuzhou: Fujian renmin chubanshe.

Yan, Huo 彦火, 1993. "Gu Cheng: yige weixiao er tongku de linghun" 顾城: 一个微笑而痛苦的灵魂 (Gu Cheng: A smiling and agonized soul). In Chen Zishan 陈子善, ed., *Shiren Gu Cheng zhisi* 诗人顾城之死 (Death of poet Gu Cheng), 79–85. Shanghai: Shanghai renmin chubanshe.

Yan, Li 严力. 1999. *Duomian jing xuanzhuanti* 多面镜旋转体 (Spinning polyhedral mirror). Xining: Qinghai renmin chubanshe.

———. 2003. *Yan Lin Shi Huaji* 严力诗画集 (Poetry and art of Yan Li). Xining: Qinghai renmin chubanshe.

———. 2004. *Huanggei Wo: Yan Li Shixuan 1974–2004* 还给我：严力诗选 1974–2004 (Give it back to me: Yan Li's selected poems 1974–2004). Kingsbury: Yuanxiang chubanshe.

Yan, Li 严力, and Denis Mair. *Shi tiankong* 诗天空 (Poetry sky—online, bilingual poetry journal). <http://www.poetrysky.com/quarterly/quarterly-1-yanli.html>. Accessed November 18, 2006.

Yan, Yuejun 阎月君, ed. 1985. *Menglongshi xuan* 朦胧诗选 (An anthology of misty poetry). Shenyang: Chunfeng wenyi.

Yang, Lian 杨炼. 1998. *Guihua. Zhili de kongjian* 鬼话. 智力的空间 (Ghost-talks, space of mind). Shanghai: Shanghai wenyi chubanshe.

———. 2003. *Xingfu guihun shouji* 幸福鬼魂手记 (Notes of a happy ghost). Shanghai: Shanghai wenyi chubanshe.

Yang, Mu 楊牧 (C. H. Wang). 1974. "Zheng Chouyu chuanqi/daixu" 鄭愁予傳奇／代序 (The legend of Zheng Chouyu/in lieu of a preface). In Zheng Chouyu (1974) 1993, 11–46.

Yang, Mu 楊牧, and Zheng Shusen 鄭樹森, eds. 1989. *Xiandai Zhongguo shixuan* 現代中國詩選 (Anthology of modern Chinese poetry). Taibei: Hongfan.

Yang, Xiaobin. 2002. *The Chinese Postmodern: Trauma and Irony in Chinese Avant-Garde Fiction*. Ann Arbor: University of Michigan Press.

Yeh, Michelle (Xi Mi 奚密). 1987. "Circularity: Emergence of a Form in Modern Chinese Poetry." *Modern Chinese Literature* 3 (Spring/Fall): 33–45.

Yeh, Michelle (Xi Mi 奚密). 1991a. *Modern Chinese Poetry: Theory and Practice since 1917*. New Haven and London: Yale University Press.

————. 1991b. "A New Orientation to Poetry: The Transition from Traditional to Modern." *Chinese Literature: Essays, Articles, Reviews* 12: 71–94.

————. 1991c. "Nature's Child and the Frustrated Urbanite: Expressions of the Self in Contemporary Chinese Poetry." *World Literature Today* (Summer): 405–409.

————. 1992. "Light a Lamp in a Rock: Experimental Poetry in Contemporary China." *Modern China* 18 (October): 379–409.

————. (1992) 1994. "From the Margin: An Introduction." In *Anthology of Modern Chinese Poetry*. New Haven: Yale University Press; Paperback Reprint.

————. 1996. "The 'Cult of Poetry' in Contemporary China." *The Journal of Asian Studies* 55.1 (February): 51–81.

————. 1999. "Chinese Postmodernism?—the Cultural Politics of Modern Chinese Poetry." In Wen-hsin Yeh, ed., *Cross-Cultural Readings of Chineseness: Images, Narratives, and Interpretations of the 1990s*, 100–127. Berkeley: University of California at Berkeley, Institute of East Asian Studies.

————. 2000a. "From Surrealism to Nature Poetics: A Study of Prose Poetry from Taiwan." *Journal of Modern Literature in Chinese* 3.2 (January): 119–156.

————. 2000b. "International Theory and the Transnational Critic: Chinese Studies in the Age of Multiculturalism." In Rey Chow, ed., *Modern Chinese Literary and Cultural Studies in the Age of Theory: Reimagining a Field*, 251–280. Durham and London: Duke University Press.

————. 2003. "Misty Poetry." In Joshua Mostow, ed., *The Columbia Companion to Modern East Asian Literature*, 520–526. New York: Columbia University Press.

Yeh, Michelle, and N. G. D. Malmqvist, eds. 2001. *Frontier Taiwan: An Anthology of Modern Chinese Poetry*. New York: Columbia University Press.

Yi, Hushui 伊湖水 2006. "Makesi gongguo" 马克思功过 (The merits and faults of Marx). <http://club.cat898.com/newbbs/dispbbs.asp?BoardID=1&ID=1373723>. Online posting accessed December 3, 2006.

Yi luntan 翼论坛 (Wings forum). <http://bbs.poemlife.com:1863/forum/list.jsp?forumID=60>. Accessed December 3, 2006.

Yip, Wai-lim 葉維廉. 1970. *Modern Chinese Poetry: Twenty Poets from the Republic of China 1955–1965*. Iowa City: University of Iowa Press.

Yu, Guangzhong 余光中, tr. 1960. *New Chinese Poetry*. Taibei: Heritage Press.

Yu, Jian 于坚. 1999. "Shigezhishe de yingyuruan: guanyu dangdai shige de lianglei yuyan xiangdu" 诗歌之舌的硬与软: 关于当代诗歌的两类语言向度 (The hard and the soft tongues of poetry: On two different directions in the languages of contemporary poetry). In Yang Ke 杨克, ed., *1998 nian*

Zhongguo xinshi nianjian 1998 年中国新诗年鉴 (1998 yearbook of Chinese new poetry), 1–17. Guangzhou: Huacheng chubanshe.

———. 2003. *Shiji yu tuxiang 2000–2002* 诗集与图像 2000–2002 (Anthology and image 2000–2002). Xining: Qinghai renmin chubanshe.

———. (2001) 2004a. "Dangdai shige de minjian chuantong" 当代诗歌的民间传统 (The popular tradition in contemporary poetry). In Tan Wuchang 2004: 548–555.

———. 2004b. "Two or Three Things from the Past." Ping Wang and Ron Padgett, trs. *Words Without Borders—The Online Magazine for International Literature* (May). <http://www.wordswithoutborders.org/article.php?lab=Things>. Accessed June 30, 2005.

Zarrow, Peter. 1999. "Meanings of China's Cultural Revolution: Memoirs of Exile." *positions: east asia cultures critiques* 7.1: 165–191.

Zhai, Yongming 翟永明. 1989. "'Nüxing shige' yu shigezhong de nüxing yishi" "女性诗歌"与诗歌中的女性意识 ("Women's poetry" and female consciousness in poetry). *Shikan* 诗刊 (Poetry monthly) 241 (June): 10–11.

———. 1994. *Zhai Yongming shiji* 翟永明诗集 (The collected poems of Zhai Yongming). Chengdu: Chengdu chubanshe.

———. 1997. "Jiandaoshou de duihua" 剪刀手的對話 (Scissor cutter's dialogue). *Jintian* 38.3: 119–123.

Zhang, Jiayan 张嘉谚. 2004. "Dishige yundong—wangluo huayu genming de qianchao" 低诗歌运动—网络话语革命的前潮 (The low poetry movement—forerunner of the Internet discourse revolution). <http://www.boxun.com/hero/zhangjy/11_1.shtml>. Online posting accessed December 3, 2006.

———. 2005. "Zhongguo wangluo fanjiquan de 'getixianfeng' shige xiezuo" 中国网络反集权的"个体先锋"诗歌写作 (Poetry writing of the "individual avant-garde" against centralized state power on the Internet in China). <http://www.2008red.com/member_pic_56/files/dpoem/html/article_6069_1.shtml>. Online posting accessed December 13, 2006.

Zhang, Meifang 張梅芳. 2001. *Zheng Chouyu shi de xiangxiang shijie* 鄭愁予的想像世界 (The imaginary world of Zheng Chouyu). Taibei: Wanjuanlou.

Zhang, Mo 張默, ed., and Yu Guangzhong, series ed. 1989. *Zhonghua xiandai wenxue daxi: Taiwan 1970–1989* 中華現代文學大系 (A compendium of modern Chinese literature: Taiwan 1970–1989). *Shi juan* 詩卷 (Poetry volume), 1–2. Taibei: Jiuge chubanshe.

Zhang, Qinghua 张清华. 1999. "Yici zhenzheng de shige duihua yu jiaofeng" 一次真正的诗歌对话与交锋 (A true poetic dialogue and exchange). In Tan Wuchang 2004: 442–449.

Zhang, Shuguang 张曙光. 1999. *Yuyan: xingshi de mingming* 语言: 形式的命名 (Language: The naming of forms). Beijing: Renmin wenxue chubanshe.

Zheng, Chouyu 鄭愁予 (Zheng Wentao 鄭文韜). (1974) 1993. *Zheng Chouyu shi xuanji* 鄭愁予詩選集 (Selected poems of Zheng Chouyu). Taibei: Zhiwen.

———. (1979) 2003. *Zheng Chouyu shiji I: 1951–1968* 鄭愁予詩集 I: 1951–1968 (Collected poems of Zheng Chouyu I: 1951–1968). Taibei: Hongfan.

Zheng, Min 鄭敏. 1949. *Zheng Min shiji* 鄭敏詩集 (Collected poems of Zheng Min). Shanghai: Wenhua shenghuo chubanshe.

———. 1991. *Zaochen, wo zai yuli caihua* 早晨, 我在雨裏採花 (In the morning, I pick flowers in the rain). Hong Kong: Tupo.

———. 1993a. "Four Poems by Zheng Min." John Balcom, tr., *Renditions* (Spring): 120–127.

———. 1993b. "Shijimo de huigu: Hanyu yuyan biange yu Zhongguo xinshi chuangzuo" 世纪末的回顾: 汉语语言变革与中国新诗创作 (Looking back at the century's end: Chinese language reform and the practice of modern poetry). *Wenxue pinglun* 3: 5–20.

———. 1994. "Journey in a Labyrinth." *Chinese Literature* (Winter): 133–136.

———. 1995. "Zhongguo shige de gudian yu xiandai" 中国诗歌的古典与现代 (Classical and modern in Chinese poetry). *Wenxue pinglun* 文学评论 6: 79–90.

Zhong, Ling (Ling Chung) 鍾玲. 1989a. *Xiandai Zhongguo miusi: Taiwan nüshiren zuopin xilun* 現代中國繆司: 臺灣女詩人作品析論 (The modern Chinese muse: An analysis of the works of Taiwan's women poets), 353–370. Taibei: Lianjing.

———. 1989b. "Xia Yu de shidai jingshen" 夏宇的時代精神 (Xia Yu's zeitgeist). In Li Ruiteng 李瑞騰, ed., and Yu Guangzhong, series ed. *Zhonghua xiandai wenxue daxi: Taiwan 1970–1989* 中華現代文學大系: 臺灣 1970–1989 (A compendium of modern Chinese literature: Taiwan 1970–1989). *Pinglun juan* 評論卷 (Criticism volume). 15: 1245–1259. Taibei: Jiuge chubanshe.

Zhong, Xueping, Zheng Wang, and Di Bai. 2001. *Some of Us: Chinese Women Growing Up in the Mao Era*. New Brunswick, NJ and London: Rutgers University Press.

Zhongguo dishichao. 中国低诗潮 (China low poetry tide). <http://xz.netsh.com/eden/bbs/666023/>. Accessed December 3, 2006.

Zito, Angela, and Tani Barlow, eds. 1994. *Body, Subject, and Power in China*. Chicago: University of Chicago Press.

Index

PL
2333
.N49
2008